Early Canadian Gardening
An 1827 Nursery Catalogue

EARLY CANADIAN GARDENING

AN 1827 NURSERY CATALOGUE

Eileen Woodhead

Illustrated by the author

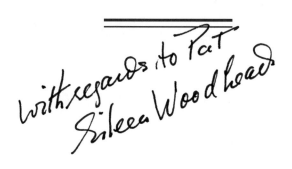

with regards to Pat
Eileen Woodhead

McGill-Queen's University Press

Montreal & Kingston · London · Ithaca

Legal deposit third quarter 1998
Bibliothèque nationale du Québec

Printed in Canada on acid-free paper

Toronto Nursery catalogue published by permission
of the Metropolitan Toronto Reference Library

This book has been published with the help
of a grant from the Humanities and
Social Sciences Federation of Canada,
using funds provided by the Social Sciences and
Humanities Research Council of Canada.

McGill-Queen's University Press acknowledges
the support of the Canada Council for the Arts
for its publishing program.

Canadian Cataloguing in Publication Data

Woodhead, Eileen
Early Canadian gardening: and 1827 nursery catalogue
Includes bibliographical references and index.
ISBN 0-7735-1731-6
1. Horticulture–Ontario–History–19th century.
2. Gardening–Ontario–History–19th century.
3. Botany–Ontario. 4. Ontario–Social life and customs.
5. Seeds–Catalogs. 6. Plants–Catalogs. I. Title.
SB451.36.C3W66 1998   655'.09713'09034   C98-900334-5

This book was typeset by Typo Litho Composition Inc.
in 10.5/13 Bembo.

Contents

Introduction

═══════════════

Trade catalogues are generally overlooked as sources of historical information, yet they contain details about the past that few other documents provide. Commercial trade catalogues began in the eighteenth century as pattern books that manufacturers supplied to their travelling salesman, listing assortments of goods with details of sizes and styles from which retailers could place orders. Many of these books were illustrated, especially those for hardware and furniture. The advantages of catalogues were soon realized by the retailers themselves, who began to use the method to attract customers.

Nurserymen in England started publishing catalogues in the eighteenth century, and the practice was initiated by American nurseries early in the nineteenth century. Those that have survived provide us with a reliable record of the plants available at a particular place and time.

The *Catalogue of Fruit & Ornamental Trees, Flowering Shrubs, Garden Seeds and Greenhouse Plants, Bulbous Roots & Flower Seeds Cultivated and for Sale at the Toronto Nursery* was printed in York by William Lyon Mackenzie in 1827. The Toronto Nursery on Dundas Street in the township of Toronto was owned by nurseryman William W. Custead. The only known copy of this catalogue is in the Baldwin Room at the Metropolitan Toronto Reference Library. It was originally owned by Dr William Warren Baldwin, who had it bound with other pamphlets for his library.

The catalogue's contents and format closely resemble those of contemporary American catalogues. A detailed examination of the plants and seeds it offered presents us with an historical perspective on horticulture in the nineteenth century and on the gardens of Upper Canada during that the period. Studying the plants selected, their function, and their diversity, we gain meaningful insights into Canadian social history.

When I came upon the catalogue in the Toronto Library, I felt challenged to reproduce in my own garden the plants it listed. Locating sources would become an adventure that took me around Canada and the United States; before that could be done, however, all the plants had to be identified through searches of other early catalogues and contemporary botanical sources.

The most influential garden book of the early nineteenth century was Philip Miller's *The Gardener's Dictionary*, reissued many times since its original publication in 1724. Miller often recommended plants "for the curious garden." The word "curious" was at that time not limited to the meaning of "odd" or "inquisitive": an eighteenth-century dictionary defined it as "attentive, careful, subtle, artful, elegant, neat or finished." These are terms that would apply to a garden managed by an experienced and discriminating gardener. From the lists of plants offered in the Toronto Nursery catalogue, it is obvious that even among the early settlers in Upper Canada there were already a number of "curious" gardeners.

The chapters that follow place the Toronto Nursery in time through a brief survey of horticulture at the beginning of the nineteenth century. The plant descriptions, many accompanied by botanical drawings made from live plants, include brief histories of their cultivation, emphasizing the role each played in early Upper Canadian life and tracing its present-day status as a garden plant.

Early Canadian Gardening
An 1827 Nursery Catalogue

The Toronto Nursery

The *Catalogue of Fruit and Ornamental Trees, Flowering Shrubs, Garden Seeds and Greenhouse Plants, Bulbous Roots & Flower Seeds*, published in 1827 by the Toronto Nursery, near York in Upper Canada, was one of the first nursery catalogues in Upper Canada. The eighteen-page Toronto Nursery catalogue was printed by William Lyon Mackenzie, "Printer to the House of Assembly," and editor of the newspaper the *Colonial Advocate*; Mackenzie was later to find a place in Canadian political history as one of the leaders of the Reform Party in Upper Canada, and later as an instigator of the 1837 Rebellion. The catalogue is perhaps the earliest of its kind extant, and the only copy known to exist is in the history department of the Toronto Metropolitan Reference Library. It is one of the few records available for the study of garden plants in Upper Canada during the first decades of the nineteenth century. Small in size, 10 cm by 18 cm, it is bound with several other pamphlets on widely divergent subjects, none dated later than 1828. Several of these are treatises dealing with political and religious subjects; an exception is one directed toward "Those who raise Tobacco in this Province." The longest document included in the binding is an English translation of Jean Jacques Rousseau's *Social Contract*, printed in Dublin, dated 1791.

Printed catalogues from domestic nurseries are the earliest documents providing a detailed record of the cultivated plants available to Canadian gardeners. The extensive itemized list of plants and seeds in the Toronto Nursery catalogue makes it a particularly valuable resource for the study of garden history in Canada. From the number and range of the plants and seeds it is evident that the nursery intended to serve the needs of a widely diverse market, from the simple practical needs of the farmer to the esoteric demands of the plant collector.

Prior to the existence of Canadian nurseries, imported garden material was offered for sale or by auction to the public advertised in newspapers and broadsheets. Advertisements for seeds and bulbs usually appeared in the spring or early summer months, as soon as weather conditions permitted the arrival of goods by sea from Great Britain or overland from the United States. Seeds for grains and edible vegetables were frequently listed by name, but the occasional mention of "flower seeds" inevitably failed to list individual species. Shipments of flowering bulbs were often announced in more detail, and we learn that hyacinths, tulips, and daffodils were among these imports. Plants in a verdant condition were noticeably absent.

Advertisements listing seeds of native plants were intended to attract the attention of exporters, as the popularity of North American plants was growing in Europe. The earliest of these was a broadsheet published in Quebec City in 1767 by John Wright, "collector of seeds for a Society of Noblemen and Gentlemen of Great Britain." The seeds he offered were predominantly those of woody species, particularly trees and shrubs that were gaining international recognition from botanists and nurserymen and serving to enrich the European landscape.

The volume in which the Toronto Nursery catalogue is bound bears the bookplate of Dr W.W. Baldwin of Spadina, a gentleman who settled in York (Toronto) in 1802 and became one of its leading citizens. He was educated at the University of Edinburgh as a physician, and was one of two medical practitioners in York before 1812. He was also licensed as a lawyer in 1803 and served as a judge in the Home district court from 1809 to 1836. His political career was illustrious, as a member of the House of Assembly from 1820 to 1824 and from 1828 to 1830, a leader in the Reform movement, and an earnest believer in the responsibility of the government to the people. Through his own dealings and by inheritance, he was a large landowner in the Toronto area.

His first home in York, named Spadina, was built on a rise of land above the present Davenport Street. This house was destroyed by fire in 1835, but a second Spadina was built in the same location. He owned a large tract of land in what is now downtown Toronto, part of which he laid out in a grand fashion and donated to the city, including the 160-foot-wide street now known as Spadina Avenue. He had many business dealings with one of the area's largest importing merchants, Quetton St George, who in turn dealt in trade with John Jacob Astor in New York City. As a physician, Baldwin would have had a thorough knowledge of botany and may have been one of the patrons acknowledged in the preface of the Toronto Nursery catalogue.

It was fortunate that he chose to include the Toronto Nursery catalogue when having his books bound, for this act was responsible for saving it for posterity. A very small number of trade catalogues have survived from this period. Among them are several from American nurseries that show the increase in the number of plant growers south of the border. The outstanding example was Prince's Nursery on Long Island, New York, which led all others in the extent of species and varieties offered and "was the first in America to advertise ornamental plants in a large way" (Hedrick 1950:72). Established in 1737, it prospered for over a century. The nursery's first known advertisement is dated 1767, and a broadsheet catalogue (now in the Library of Congress) is dated 1790. All the plants listed are woody species of fruit trees and shrubs, ornamental trees, flowering shrubs, and roses (Leighton 1986:308).

The Prince Nursery had agents who received orders and delivered nursery stock, and its distribution extended into Upper Canada early in the nineteenth century. In *The Gleaner and Niagara* dated 28 October 1825, the following advertisement was placed by an agent:

Fruit and Ornamental Trees, &c.
Mr. Prince, proprietor of the Linnaean Garde and Nurseries near New York, offers to the public his very extensive collection of Fruit Trees of the choicest kinds ... Thomas Butler, Agent, Niagara.

On the same date, a similar advertisement was placed by another agent:

FRUIT AND ORNAMENTAL TREES
The subscriber offers for sale at the old American Nursery on Long Island, their usual extensive assortment of Fruit and Ornamental Trees, Flowering Shrubs, & Plants, also Tulips, Hyacinths and other Bulbous Flowers, a very large collection of the finest Grape Vines; about two hundred kinds of Roses, and a great variety of Oranges, Lemons & Citron Trees, Geraniums, Japan Roses, and other Greenhouse plants, a catalogue with the prices of the plants and trees respectively, may be seen at the office of the *Gleaner*. All orders will be promptly executed and the trees forwarded with the greatest care. The subscribers have requested R. Dickson, Esq. of Niagara to receive payment on behalf of the firm Stephen F. Mills & Co. late Prince and Mills, Niagara.

An advertisement placed in the *Montreal Gazette* the following year by the Blink Bonny Nursery is worded in much the same manner: "Fruit and Ornamental Trees, Flowering Shrubs, Plants and Bulbs, Greenhouse Plants and Garden Seeds ... general catalogue may be had by Application to H. Cleghorn" (*Gazette*, 15 March 1826).

The title pages of the catalogues advertised above are worded almost identically to that of the Prince catalogue, and the Canadian nurseries may well have based their publicity on the example set by the well-established American nursery. The surviving Toronto Nursery catalogue lists a system of agents throughout the southern part of the province. These were, for the most part, shopkeepers who would have had copies of the catalogue available to the public. The agents were responsible for receiving and delivering orders. In this way the nursery could take advantage of the expanding markets in settlements at a distance from the town of York.

Incidentally, in 1827, the year the Toronto Nursery catalogue was printed, the Prince catalogue was in its twenty-fourth edition and 171 pages long. William Prince, "Proprietor," was a "charter member of the Linnaean Society of Paris, of the Horticultural Society of London, of the Imperial Society of the Georgofilii at Florence, &c, &c." The plants were identified by "Botanic Names generally according to Pursh's Flora of North America and others, e.g. Michaux, Nuttall, Torrey, Elliott, Hortus, Britannicus, &c." If these were the models aspired to, nurserymen were emulating the most recent and accredited horticulture authorities of their day.

The Toronto Nursery was owned and operated by William Ward Custead, who arrived in the Toronto Township in 1811 when settlement in Upper Canada was sparse. In the period between Custead's arrival and the publication of the catalogue the province saw rapid growth. Nearby York, a mere village in 1811, was a town of almost 9,000 by 1833. A lady traveller described the town in 1827: "York, which, though the Capital of the Province, is no more than a small Hamlet, covering a good deal of ground, for each house has some garden attached to it" (Hall: NA MG24 H13). When Anna Jameson arrived there from England a few years later, she noted that her new home was "surrounded by a garden of some extent − or, rather, what will be a garden at some future time" (Jameson 1838/1972 1:258). York soon became the largest town in Upper Canada, a centre for all services and trade as well as the seat of government. The surrounding Home District had a population of 21,329 in 1827, which grew to 40,000 in 1833. The area provided a rapidly growing market for entrepreneurs.

Few historical records provide a satisfactory description of early Canadian gardens. Travellers and diarists writing about the Canadas commented on novel experiences rather than on familiar sights. Remarks on native flora were common, but little attention was given to cultivated plants. Elizabeth Simcoe, wife of the governor of Upper Canada, left an interesting account of her years in Upper Canada at the end of the eighteenth century. However, her writings are frustrating for a gardener to read, for she frequently referred to a "Garden," yet never described one nor mentioned by name any of the plants that were growing there. She "walked in the garden in the moonlight," and when the weather was mild, took breakfast "with the door open into the garden." She admired the cherry and peach trees in the orchard at Navy Hall when they bore prolific fruit in 1793 and told how she enjoyed the covered walk in Mr Hamilton's garden at Queenston (Innis 1983:76, 97, 129). Perhaps garden plants were too familiar to her to require documentation, for there is no doubt she had a genuine knowledge and appreciation of botany. Her diary describes in some detail many of the native plants she encountered in her travels.

Anna Jameson, wife of a Toronto lawyer, offered many details in her writings of life in Upper Canada in the 1830s. She admired the native plants and was intrigued by their colours and shapes. In her travels she stopped her carriage to gather purple and scarlet iris, blue larkspur, "elegant Canadian columbines, scarlet lychnis and white and yellow cyprepediums," to make a wreath so that she might "enjoy at leisure their novelty and beauty." She once tore open the blossom of the lady's slipper orchid to discover a "variety of configuration, and colour, and gem-like richness of ornament, enough to fashion twenty different flowers" (Jameson 1838/1972 2:116–17). During her stay in Upper Canada she visited many of the leading figures of the day; almost immediately upon her arrival at Colonel Talbot's estate, she was shown the garden which occupied two acres, "very neatly laid out and enclosed. It abounds in roses of different kinds" (Jameson 1838/1972 2:197–8).

The town of York had a number of citizens who, like Dr Baldwin, had substantial homes and gardens. Some residences had greenhouses, hot houses, and conservatories as well as spacious grounds. Driving through the Home District, Mrs Jameson remarked on the "most prosperous estates in Upper Canada, a succession of well-cultivated farms ... some of the farmers are reputed rich men" (Jameson 1838/1972 3:334). During a winter illness she received a bouquet of hothouse flowers from a friend. She met two women whose homes had conservatories, "a proof of advancing wealth, civilization and taste" (Jameson 1838/1972 1:144). These wealthier establishments formed an educated and discriminating sector of the population who could demand a degree of elegance in their environment. For such a clientele there was added prestige in the fashionable pastime of acquiring collections of botanical specimens. Some households employed professional gardeners to keep their grounds in order and operate the greenhouses. Sheriff William Botsford Jarvis, who bought the property he named Rosedale on Yonge Street in 1824, had a gardener, John Gray, living on the premises in 1836. The gardens at Rosedale, so-called because the hillside was originally covered with wild roses, became well known and admired, laid out in the English manner with gravel pathways and arbours, rose beds and orchards. There were several such estates in the York area serviced by a growing number of horticultural tradesmen. The 1833 *York Directory* listed three "Nurserymen, Seedsmen and Market Gardeners" and a seed warehouse. Four years later the city (now named Toronto), with a population of just under 10,000 people, had sixteen professional gardeners listed in the directory.

Mr Custead's Toronto Nursery offered a wide-ranging variety of plants which, in addition to supplying material for the fashionable gardens of the affluent, also fulfilled the elementary and essential needs of settlers for fruit plants and seeds for vegetables and herbs. Although many immigrants and newcomers to the Canadas lived in shanties or log cabins in densely wooded landscapes, this type of homestead was generally regarded as temporary, a first step towards establishing a more permanent home. Travellers in the Niagara area (settled by Loyalists in the 1780s) noted by the 1830s that few shanties were left – by this time most homes were wood-framed or of masonry structure (NA MG24 H16 Rev. Patrick Bell, Nov. 1833). But no matter what their economic status, settlers often turned to their gardens in their efforts to create a civilized appearance. In doing so they could feel closer to the established homes and traditions they had left behind in Great Britain or the American states. They attempted to re-create gardens as they knew them, in a climate and environment with very different characteristics. The entries in Custead's catalogue reflect this aspect of early Canadian life, as many of the selections, popular as they may have been elsewhere, were quite inappropriate for the often hostile climate of Upper Canada.

The Toronto Nursery catalogue provides us with a reliable list of plants available in Upper Canada in the early nineteenth century. It includes fruit plants of various species, and seeds for vegetables and herbs to supply the basic need for food plants. In addition there are ornamental trees and flowering shrubs, many of North American origin. Most remarkable is the range and selection of nursery-grown herbaceous plants that Custead had to offer. The list includes biennial and perennial plants, roses, bulbs, and seeds for annual herbs and flowers. Custead meticulously named all the plants by their accepted common names, sometimes providing a second term where there may have been confusion in nomenclature. While many of the plants were familiar favourites of the period, some were suitable only for those with sophisticated tastes and greenhouse facilities. A number of American species included had been introduced earlier to Europe and were being re-introduced to America, albeit to a different environment and often as improved varieties. In spite of the difficulties of communication and transportation associated with a young and relatively undeveloped country, those who were interested in horticulture appear to have been well informed of the trends and discoveries being discussed in more cosmopolitan centres.

The Toronto Nursery was located on Lot 5, Concession 1 north of Dundas in Toronto Township. William Ward Custead purchased the property on 8 November 1810, registering the deed on 4 July 1811. The land was originally granted to Daniel House in 1807, but he promptly sold to A.T. Grant in March of the following year. The deed described the property at that time, which included a "house erected on the aforesaid lot 16 by 20 feet ... one half of the road in front of aforesaid lot is cleared" (AO RG1-C-IV, #1097). This description need not be take too literally for it simply indicated that the minimal improvements required had been met, as prescribed by the 1798 settlement duties.

When William Custead made his purchase, he was identified in the deed as a shoemaker from the township of Willoughby, Lincoln County, Upper Canada (now part of the city of Niagara Falls). Lots adjacent to his were settled when he arrived, and one of the deeds to these properties mentioned that there was a good road for travellers "North of the Lot" (AO RG1-C-IV Township Papers). The road in front of the lots was Dundas Street, the main route from York to Dundas laid out by Governor Simcoe in 1793. In 1827, the year Custead published his catalogue, a vivid description of travel conditions along this road was given by Mrs Margaret Hall in her letters home to England (NA MG24 H13). Approaching York from the west she found that "for six miles [the road] was through forest as before and bad enough but when we came into more open country it was worse, over logs without any earth whatsoever over them with occasional gaps between the logs big enough for a horse to break a leg in ... we had twenty miles of this before we reached York." Ten years later Anna Jameson declared that it was still a "very rough road for a carriage, but a most delightful ride" (Jameson 1838/1972 2:7).

The land purchased by Custead would have been a good choice for a nursery. It slopes gently toward Lake Ontario, with a favourable southeasterly exposure. The climate is tempered by the nearness of that expanse of water only four kilometres away. A stream ran through the property from half-way north on the west side to the southeast corner. In his "Prefatory" to the catalogue, Custead described how the nursery began as a result of his frustration in finding plant material he wanted for his land and the difficulties he had with existing sources which lacked proper nomenclature. He assured his customers that every attempt would be made to identify his plants correctly. He explained how he began his nursery by raising "a few trees" for his own use, and finding this to be an enjoyable task, he expanded his efforts to become a nurseryman. He acknowledged the contributions of his patrons who supplied plants and seeds "which perhaps he could not otherwise have obtained" and stated that he would be personally accountable for any mistakes made in the nomenclature of the plants he supplied.

From the time Custead purchased the Dundas Street property until the publication of the catalogue, a period of sixteen years, he created a nursery in which there were nearly 20,000 apple trees, many varieties of pear, plum, cherry, peach, and nectarine trees, and a quantity of small fruits including grapes, currants, gooseberries, raspberries, and strawberries. He also grew ornamental trees and shrubs, perennial garden flowers, herbs, and greenhouse plants. He could supply seeds for herbs, annual flowers, and "esculent" or edible vegetables.

The prices charged for nursery-grown stock ranged from 7 1/2d for most selections to 2s to 5s for rare dahlias. Bulbs were priced between 7 1/2d for common sorts to over two pounds for greenhouse species. Woody plants, shrubs, and trees varied from 1s 3d to 2s 6d. Greenhouse plants were considerably more expensive because of their rarity and the careful cultivation required. Most were priced between 2s and 4s, but prized kinds of roses cost as much as 7s 6d. (There were no prices supplied for seeds.) To compare these prices to those of other merchandise, the average cost of a pound of butter in 1827 was 1s 2d, about the same as an apple tree; a barrel of flour cost between 13s and 16s.

Custead's sources of plant material were diversified. The fruit trees he grew were "approved" varieties from England and the United States. He referred more than once to his prices being the same or cheaper than those charged in New York. His repeated reference to New York encourages the thought that this was a market he was familiar with, and that his sources were primarily American. He stated that the bulbous plants "have been ordered from New York and will be for sale as soon as they can be increased." At this time nearly all the flowering bulbs offered for sale originated in the Low Countries in Europe, and Custead's supply would have been obtained from New York importers. The duties and shipping charges through American routes to Upper Canada were probably more advantageous than through the Montreal/St Lawrence corridor. Upper Canada merchants complained frequently of the high costs of importing goods through Montreal merchants because of high freight charges and import duties.

The routes from New York to central Canada were well established by the 1820s. Sixteen steamboats operated between New York and Albany on the Hudson River in 1816, and stagecoach lines ran on both sides of the river in winter. In 1817 the ground was broken for the Erie Canal, and in 1825 the canal was opened for traffic. It was an instant success: during the first year up to fifty boats a day were recorded leaving Albany for the western part of the state. Goods moved in both directions along the canal, opening the markets of New York City to producers and consumers in the western parts of the state and in Upper Canada.

American merchants quickly took advantage of this route to export their merchandise into Upper Canada. Nurseries such as the Prince Nursery of Long Island placed their catalogues with agents in towns in the York-Niagara area and advertised in local newspapers. The catalogues and advertisements began with a list of fruit trees, for these were in great demand in early settlements; apple trees were particularly sought after. As most of the crop was used in making cider, the quality of the fruit was not a vital consideration. It was at this time, from about 1800 until 1828, that Jonathan Chapman, better known as Johnny Appleseed, obtained apple seeds from the pomace of cider mills in the east and distributed them from Pennsylvania to Indiana. The seeds were given to settlers who would promise to grow and care for orchards. The resultant trees were diversified, as apple seeds do not reproduce their parent trees. Only a few seedling trees were eventually to become desirable varieties.

Growing fruit trees had developed into a business of some proportion by the 1830s in western New York State. The first commercial orchard in that part of the state was established in 1827 on Grand Island in the Niagara River (Hedrick 1950:238). Customs records show many barrels of apples imported into Upper Canada in this period. A number of these American orchards also exported apple trees, on which a duty of 15 per cent was imposed. There is no record of duties being charged on scions for grafting, however, and growers in Upper Canada, such as Custead, may have received many of their fruit varieties in that form from the United States. In May 1801, an advertisement in the *Upper Canada Gazette* offered fruit trees for sale "grafted from the best fruit of Mr. Prince's garden Long Island" (Crawford 1985:30). The advertisement reveals that grafting was in practice very early and that grafted varieties from Prince's nursery were held in high esteem. Itinerant grafters travelled the countryside each spring, offering their services and supplying scions of the better varieties to graft on hardy rootstock. In the *Gore Gazette*, Ancaster, 17 March 1827, an advertisement announced:

Philip Peaslee informs the public that he is now on his annual journey for the purpose of grafting orchard Trees, that he has with him a fine selection of Grafts; plums, pears, cherries and apples, and that he is ready to wait on any one who may require his services, upon his usual terms.

In the early nineteenth century many of the named varieties originated as seedlings selected for their "improved" qualities. The famed McIntosh apple, which presently forms a large part of the apple trade, was one such seedling found growing on a farm in eastern Upper Canada in 1795 and named for its grower. All the McIntosh apple trees in the world are descended from scions taken from this one tree.

In the Toronto Nursery catalogue, Custead made the point that all his fruit trees were "inoculated" (budded) or grafted with named varieties. By doing so, he demonstrated his professionalism in recognizing the desirability of improved stock and the most approved way of accomplishing this end. The catalogue claimed to have 20,000 fruit trees for sale.

But the nursery was not without competition. John Boardman, a nurseryman from Rochester, New York, wanted to bring fruit trees into Upper Canada duty free. He addressed a petition to Lieutenant-Governor Peregrine Maitland, and on the advice of Inspector-General James Baby, and in doing so confirmed the existence of Custead's nursery and the absence of other suppliers in Upper Canada. The letter was dated 19 November 1827, the same year as the publication of the Toronto Nursery catalogue:

By advice of the Honorable James Baba [sic] and other Gentlemen of distinction in the Province, I am induced to petition your honor for the priviledge [sic] of transporting to and introducing into your Province of Upper Canada free of duty, Fruit trees of the most choice collections principally apple trees all of which are ingrafted and warranted (to the satisfaction of all purchasers) to be genuine & of the very kinds I represent them to be, being selected from the best gardens & orchards both of Europe and America which I am now cultivating in the State of N. York near Rochester. And I do further petition for a remittance of such duties as have been required of me of 15 per cent in this place and also for a quantity of fruit trees landed at Port Hope the duties of which is suspended by the Customs House officer of this place until a decision of your Honor ... all men with whom I have consulted on the subject (which have been many) when considering the scarcity of that article in the Province & knowing the other side of the Lake to be more congenial to the growth of the young plant until suitable size for transplanting for an Orchard. And Sir permit me to solicit your Honor to consider that there is no flourishing or extensive establishment of this kind in the Province notwithstanding the country has been so long settled. Mr. Costard [sic] of Toronto a few miles distant has a small establishment of the kind which is the only one of any note and I do presume to say he has not half enough at this late period to supply a township ... An immediate answer to this I humbly ask ... [signed] John Boardman (NA RG16 A-1 353).

The note on the back of the document reads "cannot be acceded [sic] to Contrary to Law."

Seeds for annual flowers, herbs, and vegetables were available from a number of sources in 1827. Seedsmen in Great Britain and the European continent exported garden seeds to America through agents in the larger cities. One of the first seed-raising enterprises in America was begun in 1780 by the United Society of Believers, better known as the Shakers. The business was well established by 1800 and continued to grow to its peak in 1879. Members of the society travelled the countryside, leaving seeds with merchants as agents in small towns. The merchants in turn placed advertisements such as the following in local newspapers:

Garden Seeds for Sale
By the subscribers at the Niagara Apothecary Store a quantity of FRESH GARDEN SEEDS of all descriptions; put up by the Shakers in New Lebanon, New York, and warranted of the growth of 1825. Starkwather & Brown, Niagara (*Colonial Advocate*, 18 March 1826).

A later advertisement:

FRESH SEED
Shaker's Garden Seeds of 1827
Flower and Clover Seeds for sale by
E. Lesslie & Sons, York (*Canadian Freeman*, 19 March 1828).

The seeds offered by the Shakers were for useful plants, herbs and vegetables rather than ornamentals, as their religious convictions did not permit frivolity. The seeds had the reputation of being "the best to be had in America" (Hedrick 1950:205). Part of the Shakers' success was their insistence that all unsold seeds were to be removed from sale at the end of each season, ensuring a fresh supply at the beginning of the following year. The Shakers are recognized as being the first seedsmen to put seeds in paper packets; prior to packaging, seeds were sold by weight or volume, taken from bulk containers that permitted contamination and encouraged deterioration through exposure to insects and fungus growth.

It was a general practice for seeds to be saved from year to year. Some professional gardeners began their own seed businesses in Upper Canada in competition with the importers:

GARDEN SEEDS
William Adam, Gardener and Seeds man
Thankful for past favours, respectfully informs his customers and the public in general, that he has for sale
A choice selection of Garden Seeds
of the growth of 1826, saved by his own hand and warranted, as usual, of true kinds and good quality, which he offers on reasonable terms. He has likewise forwarded Seeds to Kingston, Port Hope and Dundas, which may be had at the Store of Mr. Noble Palmer, Druggist, Kingston; at the Store of Mr. D. Smart, Port Hope; and at the Store of Mr. J. Patterson, Dundas.
N.B. He will be in readiness to attend to his customers at his Seed shop opposite Mr. G. Munro's Store, where a catalogue of the Seeds may be seen. York (*Canadian Freeman* 2, no. 42, 14 March 1827).

By 1827 several American seedsmen had established successful enterprises around the cities of Philadelphia, New York, and Boston, marketing both imported and domestic-grown seed. In Philadelphia, the Landreths, father and son, founded a business in 1784, followed by Bernard M'Mahon in 1802. Grant Thorburn had his seed house in New York by 1805, and Joseph Breck was established in Boston by 1818. These major seed houses offered most of their seeds in packages priced at five or six cents each. Unfortunately Custead did not list the prices of seeds in his catalogue for comparison.

Custead invited his clients to visit his nursery and select their choices of stock in person. For those in the vicinity of York, he offered a service in planting the trees and insuring their viability for a limited time. For customers living at a distance, he established agents in Richmond Hill, Gwillimbury, Esquesing, Dundas, Niagara, Queenston, Cobourg, Port Hope, Waterloo, Oxford, and Lewiston. These agents, most of whom were merchants, could supply catalogues and take orders. However, clients dealing with the agents were expected to have a reference in York who "could be responsible for the payment." Plants were to be delivered carefully packaged in boxes or matts, each kind "kept by itself, tied together and carefully labelled." While a small additional charge would be made for such shipping, Custead insisted his prices would be found to be up to one third less than nurseries in New York. He informed his customers that they could transplant fruit trees in the spring "as soon as the frost was out of the ground, which often happens before the snow is quite gone"; thus "persons in the new settlements [could] have the opportunity of bringing out produce and returning with fruit trees before the roads break up."

Custead was willing to barter with new settlers in return for nursery stock, which suggests he also was a dealer in farm produce. It was common practice at this time, when specie was in short supply, for merchants to exchange one sort of goods for another. In this manner many country items found their way to manufacturers: feathers and horsehair, for example, were collected by agents and shipped to distributors for use in making mattresses and upholstered furniture. In 1836 Custead, with others, petitioned for a title to property on the waterfront in the city of Toronto for the Farmers' Storehouse Company, which had been operating a warehouse on the site since 1824 (NA RG1 Land Book S: 33). No details about the operations of this company could be found, but it is likely it was a clearing house for farm products.

In the years between 1836 and 1838 Custead gradually sold off parcels of his Dundas Street property and left the country. These years were trying times in Upper Canada, for the political struggle between the Reformers and the establishment was not restricted to governmental debates. The conflict reached into personal life, and harassment of Reformers and their sympathizers was rampant in the area around Toronto. Several of Custead's agents and his associates in the Farmers' Storehouse Company were known Reformers, and Custead himself may have had Reform leanings.

In a deed dated 1836, Custead and his wife, Elizabeth, sold 1 1/6 acres to John Hunt. In 1837 the southern half of the lot was sold to John Barnhart. This piece of land was probably the prime nursery area on the property, as a newspaper advertisement in the same year named Barnhart as the owner of the Toronto Nursery. The 1837 deed identified Custead and his wife as residents of the Township of Cleveland, Cayahoga County, of the State of Ohio, "one of the United States of America." In this deed Custead is recorded as a nurseryman. In 1837 and 1838 two more deeds record the final sales of Custead's holdings in Toronto Township.

The 1838 deed referred to Custead as a horticulturist of Cleveland. If it seems strange today that Custead the shoemaker could become Custead the horticulturist, it must be remembered that there were many self-made men in the early nineteenth century. The most remarkable contribution to the knowledge of American flora in the eighteenth century was the work of a farmer, John Bartram, and one of the most outstanding botanists of the day was Thomas Nuttall, who began his career as a printer's devil.

A new catalogue for the Toronto Nursery published in 1837 identified a Charles Barnhart as the proprietor. In 1842 another Toronto Nursery was opened by George Leslie on King Street East (also known as Kingston Road) in the city of Toronto. Leslie had been one of the first members of the Toronto Horticultural Society, founded in 1834. There does not appear to be any link between Leslie's nursery and that of Custead or Barnhart. During the 1840s Charles Barnhart began selling parts of his land, and there are no further references to a nursery on this site.

The Toronto Nursery Catalogue

The 1827 Toronto Nursery catalogue is reprinted here in its entirety. In his "Prefatory Remarks" nurseryman William Custead puts forth the history of his enterprise, declares his intention to satisfy his customers, and outlines the means by which he proposes to provide service and advice. Some of the personality of the man comes through his writing: his enthusiasm, his ambitious goals, and his desire to share his knowledge and experience.

The plants and seeds to be supplied by the nursery are listed under headings according to the nature of the plants: fruit trees, ornamental trees and shrubs, biennials and perennials, vegetables, herbs, and annuals.

Identifying the plants named in the Toronto Nursery catalogue involved translating Custead's common names into the Latin nomenclature of the early nineteenth century and bringing it up to date. Common names for plants differ from time to time and from place to place, and thus are generally not a reliable identification. With changes in the Latin nomenclature as well, many plants have acquired a number of synonyms in both their common and Latin names. Fortunately contemporary British and American sources are available to compare with and confirm Custead's nomenclature.

Linnaeus's work in the eighteenth century on classification of the natural world eventually came to be the accepted system in botany. The botanists who studied the innumerable plants introduced by global exploration placed them in this scheme. Oftentimes a single plant received more than one scientific name as botanists working in different places or seeing a plant at a different stage of its growth named a plant already identified by another botanist. Many initial identifications, made from herbariums (dried examples) or from plants that were not in a flowering phase were understandably inaccurate. Species names were given to plants in recognition of their origin, particular characteristics, and uses, or to honour a scientist or public figure. Names of plants from foreign places were sometimes given an angli-cized form of the name assigned to them in their native environment. With such confusion in methods of nomenclature, Custead was not alone in his criticism of suppliers who did not correctly identify their plants.

In this work the current nomenclature is taken from the Royal Horticul-tural Society's *Index of Garden Plants*, published in 1994. Each Latin desig-nation is accompanied by an abbreviation of the name of the person who made the identification; for example, plant names given by Linnaeus will be followed by L., and those by Miller, Mill. The present philosophy of nomenclature is to give a plant the name first assigned to it, if that name correctly fits the criteria for the genus.

In recent years more scientific tools and knowledge have become avail-able, not the least of which are the electron microscope and the discovery of the DNA molecule. The classification of plants, the work of the taxono-mist, has become increasingly complex. Genetic work on plants has also been valuable in the development of economic plants such as grains and food crops, and the new field of genetic engineering will bring even more changes in the future. Some have already been so dramatic that the need for gene banks of original species has become critical. A plant list from the early nineteenth century, such as the Toronto Nursery catalogue provides, helps to identify species and varieties available in Upper Canada before extensive hybridization took place. It also reflects the desires and tastes of the period – a part of our cultural heritage.

CATALOGUE

OF

FRUIT & ORNAMENTAL TREES,

Flowering Shrubs,

GARDEN SEEDS AND GREEN-HOUSE PLANTS,
BULBOUS ROOTS & FLOWER SEEDS,

CULTIVATED AND FOR SALE AT THE

TORONTO NURSERY,

Dundas Street, near York,

BY

WILLIAM W. CUSTEAD.

YORK:
Printed by William Lyon Mackenzie, Printer to the House of Assembly.

1827.

Agents for receiving orders.

MR. JESSE KETCHUM.............. *York.*
MR. BENJAMIN BARNARD......... *Richmond Hill.*
MR. GEORGE LOUNT.............. *Gwillimsbury.*
MR. STEVENS.................... *Esquesing.*
MESSRS. LESSLIE & SONS........ *Dundas.*
MR. JAMES CRYSLER, (Merchant) *Niagara.*
MR WYNN....................... *Queenston.*
MR. JONES .... *Near Cobourg.*
MR. JOHN SMITH .... *Port Hope.*
MR.   .... *Guelph.*
MR. ABRAHAM ERB.............. *Waterloo.*
MR. CHARLES INGORSOLL,....... *Oxford.*
MR. LEMING,................... *Lewiston.*

PREFATORY REMARKS.

THIS establishment was commenced in 1811 by the proprietor's raising a few trees for his own use, and would perhaps never have been thought of, had there not been such a difficulty in obtaining good kinds by purchase.

Finding his efforts crowned with success and the business delightful, he resolved to extend his nursery, and devote the most part of his time to it, not only from a consideration of the pleasure and advantage he might himself derive, but also from a desire of placing the bountiful gifts of nature within the reach of his friends and neighbours.

It will be seen by the catalogue, that my greatest attention has hitherto been paid to apple trees, because I considered the apple the most congenial fruit to this climate, and the most useful in new countries : there is now in the nursery nearly 20,000 apple trees, the greater part of which are grafted or inoculated with the best and most approved European and American kinds, and are from one to seven years old, and from one to nine feet high. Gentlemen by calling at the nursery can select for themselves---no difference is made in price on account of age or size.

The nursery business is attended with difficulties and disappointments which ought carefully to be guarded against ; mistakes are often made in the proper names of trees, plants &c. by the ignorant and careless, to the great mortification of the purchaser. I have been disappointed in this way myself, but the public may rest assured that the greatest care will be taken to prevent such disagreeable occurrences in this establishment, all the business is done by my own hands and I will be accountable for all mistakes of my own making, but there is one cause of disappointment with which the nursery-man has nothing to do, and for which he is often unjustly blamed. A person gets a fine apple and enquires its name---a wrong one is given, he sends to the nursery and gets trees by this wrong name---after careful culture the fruit appears, and is not what he expected : to prevent disappointments of this kind a person should be very certain that he has got the proper name of his favourite fruit, before he orders trees from the nursery.

From many experiments I am fully persuaded that the fall is the best time for transplanting fruit trees---the work may be performed any time from the middle of October until the ground freezes.

Transplanting in the spring often succeeds well also, and may be begun as soon as the frost is out of the ground, which often happens before the snow is quite gone, by which means persons in the new settlements have an opportunity of bringing out produce and returning with fruit trees, before the roads break up : spring planting may be continued to the first of May. Produce delivered at the nursery, will be taken from the new settler for trees &c. at cash prices.

The best season for removing bulbous flower roots is from July to October inclusive.

Greenhouse plants may be removed at any time when the weather is warm.

When fruit trees &c. are ordered from a distance they will be carefully packed in boxes or matts so as to arrive safe in any part of the Canadas or the adjoining states ; in this case a small additional charge will be made for package.

Every thing in my line will be delivered at York free of carriage, and every kind kept by itself, tied together, and labelled.

Scions of fruit trees for grafting packed in the most secure and portable manner at two shillings per dozen, no less than half that number can be furnished of any one kind. The prices will in no case exceed those of the nurseries at New York, and in general will be found one third less.

The proprietor has appointed agents through the country, of whom catalogues may be had, and by whom orders will be received and forwarded, it is expected that gentlemen at a distance sending orders otherwise than through an agent, will name some person in York who will be responsible for the payment.

Purchasers residing in York or its vicinity or within the same distance of the nursery in any other direction, may have trees planted and insured for a limited time, on such terms as may be agreed upon, taking into consideration the number of trees wanted and the distance from the nursery.

An allowance equal to ten per cent will be made to those who purchase by the quantity at the nursery.

Very considerable additions have been lately made to this establishment by importations from some of the foremost nurseries and seed shops in the United States and in England, and it
is intended that neither pains nor cost shall be spared in making
annual additions of such trees, shrubs, plants &c. either ornamental or useful as may best agree with our climate.

The proprietor embraces with pleasure the present opportunity of returning his thanks to those gentlemen who have fostered
his establishment by presents of plants, seeds, &c. which perhaps he could not otherwise have obtained: to his customers he
is grateful for former favours, and hopes to render his nursery
still more worthy of *public patronage*.

WILLIAM W. CUSTEAD.

DIRECTIONS FOR PLANTING FRUIT TREES.

In planting out trees, let the hole be dug sufficiently large to
admit the roots in their natural position; particular attention
should be paid, that all the wounded parts of the roots are cut
off; if a hard marly soil, it would be advisable to have the hole
much larger than is required to receive the roots. Then fill in
good earth from the surface up to the proper height. Before
introducing the tree especially if tall it is advisable to drive down
a stake, placing the tree close to it on the north east side to
which let the tree be securely tied after planting. Care must
be observed not to plant the trees too deep; the upper roots
when planted, should have about three inches of earth over
them, which will generally make it about two inches deeper
than it stood in the nursery. Fill in the hole with rich mould,
and if required, some well rotted manure. After covering the
roots, shake the tree, that the earth may be admitted among
all the small roots; then fill up, treading round the tree, leaving
a basin round it to conduct the water to the roots. In dry seasons, watering will be of service: the head of the tree should
be cut off in proportion to the size, say one third though not
until May. Much of their doing well depends upon attending
to this.

I would recommend to those planting out young trees, to
keep the ground cultivated for a few years in succession. From
observation, I have found that trees thrive much better in cultivated ground, than if planted in grass or uncultivated: a few

years, say four or five, of cultivation, will richly pay the plan-
ter. as the trees in that time will generally get in a thrifty growing state : after which they will only require ordinary care.---
Experience has proved the utility of soft soap to trees, and I
highly recommend the washing of the bodies and branches, as
high as can be conveniently got at, of all sorts of fruit trees.---
The soap may be diluted with water, to the consistency of
thick paint, and applied with a brush. The effect is very evident, making the bark smooth and pliable, trees thrifty, destroying any small insects that may be feeding on the sap, to
which the apple and the pear tree are particularly subject.

DIRECTIONS TO PRESERVE PEACH TREES IN A HEALTHY STATE.

Let every tree which has been known to produce its fruit
prematurely, be immediately removed ; and if it is desired to
have a peach tree planted in the same place where a diseased
tree has been removed from, let a large hole be dug, so as to
remove all the roots, that the roots of the new planted tree
may not, in one season, come in contact with them. But new
ground is to be taken, in preference to that on which peach
trees have been. Let the greatest attention in summer, be paid
to the ripening of the fruit, and where fruit is found to ripen
two, three or four weeks before the usual time, you may con-
clude that the tree has taken the infection ; and as it gives you
notice one whole season previous to its power of spreading the
contagion, you can, by removing it, prevent its injuring the other trees ; or if the tree has taken the infection when in blossom,
and has lost its fruit before it ripened, it will show that it has
become diseased, by pushing out small slender shoots, and frequently in bunches of a pale yellow colour, from the body and
branches ; and by observing the same appearance on those
trees that have ripened their fruit prematurely, you will soon
be able to distinguish the trees that are diseased, from those
which are in a healthy state, and by removing them before they
blossom, prevent their spreading the infected farina.
Ashes and lime, a small quantity placed as near the trunk of
the tree as possible, have been used with good effect, in preventing and destroying the worms at the roots of peach trees. Tobacco leaves and stems, put round the trunks of peach trees

at the roots, have also been found beneficial in destroying the worms, as well as preventing their getting in the trees.

To have thrifty peach trees, and fine fruit, the ground should every year be kept cultivated, by planting it with corn, potatoes, or other vegetables, and every autumn or spring, have some rotten manure dug in round the trees. Peach trees remaining more than one year in grass or sod ground, become unthrifty and yellow, it is therefore easier to distinguish the diseased from healthy, in cultivated ground.

N. B. To those that order fruit trees &c. who are not acquainted with the different sorts of fruits by name, I would recommend that their orders specify the number of the different species of trees wanted, and leave the selection to me, as in all such cases I should feel myself bound to send none but what I know to be of approved sorts, and that ripen in succession, or as may be requested.

CATALOGUE.

APPLE TREES,
1s. 3d. each except otherwise marked.

No.	when ripe.	No.	when ripe.
1 Yellow Harvest--July&Aug.		27 Proud Pippin,	do.
2 Small Early,	do.	The fruit of the 2 last will keep	
3*Early Red Streak,	do.	from Oct. to Jany.	
4 Coult's Early,	do.	28 Land's Fine Yellow,	Oct.
5*Juneting,	do.	29 Small's Russet,	do.
6 Early Sweet Bough,	do.	30 Winter Codlin, large,	do.
7 Sweet Pippin,	Sept.	31 Black Vandevere, fine flavor	
8 Gaitzor, very soft and a		32*English Crab,	Oct.
great bearer,	do.	33*Wine Apple,	do.
9 English Codlin,	Oct.	The last 6 will keep from Oct.	
10 Yellow Pippin, very fine		to February,	
cooking apple,	do.	34†Seedless Pippin,	Oct.
11 None Such,	do.	35 Red Streak Vandevere,	do.
12 Summer Sweeting, large &		36†Hertfordshire Red Streak,	
fine,	do.	37†Seek no Further,	do.
13*Mammoth Apple,	do.	38†Harrison's Apple	do.
14*Lemon or Orange Pippin	do.	39†Bell Flower,	do.
15*Large fair soft & white,	do.	Last 6 will keep from Oct. to	
16*Large Green Streaked,	do.	March.	
17*Large Green Sweet,	do.	40 Ribston's Stone Pippin,	Oct.
[15, 16 & 17 are very fine fruits		41 King Apple,	do.
from Mr. Cooper's famous		42 May Bloom,	do.
Orchard, not having the pro-		43 Queen's Apple,	do.
per names at present I have		44 Nonpareil,	do.
given this description.]		45 Davenport Gooseberry,	do.
18 Large Fall Pippin,	Oct.	Last 6 will keep from Oct. to	
19 Farmer's Profit,	do.	April.	
20 Spitzenburgh Yellow,	do.	46†English Pearmain,	do.
21 Holland Pippin,	do.	47 Bambo or Romanites, very	
22*Rose Apple,	do.	fine,	do.
23*Russet, large and fine,	do.	48 Spitzenburgh Red,	do.
24 White Russet,	do.	49 Barussau's Apple from L. C.	
25 McKay's Apple, fine,	do.	50 Winter Pearmain,	Oct.
26 Snow Apple,	do.	51 Red Pippin,	do.

No.   when ripe.
52 Spitzenburgh,   Oct.
Last 4 will keep from Oct. to
  May.
53 Talman's Sweeting,   do.
54 Rhode Island Greening, do.
55‡Black Apple,   do.
56‡Jelly Flower Apple,   do.
Last 4 will keep from Oct.
  to June.
57‡Green Everlasting,   do.
58‡Red Everlasting,   do.
59‡Millar's Long Keeping, do.
It is said these last 3 will keep
  a year.
60 Golden Pippin,   Oct.
61 French Crab,   do.
62†English Russeting,   do.
63 Hopkin's New Sown Pippin,
64 Phœnix Apple,   Oct.
65 Small's Best Keeping, do.
66‡Golden Russeting,   do.
67‡Green New Sown Pippin,
68‡Montrous Pippin, very large
69†Yellow New Town Pippin,
70‡Cart House or Gilpin, Oct.
71‡Hugh's Virginia Crab, do.
72‡Tewksbury Winter Blush,
Last 13 will keep from Oct. to
  June.
73‡Pennock's large Red Winter, will keep from Nov. to
  April.
74‡Wine Sap, keep from Oct.
  to January,
75 Paradise Apple, very dwarf,
  fruit of no estimation.
76 Siberian Crab,
77 Cherry Crab-----these are
  both ornamental and useful,
  valuable for preserves.
78‡Paradise Apple---tree small,
  fruit large and fair---price 2s.

No.   when ripe.
79 Double Flowering Chinese--
  said to be the most beautiful
  of flowering trees---price 2s.
  Several choice varieties of the
Apple will be cultivated on Paradise stocks for dwarfs or espaliers at 2s. each.

PEAR TREES.
1s. 10d. each except otherwise
         marked.
1 Early Musk,   July.
2‡Chaumontelle M.   August.
3 Jargonelle M.   do..
4‡Cuisse Madame M.   Sept.
5 Summer Bon Cretion, Aug.
6 Skinless M.   do.
7‡Early Catharine,   do.
8 Great Mouthwater M. Sept.
9 Late Catharine M.   do.
10‡English Red Cheek M do.
11 Large Bell M. (fine)   do.
12 Red Butter Pear M.   do.
13‡Seekle Pear,   Oct.
14‡Cap Sheaf M.   do.
15 Cresane M.   Decr.
16 Rushmore M.   do.
17 Colmar M.   Decr. & Jan.
18 King's Bon Cretion M. fm.
  Decr. to March.
19 Vergalue, M.   Oct.
20 St. Germain M. fm. Decr.
  to April.
21 Pound Pear B.   Decr.
22 Winter Bon Cretion B. fm.
  Jan'y to April.
23‡Orange Red,   Augu
24‡Green Chissel M.   do.
25 Small Bergamot,   Oct.
  A few choice varieties of the
above will be propagated on
Quince stocks at 2s. 6d.

M. signifies melting pears. | No.   when ripe.
B.   baking do. | 6 Ox Heart,   do.

PLUMS.

At 2s. each except otherwise
marked.

No.   when ripe.
1*Early Scarlet or Myrobo-
lans S.   July.
2 Yellow Gage S.   August.
3*Purple Gage S. do. & Sept.
4*New Green, or Flushing
Gage L & S. 3s. 9d.   do.
5 Red Orleans L.   do.
6 Little Black Denmark S. do.
7*Bolmar's Washington,
L & S. 3s. 9.   Sept.
8*Smith's Orleans L & S. do.
9*Drap's D'or, or cloth of
Gold S.   do.
10 Yellow Egg or White
Magnum Bonum L.   do.
11*Cooke's Large, double the
size of the Egg Plum,   do,
12*Fotheringham,   do.
13 St. Catharine,   do.
14*Cooper's Large Red,   do.
15 Large Blue,   do.
16*Green Gage S.   do.
17 Red Magnum Bonum L. do.
L signifies large.
S superior flavour.
L & S large size and superior
flavour.

CHERRIES.

2s. 6d. each except otherwise
marked.

1 May Duke,   June.
2. White Heart,   do,
3 Black Heart,   do.
4 Carnation,   do.
5 Kentish,   1s. 3d.   do.

PEACHES.

1s. 3d. each.
1 Red Rare Ripe,   August.
2 White Rare Ripe,   do.
3 Yellow or Red Cheek
Malagatune,   do.
4 Columbia,   do.
5 Old Newington, cling   do.
6 Noblesse,   [stone. do.
7 Lemon Peach,   do.
8 York Toland   do.
9 Orange, cling stone.   do.

NECTARINES.

1s. 3d. each.
1 Early Yellow,   Sept.
2 Temple,   do.
I would recommend that
Peaches and Nectarines be
planted in a dry and sheltered
situation, and by no means in a
rich soil---My Peaches and Nectarines will not be fit for transplanting until the fall of 1828.

GRAPES.

1†Early White,   price 1s. 9d.
2†Boston Sweet Water, do.
3 Bland's Virginia,   do.
4†Isabella Grape,   do.
5 White's Sweet Water, 1s. 3d
6 Jersey Grape,   do.
7†Black Frontenac,   1s. 9d.
8 French Chocolate,   2s. 6d.
Grapes require an open sunny
situation and some protection in the winter.

CURRANTS.

1s. each except otherwise

marked.
1 Red,
2 White,
3 Black,
4†Large Dutch Red,   1s. 3d.
5†   do.   White,   do.
6†Large Champaigne Red, do.
7†Lewis' Fragrant,   2s.

GOOSEBERRIES.
1s. each.
1 Smooth Green,   green.
2 Rough Green,   do.
3 Green Gascoign, do.
4 Reed's Satisfaction, do.
5 Large Amber,   Red,
6 Royal Oak,   do.
7 Farmers' Glory, do.
8 Rambulion,   do.
9 Ironmonger,   do.
10 Golden Globe,   Yellow.
11 Hercules,   do.
12 Livingstone,   Large White.
Gooseberries require a deep
rich soil and regular pruning.

RASPBERRIES.
1 English White, price 7½d
2 English Red,   6d
3 Large White Antwerp, 1s.
each or 7s. 6d. per dozen.

STRAWBERRIES.
1 Hautboy, price 1s. per doz.
2†Large Hudson, do. do. do.
3†Alpin Monthly, 2s. per do.

ORNAMENTAL TREES.
1s. each.
1 Lombardy Poplar,
2 Yellow or Ship Locust,
3 Black Walnut,
4 Honey Locust or 3 thorned

Acacia,
5 Glutinous Acacia or Italian
Locust,
6 American Chesnut,
7 Horse Chesnut,
8 New England Walnut, or
Hickory,
9 Mountain Sole,
10 Yellow Willow,
11 Sleeping Willow,   1s. 3d.
12 Catalpha,   do.

FLOWERING SHRUBS.
1s. each.
1 European Syrango,
2 Hypericum Frutex.
3 Snowy Medlar,
4 English Linden,
5 Large Cole Nut,
6 English Filbert—these last
two are good and produc-
tive Nuts,
7 Cranberry Tree or Moun-
tain Viburnum,
8 Candleberry Myrtle,
9†Red double flowering Althea Frutex,   1s. 3d.
10†Single Red   do.   1s.
11†Single White do.   do.
12 Snow Ball or Gilder Rose,
1s. 3d.
13 Purple Lilac,   1s.
14 White do.   do.
15†Purple Persian Lilac, 2s.
16 Brown Flowering Caly-
canthus,   do.
17 Calycanthus or sweet scented shrub,   1s. 3d.
18†English Passion Flower, 2s.
19 Bladder Sena,   1s.
20†Mezerion,   do.
21†Cletha,   do.
Barberry,

22 Strawberry Tree, 1s.
23 Scarlet trumpet flowering Creeper, do.
24 Laburnam, do.
25 Red berried spindle tree do.
26 Pyracantha or Ever
Green Thorn, do.
27†Double flowering Al-
mond do.
28 Venitian Sumack 1s. 3d.
29†European Hawthorn, do.
30†St. John's Wort, 1s.
31 French Tamarisk, do.
32 Southern Wood, do.
33 English Nightshade, do.
34 Periwinkle or ever Green
Myrtle, do.
35 Rose Acacia, do.
36 New Jersey Tea. 2s.

HONEYSUCKLES.

Early sweet Italian,
English White,
Scarlet Monthly Trumpet,
English Woodbine,
Striped Monthly,
Variegated leaved.

BIENNIALS & PERRENNIALS,
Ornamental and useful.
Price 7½d each, except
otherwise marked.
Double crimson Peony,
Tart Rhubarb, 2s.
†Turkey Rhubarb, do.
Leeks,
Shallots & Scives,
Hops,
Sage,
Wormwood,
Hyssop.
Purple Perrennial Convolvo-
lus,
Dyers' Madder,

Italian Spiderwort
Purple Fox Glove,
White Fox Glove,
Tarragon,
Chamomile,
Rose Campion,
Black Antwerp Holyhock,
Double Yellow, do.
Double Chinese, do.
Snap Dragon,
Double Columbine, 5 varie-
ties.
Caledonian Thistle.
Blue Canterbury bell purple.
White do. do.
Ribband Grass.
Wall Flower,
†Sweet scented Virgin's Bow-
er, 2s.
†Virginian, do. 1s.
†Traveller's Joy, 2s.
†Dahlies from 2s. to 5s.
Pinks, Fine, Double, Various
Colours 1s.
Broad Leaved,
Pheasant eyed,
Chinese,
†Clove,
†French Honeysuckle,
Sweet Rocket,
Moss Pink,
Everlasting Pea,
Scarlet Lychnis,
†Scarlet Cardinal Flower,
Blackberry Lily,
Iris, or Flower De Luce,
large Purple German.
—— Dwarf Purple,
Polyanthus, many varieties,
1 shilling,
Cowslip,
English Daisy,
†English Primrose,

†White Sophora, 1s.
†Blue do.   do.
White Broom,
Yellow do.

RUE.

Asparagus, 5s. per hundred,
Capus Spurge,
Crimson Menardi,
Maryland Cassa.

ROSES.

†Moss Rose,	5s.
†Rosa Multifloræ or Garland,	2s.
Thornless,	1s. 3d.
Burgundy,	1s.
Double Velvet,	1s. 6d.
Red Damask,	do.
Copper Coloured,	do.
Cabbage Rose,	do.
†Rosa Mundi varigated,	1s. 3.
†Hundred Leaved,	do.
Large Provence,	do.
Rose of Sharon,	2s.
White Monthly,	3s. 9d.
Crimson Dwarf,	1s.
Maidens' Blush,	do.
Portland Rose,	do.
Large Crimson,	1s. 3d.
†Mottled Rose,	do.
†Michigan Rose,	do.
Single White do.	do.
Double do. do.	do.
Sweet Briar, do.	1s.

BULBOUS ROOTS.

TULIPS.

Briggette---Bizarre.	1s. 3d.
Queen of England---Rosy and White,	4s.
Duke of Richmond---Bizarre,	1s. 3d.

Chailon New--Bizarre,	1s. 3d.
Perfecta---Parrot,	2s.
Yellow Crown,	1s. 9d.
Pain d'Epice,	1s. 3d.
Dw Van Toll---dble.	do.
Duc de Bouflers' Bibloem,	do.
Prince Kaiel---dble.	2s.
Queen of the Moors--Bib :	2/6
Violette ma fovorite	3s.
Grand Tamerlane--Bib :	1/3
Prosperine---dble.	2s.
Blanc Corde bleu--dble.	1/3
Courone d' Or--dble.	do.
Rose Agatha,	4s.
Duc d'Holstien, early.	1s. 3d.
Adml. Kingsbergin--dble.	2s
Yellow Rose---dble.	1s. 3d.
Claremond---early	do.
Prince Maurity--Bib :	do.
Grand Alexander--dble.	1/6
Tucarnate grisdelin--dble.	1/3
La Fidelle---dble.	1s. 3d.

This assortment of Fine Tulips in 25 varieties may be had for 40s. being less than the N. York prices for the same.

HYACINTHS.

Passe tout blue.	1s. 3d.
Prince Henri de Prussia blue	2s
La Rosse Blue,	1s. 9d.
Duc de Berri Yellow,	do.
Phœnix Red,	do.
La Fidelle Red,	1s. 6d.
Rose Sarre Red,	
Rose Surpassant Pink,	1s. 3d.
Nannette White,	1s. 9d.
Prince Wm. Frederick, white	5s
Don Gratuit, white.	1s. 9d.
Belle ferme, do.	do.

This assortment of 12 double hyacinths may be had for 20s. being less than the New York prices for the same.

NARCISSUS.

Double Narcissus--daffodil, 7½d
  do. Orange Phœnix, do.
  do. Albo pleno oderato, do.

LILIES.

White Lily,   7½d.
Yellow day Lily,   1s.
Sword Lily,   7½d.
Lily of the Valley,   7½d.
†Martigon or Turk's cap, 1s.
Jonquils, from 7½d. to 1s.
†Amaryllis in sorts, do. do.
†Rannunculies in sorts, 1s.
†Anemonies in sorts, do.
Tube Roses double,   7½d.

GREENHOUSE PLANTS.

China ever blooming roses,
several varieties price 2/6 each.
American Century Aloe, some
varieties, price 3s.
Coloured Indian Fig, 3s. 9d.
Indian Fig,   3s. 9d.
Creeping Cereus,   3s. 9d.
Silver leaved Wormwood, 3/9
Rosemary,   2s
Chinese Chrysanthemum, 2/6
Carnations several varieties, 2s.
  to 3s. 9d.
Stock Jilly-flowers 6 varieties,
  2s. each.
Wall Flower,   2s.
Scarlet & Blush Horse Shoe
  Geraniums, 2s. each.
Silver edged, do.   3s. 9d.
Rose scented, do.   2s.
Strawberry leaved, do. 2s.
Sweet scented, do.   2s.
  Oak Leaved Geranium, 2s.
  Jerusalem Cherry,   2s.

Multiflora Rose,   2s. 6d.
Chinese Changeable
  Hydrangea,   2s. 6d.
†Guernsey Lily,
†Broad leaved Myrtle,
†Box   do.   do.
All of which will thrive in a
  comfortable sitting room du-
  ring winter, they are in ei-
  ther Pots or Boxes, and the
  prices are inclusive.

SEEDS OF ESCULENT VEGETA-
BLES, & plants in their season.
CABBAGE, Early York,
       do. Heart shaped.
    "   Savory,
    "   Drumhead,
    "   Red Dutch,
CELERY, White Solid,
    "   Rose Coloured,
PARSNIPS, Hollow Crowned,
CARROTS, Early Horn,
    "   Long Orange,
    "   Blood Red,
BEETS,   Blood Red,
    "   White or scarcity,
TURNIPS, Common Field,
    "   Swedish or Rutabaga.
    "   French.
ONIONS, Red,
    "   White,
    "   Top or Tree,
LEEKS, London,
BEANS, Early Mohawk, ⎱
    "   do. Six Week, ⎰ Dwarfs.
    "   do. Dunn, ⎱
    "   do. Chince, ⎰
BEANS—Pale white or cream
      coloured,
    Purple Cranberry,
    Scarlet Runners,
    White Dutch do.

BEANS–Asparagus or y'rd long
Brussels sprouts,
   Asparagus
PEAS---Early Frame,
   do. Hotspur,
   Dwarf Green,
   Prussian Blue,
Dwarf Prolific, or Strawberry,
   Knight tall Marrow, or
   Honey pea, extra fine
   Tall Grey Sugar,
   Dwarf Sugar or White,
PARSLEY---Curled or double,
   Hamburgh or large rooted,
   Nasturtium, a fine pickle,
   Egg Plant, Purple,
   do. do. White,
   Mustard White or English,
   Cress or Pepper Grass,
   Salsify or Vegetable Oyster,
PEPPER---Long or Cayenne,
   Tanatoe Shaped,
   Cherry Shaped,
SPINAGE---Prickly or Fall,
   Round leaved,
   Sorrel English or Garden,
SQUASH---Early Bush,
   do. Crook Neck,
   Large Green do.
Tomatoe or Love Apple.
LETTUCE---Early,
   Long leaved or Cabbage,
   Ice Coos,
   Brown Dutch,
   Grand Admiral.
CUCUMBERS, Early Frame,
   "   Long Prickly,
   "   Short   "
   "   Serpentine,
MELONS, Pine Apple,
   "   Nutmeg,
   "   Paradise,
   "   Green Citron,

MELONS, Burnet,
POTATOES, English White,
   "   Some other choice
   varieties,
   Indian Corn & Grass Seeds.
RADISH, Short topt scarlet.
   "   Black fall.

POT & SWEET HERB SEEDS.

Carraway,
Marygold,
Sweet Basil,
Sweet Marjorum,
Anise,
Common Sage,
Red Sage,
Summer Savory,
Thyme,
Lemon Thyme,
Nutmeg, good substitute for
   spice,
Tarragon.

MEDICINAL HERB SEEDS.

Marsh Mallows,
Sweet Fennel,
Dill,
Saffron,
Coriander,
Purple Fox Glove,
Moldavian, or Lemon Balm.
Hyssop.
Elecampane,
Dyers' Wood,
Lovage,
Horehound,
Balm,
White Officinal Poppy,
Palma Christi,
Rue,
Virginian Speedwell.

Bene,
Comfrey.

ANNUAL FLOWER SEEDS.
Flos Adones,
Princes' Feather,
China Aster, White,
    "   "   Purple,
    "   "   Blush or Rose,
    "   "   Red striped,
    "   "   Purple striped,
    "   "   Red,
    "   "   Mixed all colors,
Sweet Sultan Purple,
    "   "   White,
Cock's Comb Red,
    "   "   Yellow,
    "   "   Crimson velvet,
Chrysanthemum White,
    "   Yellow,
Job's Tears,
Convolvolus Minor, White,
    "   "   Pale Red,
    "   Major, Purple,
    "   "   Pink,
    "   "   White,
" Blue & White striped,

Lark's Spur, large Purple,
Hyacinth Bean, Purple,
Horn Poppy,
Globe Amaranthus, Purple,
Balsamine, Fine double,
Cyprus Vine,
Sweet Peas,
Broboscis Flower,
Caterpillar's Flower,
Snail Flower,
Ice Plant,
Sensitive Plant,
Marvel of Peru,
Scarlet Flowering, Havanah Tobacco.
Love in a Mist,
Evening Primrose,
Carnation Poppy,
Scarlet Flowering Bean,
Red Persicaria,
Sweet scented Trefoil,
African Marygold,
    "   "   Orange
Quilled.
Heart's Ease.
Mexican Ximensia,

Trees and Plants marked * † ‡ throughout this Catalogue, will not be a proper size for transplanting until the Autumn of 1823.

FINIS.

Mackenzie printer

APPENDIX.

The following BULBOUS ROOTS and PLANTS are ordered from New York, and will be for sale as soon as they can be increased.

CROWN IMPERIALS.
Chapeau de Prince, yellow 1s. 3d.
Crown upon Crown, red 1s. 9d.
Sang de boeuf, 1s. 3d.
Yellow Striped, 2s. 6d.
Pileus Cardinal's, crim- son, 1s. 6d.

TURK'S CAP LILIES.
Caligula Scarlet, 1s. 6d.
Crown of Tunis, pur- ple, 1s. 3d.
Crown of Jerusalem, 2s.
Grand Duke, yellow, 1s. 6d.
King of Prussia, 1s. 3d.

AMARYLLIS.
Jacobean Lily, 1s. 10d.
Guernsey, 2s. 6d.
Atamasco, 1s. 3d.
Yellow flowering, 1s. 3d.

JONQUILS.
Double Fragrant, 1s.
Large Single, 7½d.
Small Fragrant. 7½d.

RANUNCULUS.
Orange, 1s.
Bright Crimson, do.
Bright red and pink, do.
Yellow, do.

Yellow striped, 1s.
Black, do.
Scarlet Turban. do.

ANEMONES.
Double rosy & crimsoned, 1s.
red and pink, do.
dark blue, do.
white, do.
scarlet. 1s. 3d.

CROCUSES.
Cloth of Gold, 6d.
Garland, do.
Large white, do.
yellow, do.
blue, do.
pink, do.
Slisfaction. do.

ROSES.
York and Lancaster, 3s. 9d.
Pearl of the East, do.
Striped Monthly, do.
Great Mogul, 7s. 6d.
Bromley Rose, 2s. 6d.
Rose de Pompone, 3s. 9d.
King of Rome, 9s.
Frankfort, 2s.
Unique white Provence, 7s. 6d.

To the GREEN-HOUSE list, please to add the following.

Rosa Semperflorens, palida Odorata,	3s. 9d.
Rosa Indica Rubra,	3s. 9d.
Myrtle leaved Geranium,	2s. 6d.
Balm scented,	2s. 6d.
Pennyroyal or rash leaved,	2s. 6d.
Pyrus Japonica or scarlet flowering Japan Apple,	7s. 6d.
Striped Rose Bay,	7s. 6d.
Starry Hydrangea,	2s.
Oak leaved do.	2s.
Hortensis do.	2s. 6d.
Frost Plant,	2s.
Nutmeg scented,	2s. 6d.
Balm scented.	2s. 6d.

Horticulture in the Early Nineteenth Century

The value of the Toronto Nursery catalogue cannot be adequately assessed without a brief review of horticultural history at the time it was published. The first decades of the nineteenth century evolved as a period of cultural transition between the eighteenth century's Age of Reason and the extravagant Victorian epoch. Worldwide explorations and scientific discoveries changed the manner in which the natural world was approached and fuelled the rapid development in science and technology that took place after Queen Victoria ascended the throne of the British Empire. These changes were felt by all who were involved in horticulture, for the field of botany was one of the first areas to be affected. By the 1840s gardens and gardening practices had been transformed. The early settlers in Upper Canada began their lives here during a time when the spirit of discovery was pervasive.

By the end of the eighteenth century exploration and colonization greatly expanded the world known to Europeans. Travel for the adventurous extended far beyond the Grand Tour of European cultural centres to foreign and unknown areas in the Americas, the Pacific, and the Far East. Far-flung expeditions brought new sources of minerals and natural materials to European markets, increasing the availability of exotic goods and reducing their cost. The initial incentive of finding new sources of spices expanded to include a search for new crops, fibres, foods, and sources of medicinal plants. Cultivation practices were changing as science examined the growth of plants, including the chemistry of soils and the effects of light and water on widely divergent species.

The discovery of the Americas by Europeans in search of spices had resulted in many strange and unfamiliar plants being taken back to Europe. The Spanish conquistadors in the sixteenth and seventeenth centuries were responsible for introducing the first plants from Central and South America. A number of these – notably the potato, tobacco, and maize (Indian corn) – eventually became crops of great economic value. Other introductions like the dahlia and the French marigold later became ornamental garden favourites. After proving their value in European gardens, many plants introduced by the Spaniards later re-crossed the Atlantic to be introduced to colonial gardens in eastern North America.

Members of the Society of Jesus, the Jesuits, played a major role in the introduction of exotic species. They were active in collecting plants and seeds encountered in their missionary work in the French colonies in America and in China during the seventeenth and eighteenth centuries. They sent plant and seed collections to the Jardin des Plantes in Paris, one of the outstanding botanical gardens of Europe. Subsequently, the exotic plants grown in Paris were exchanged with botanical gardens and nurserymen in other European countries. The Jesuits were also responsible for introducing European species to far-away places, for they took with them seeds of familiar farm crops, garden vegetables, and ornamentals for their mission gardens.

The British and the Dutch, world-wide trading nations during this period, took goods to Europe from Asia, the Pacific, Australia, Africa, and the Americas. Frequent traffic in the tea trade to and from India and China around the Cape of Good Hope provided the means by which large numbers of Asiatic and African plants found their way into European gardens. Many a ship's captain was entrusted with a botanical collection on the return trip to Europe. Eventually scientific organizations sponsored geographical expeditions specifically commissioned for the amassing of natural history collections. The men sent into unexplored territories were charged with the task of assessing and analysing their discoveries. Botanists were foremost in these ventures, and many returned to Europe with valuable collections. European gardens were enriched by innumerable exotic species, though more than a few collections were lost to storms, shipwrecks, and pillaging.

Shipping plants on overseas voyages often months in duration was fraught with problems. Controlling temperature, watering, and protecting plants from physical damage demanded more attention than could be expected from a ship's crew. At greatest risk were potted plants in full leaf. A few deciduous woody plants could be shipped bare-root during a dormant period, or as cuttings to be rooted or grafted later. The live plant material successfully introduced to Europe from distant parts of the globe consisted mainly of seeds and bulbs, which remained viable for long periods but often suffered from damp conditions, rot, moulds, and rodent damage during transport. These were a few of the difficulties facing a plant hunter in Custead's time. Nurseries experimented with various types of containers that a cooperative ship's captain might be persuaded to keep in his cabin. It was not until the 1840s that the Wardian case, an enclosed terrarium-type container in which live plants could be housed indefinitely, came into use for transporting plants over long distances (Bailey 1902:1963).

When collecting their specimens, botanists also made herbariums to document the plant and provide an example for study. The foliage, flowers, and fruit were preserved by drying them in a press. Herbarium specimens of the flowering parts were vital to the botanist, for a sample of the flower was essential in identifying the plant for classification. As we have seen, shipping live flowering plants, particularly shrubs and trees, was extremely problematic before the mid-nineteenth century. The often difficult process of germinating seeds upon their arrival in Europe, and the cultivation of a seedling to its mature flowering stage, could take years. Fortunately many early herbariums have survived and remain as an important body of historical reference for the identification of early introductions.

In addition to funding exploratory expeditions, British botany enthusiasts also supported plant collectors in foreign lands. One of the remarkable liaisons of this kind in America was the early eighteenth-century contract between collector Peter Collinson in England and John Bartram, a farmer/botanist near Philadelphia. Their correspondence has survived to document the intense interest and concern over plant collecting shared by Europeans and colonists. No doubt there were many other such exchanges, but few have left such a complete record or were carried on over a considerable period of time with such a professional attitude.

The American plants gathered by collectors and explorers were summarized by Andre Michaux in his *Flora Boreali Americana*, published posthumously in 1803. It was not long before this work was obsolete. The Lewis and Clark expedition, the first to cross North America from the East to the Pacific, took place from 1804 to 1806, commissioned by President Thomas Jefferson. Neither Lewis nor Clark were botanists, and their plant collecting was incidental to geographical exploration; yet they returned with a substantial botanical collection. Seeds gathered on the tour were given to growers such as Bernard M'Mahon in Philadelphia, but most of the collection was entrusted to the Elgin Botanical Garden in New York where Frederich Pursh was curator. In 1814 Pursh published his *Flora Americae Septentrionalis*, an impressive work of eleven volumes. Pursh had travelled extensively in America; he came to Canada in 1818, and died in Montreal

in 1820. Another enthusiastic collector was Thomas Nuttall, who set out
in 1810 for a four-year expedition through central North America. He
published the *Genera of American Plants* in 1818. These were only a few of
the men who made substantial contributions to the study of North American flora in this period.

In Great Britain the interest in newly introduced species was more than
just curiosity: there was a great deal to be gained if produce from foreign
sources could be grown domestically. During the eighteenth century the
Society for the Encouragement of Arts, Manufactures and Commerce gave
prizes to horticultural endeavours of this kind. Awards were made to those
who successfully raised domestic crops of hops, medicinal rhubarb, and
tobacco, which were then costly imports. On this side of the Atlantic the
Society for the Promotion of Agriculture, Arts and Manufacturing in
America, organized in Albany in 1791, discussed the topic of "Introduction
of Plants and Animals from Foreign Places" at one of their first meetings
(Hedrick 1933/1966:115).

In 1804 the London Horticultural Society was formed, to become the
Royal Horticultural Society some years later. John Claudius Loudon, a prolific botanical author, wrote *The Encyclopedia of Gardening* in 1822, a volu-
minous work that encompassed the history of gardening worldwide and
contained detailed descriptions of garden plants and their cultivation, virtually summing up the entire knowledge of gardening. According to Loudon, there were more introduced plants in the Low Countries at this time
than in any other nation. He attributed this phenomenon to the interests of
the ornamental lace and linen trades, which used floral patterns in their
manufacture (Loudon 1827:29). This was not the first time textile tradesmen had been associated with gardening: during the religious upheavals of
the sixteenth and seventeenth centuries, many textile workers from the
Low Countries had emigrated to Britain. These weavers and dyers had
taken with them the plants that had been part of their livelihood. As
artisan-growers they continued to practise their gardening skills, giving rise
to market-gardening, amateur horticultural societies, and seasonal flower
shows across Great Britain. Workers in textile manufacturing towns in
Scotland and northern England gained a reputation as accomplished florists.
One particularly well-known example was the town of Paisley, where the
artisans' flowers inspired the famous textile designs.

Among these tradesmen innumerable varieties of individual flower species were produced in the spirit of competition. The experienced gardener
with a sharp eye was quick to notice the slightest difference in a plant that
could be conceived as an improvement. Growers were keenly aware of

new colours or markings when they appeared among the seedlings, always hoping they had created a superior specimen. This competitive spirit spurred commercial nurserymen to produce ever-increasing numbers of varieties in the most favoured species. New varieties created in the early nineteenth century were frequently named after their growers or in honour of royalty and public figures. Many of the varieties developed during the heyday of their popularity quickly became extinct when interest in them lagged in favour of new introductions. It may never be known what many of these named varieties looked like, except in cases where drawings or paintings of the "most esteemed" flowers have survived.

In 1827, the year the Toronto Nursery catalogue was published, Loudon estimated that there were 44,000 plant species known: 7,000 native to central Europe, 2,300 from Great Britain, 3,000 from Africa, 13,000 from tropical America, 4,000 from the temperate areas of North and South America, 4,500 from tropical Asia, 1,500 from temperate Asia, 5,000 from the Pacific area, and the remainder from the Arctic, Scandinavia, and various islands around the globe (Loudon 1827:206). These figures were not static, as plant hunters were adding plants at such a rate that the number of species for a particular area could double within a few years. In North America the species of flora documented in the work of Michaux (1803) were doubled in Pursh's work (1814) and doubled again by Nuttall (1818). While it took time for newly introduced plants to reach the general market, the period saw an ever-increasing choice of plants for the gardener, and new varieties of popular species were being produced at an incredible speed.

European botanists and gardeners were becoming hard pressed to find a means of classifying the growing numbers of newly introduced plants. In 1694 and 1700 Joseph Pitton de Tournefort published two botanical works that proposed a classification of plants by genera. He created twenty-two classes of plants containing 8,000 sub-groups, based on the shape of the corolla. However, of all the scientific work on classification in the eighteenth century, no contribution was more important than that of the Swedish naturalist Carl Linnaeus, who devised a binomial classification system for all forms of life. Linnaeus published *Systema Naturae* in 1737, and *Species Plantarum* in 1753. His system was based on the sexual organs of the plants, the number of stamens and pistils, and their relationship. Before Linnaeus, plants were given Latin scientific names that were modified descriptions of the plants. For example, in 1629 John Parkinson named the common hyacinth "Hyacinthus Orientalis vulgaris diversorum colorum," which translates as "the common Oriental hyacinth of various colours" (Parkinson 1629/1991:118). In 1772 Bernard and Antoine de Jussieu, father and son, wrote *The Natural System of Plants*, another attempt to analyse the vegetable kingdom. But Linnaeus's system for plant classification gradually became universally accepted and remains in effect to the present day although it was initially regarded by many as being too facile to be truly scientific.

A plant's sexual organs interact to produce fruit, which contains the seed by which the plant reproduces itself. While the sexuality of plants had been discussed in the late seventeenth century, the science of genetics remained unexplored for almost two hundred years. The first conscious efforts to control cross-breeding were carried out by Thomas Fairchild, a British nurseryman. In 1717 he pollinated a Sweet William with pollen from a carnation, both plants in the *Dianthus* genus. The resultant seed produced a plant known as "Fairchild's Mule" that bloomed but was sterile. While the principles of plant breeding were understood in the eighteenth century, they were seldom applied in the commercial production of hybrids or varieties. Gardeners knew that plants grown from the seeds of some species reproduced their parent plant, while seeds from other species produced a variety of "new" plants. The best of the new varieties were selected from among the seedlings and named. Most new varieties or hybrids did not come true from seed and therefore required herbaceous propagation. These factors were part of the gardener's general knowledge of plants based on observation and experience, but the scientific reasons for plant variation were not understood until the principles of genetics were revealed. The science remained an unknown field until an Augustinian monk named Gregor Johann Mendel presented the results of his experiments in 1865. However, little work was done using Mendel's findings before the twentieth century.

The practice of plant breeding was in its infancy in the early nineteenth century. Until that time plants were propagated by natural pollinators. The scientific differences between a species, a variety, a hybrid, and a mutant or sport were not clearly understood. Not until the twentieth century was a species recognized as a distinct biological specimen, a variety a minor variant of the species, a hybrid a marriage between two species of the same genus, and a mutant a genetic change in a species. Nor was the influence of viruses even suspected. At the outset of the nineteenth century, a gardener's knowledge came solely from his careful observations.

Gardeners were always on the lookout for natural sports, or mutants, but few of these came true from seed. Mutants resulted from internal changes in a plant's chemistry and a redistribution of chromosomes in its genetic structure. Successful reproduction of a mutant was primarily executed by grafting techniques. The double flowers that were very popular and in great demand had transformed many of their stamens into petals. When all the stamens in a double flower were transformed, the plant became sterile and had to be propagated by cuttings or root division. If the vegetative propagation of a prized sterile plant failed, it was lost to history. Gardeners were aware that many plants did not come true from seed, and in many cases this was because the parent plant was a hybrid. A number of newly introduced exotics were natural hybrids, and the seedlings from their seeds varied greatly. In this period of garden history the dahlia, the China aster, and the French marigold were examples of plants that quickly provided the market with innumerable "varieties," doubles included. Occasionally multicoloured blooms with striking patterns in the petals were noted, quite uncharacteristic of the usual form, making these plants eagerly sought after. All too often they had short life spans, the vibrantly coloured tulips of the period being a prime example. Only twentieth century science revealed this phenomenon to be the result of viral infection.

Before artificial pollination practices were introduced, the process of selection was responsible for all the variations in garden plants. In 1629 Parkinson declared that it was erroneous to suppose that "any flower may be neads to grow double by art, that was but single by nature: And that one may by art cause any flower to grow of what colour they will: And that any plant may be forced to flower out of their due seasons, either earlier or later, by an art" (Parkinson 1629/1991:16). This was still true when the Toronto Nursery catalogue was published. An early nineteenth-century gardener would be astonished by the changes accomplished since: he would be incredulous viewing our greenhouses filled with man-made varieties of poinsettias forced into colour for the Christmas trade.

The 1827 Toronto Nursery catalogue includes many species having unusual characteristics in the shapes of their leaves, flowers, or seeds. This reflects an attitude of the time when there was a particular fascination in natural forms. The more unusual the arrangement of the petals or the intricacy of a seed pod, the more it intrigued the observer. Gardeners were eager to supply these conversation pieces to their appreciative clients. Flowers in double forms or with variations in the colours of a petal were prized above blooms of single form or one colour. Unusual seed pods were collected for decorative purposes. This inquisitiveness about natural forms was not peculiar to this period in history. The curving, twisting pods of "Caterpillars and Snails" were a curiosity in Shakespeare's time. It is hard not to sense a certain innocence in the wonderment and joy of discovery through the intimate examination of nature in this pre-scientific period.

The excitement created by new plant introductions began to demand more botanical collecting as explorers ventured more frequently into unexplored territory. The widely differing habitats in which exotic plants originated presented an unprecedented challenge for the gardener. Wealthy patrons, the sponsors of botanical expeditions, needed knowledgeable people to care for their collections of newly introduced species. Tropical exotics demanded special considerations, and heated or "stove" houses for plants became an integral part of garden complexes on large estates. One of the more interesting of new types of garden construction was the pinery, a hothouse intended exclusively for the growing of pineapples.

As more and more exotic plants were introduced, professional and experienced gardeners needed to establish and maintain suitable growing facilities. They constantly had to expand their knowledge of the requirements of new plant forms. In Great Britain gardening became a respected profession requiring at least as many years of study as other technical trades. The sphere of garden knowledge widened rapidly, necessitating intensive training in methods and techniques for growing an ever-increasing number and variety of plants. There were several distinct careers open to gardeners as a result of the changes in horticultural practices. The most esteemed position was that of landscape gardener, the professional who designed large estates and was often the head gardener of such establishments. These men supervised a staff of other gardeners, apprentices, and labourers. Smaller premises and physic or botanical gardens had chief gardeners or curators who also were required to manage a staff of labourers.

Other options open to professional gardeners were in the nursery and florist trades. In Europe commercial gardens and nurseries had become significant factors in the business of horticulture. The nurseyman, specializing in the growing of trees and shrubs, was distinct from the florist, who grew herbaceous plants. Most nursery-grown trees and shrubs were hardy species, grown from seed, cuttings, or by grafting. Each nursery grew a limited number of species; many developed a particular specialty in the trade. The florist grew flowering plants exclusively. These included annual and perennial garden plants as well as cut flowers or potted plants for indoor ornamental purposes. A group of plants including the tulip, auricula, carnation, pink, anemone, ranunculus, hyacinth, and polyanthus became known as "florists' flowers." Growers multiplied specific varieties of these plants in intense competition with one another, and unique varieties were named for their grower. Many gardeners became immortalized by the plant variety named after them; for others, such fame was short-lived. The life span of a particular plant variety depended to a degree on its popularity, which, in turn, was subject to the vagaries of fashion.

The professional gardener was expected to have a knowledge of all aspects of horticultural practices and be responsible for keeping records of sowing, reaping, trenching, produce, and weather, as well as for allotting wages and accommodation for his staff. His hours of work "ought to be at least one hour per day less than that of the common labourers ... who require no mind" (Loudon 1827:453). The gardener was advised to furnish his office with a library including an encyclopedia, Linnaeus's *Systema Naturae*, an introduction to botany, a catalogue of plants, a *Flora Britannica*, an introduction to entomology, the transactions of the London and Edinburgh Horticultural Societies, and "the best Gardener's Kalender of the time" (Loudon 1827:450).

This reference to a gardener's library is particularly interesting, as the number of horticultural books published in English before 1800 was limited. The first books written about plants were the herbals of ancient Greece and Rome, many of them available only in their original language. The earliest herbal written in English was *The Herbal or General History of Plants* by John Gerard in 1596. (This date is often given as the date of introduction for many plants as it was the first documented reference to the plant.) In 1629 (another date commonly mentioned for the introduction of a plant), John Parkinson published *Paradisi in Sole Paradisus Terrestris*, or *A Garden of Pleasant Flowers*.

In 1724 Philip Miller published *The Gardener's and Florist's Dictionary* which was to see many editions and remain the standard work on gardening well into the nineteenth century. In the preface to the 1752 edition Miller wrote, "as there has been a great Number of rare plants introduced into the English Gardens within the compass of a few Years past; and as the passion for collecting of foreign Trees and Shrubs now prevails in most parts of Europe; it was thought proper to enumerate such as have lately been brought into the English Gardens." Miller was curator of the celebrated Chelsea Physic Garden in London, the recipient of many plant collections. He was among the first to take note of the relationship between insects and plants in the pollination process. His work, with its careful plant descriptions and directions for the care and cultivation of each plant, was a landmark in English gardening literature.

These three English books remained as references for many generations and served as models for subsequent horticultural literature. They contain some of the earliest and most detailed descriptions of garden plants, with remarks on their origins and uses, helpful advice on their propagation, and instructions for the cultural practices required.

Several garden calendars were first published in Britain in the eighteenth century and continued to be popular well into the twentieth century. These contained detailed instructions for the gardener on the tasks to be performed on a month-to-month basis in the kitchen garden, the orchard, the nursery, the flower garden, the greenhouse, and the hothouse. One popular example was *Every Man His Own Gardener* by John Abercrombie (London, 1766), published in many editions throughout the nineteenth century. (Contemporary encyclopedias also included extensive articles on gardening, frequently written in the form of an almanac [e.g. Perthensis 1807: *Gardening* 10:228–55].) This form was also used by American authors: In 1829 the New York seedsman Thomas Bridgeman published *The Kitchen Gardener's Instructor*, which was sold in seed stores in New York, Boston, and Philadelphia (Bridgeman 1829/1864: preface).

The first garden calender to be written and published in America was Bernard M'Mahon's *American Gardener* (Philadelphia, 1806), judged at the time to be "by far the most comprehensive, complete and best work that has been written for America" (M'Mahon 1858/1976: preface to 11th edition). He made little use of scientific nomenclature in his work – nearly all the plants mentioned were identified by common names. It closely followed the English examples in format, and, in spite of his assertions, the English seasons. M'Mahon frequently noted that for remote places he might have made mistakes, and he recommended all gardening should be tempered by the climate, soil, and situation of the garden. While he claimed he took every effort to advise gardeners of the differences and difficulties encountered in America, and took "assiduous endeavors to make it useful in every State of the Union," few New Englanders or settlers in Upper Canada would have been able to sow seeds for annual flowers "in borders or other parts of the pleasure garden" in February (M'Mahon 1858/1976: preface & 166). M'Mahon's work was republished in many later editions.

American printers often copied English works, for at that time there was little copyright protection. This aroused comment from John Goldie during his travels in America in 1819. In New England he found many "excellent and extensive collections of books, in almost all the sciences and even some on botany, a subject on which I scarcely expected to find any. They have the London and Edinburgh Reviews and all the late popular publications in Britain. As soon as they come out to America they are reprinted in a less splendid and expensive form so that you can purchase books for almost one third of their London prices" (Goldie Papers 1819:195–6). The British garden books of this period usually included directions for the laying out and planting of gardens, the construction of garden walks, and the placement of garden beds.

Garden design reached a peak of artistry in eighteenth-century England, expressed most elegantly in large country estates. The English landscape style of naturalism continued to be popular in America in the early nineteenth century: "A grand and spacious lawn of grass-ground is generally first presented immediately to the front of the mansion or main habitation … each side embellished with plantations of shrubbery, clumps, thickets, &c., with serpentine gravel walks" (M'Mahon 1858/1976:74). The flower garden was placed to the rear, in a private area close by the house, bounded with flowering shrubs and divided into many small beds (ibid.:91). Details of garden plans were provided by the English cyclopedist Loudon, who described gardens suitable for every class of citizen from the grand villa to the labourer's cottage and from the "commodious" suburban house to the humble front beds of urban dwellings. M'Mahon and Loudon both stated that the parterre garden style was outdated but suggested formal flower beds for the landscaped area in front of the house. Other areas – flower gardens and kitchen gardens – were to be surrounded by a masonry wall, shrub hedge, or fence (Loudon 1827:1022–7).

On large estates the enclosed gardens were in secluded areas set apart from the landscaped settings of the residences. Vegetables, fruit, and ornamental plants were grown in these gardens to supply produce and decoration to the house. In small cottage homes, with limited grounds, gardens occupied whatever space was available close by the dwelling, be it only a few containers to grow the essential plants needed by the household. On the small farm, gardens were situated close to the house in relatively small fenced areas protected from wandering animals, both wild and domestic. Between the house and the barn was the most suitable location, placing the garden in a site readily accessible to the manure supply yet easily attended to from the house.

For many households, gardening was part of the housekeeping routine, carried on in a traditional manner with knowledge based on experience rather than formal training. Some skill in the growing of plants was needed by almost everyone, even in the poorest of homes, to provide part of the family's food supply. In addition to food crops, gardens were expected to supply medicinal substances, culinary flavourings, textile dyes, insect and rodent repellents, cleaning agents, and scents for perfumes and wash waters. The care of the home garden was often the responsibility of the women of the house; men looked after the field crops and the orchard. Through this familiarity with horticultural practices, it is likely that the average person in the early nineteenth century had a far greater understanding and knowledge of plants than most North Americans today. For the educated person botany was a socially approved field of study. This included young women who were encouraged to know the wild and cultivated plants. Coupling this with the study of water-colour painting, many women became admirable botanical illustrators. In Upper Canada, the botanical watercolours of Agnes FitzGibbon in *Canadian Wild Flowers* by Catherine Parr Traill is a fine example of this genre.

The study of natural history was popular during the early 1800s, and for many this was part of family life. The wonders of "Nature" were celebrated in poetry (Wordsworth's "Daffodils" was written during this period) and prose and interpreted as inspirational. Nature walks and collecting jaunts to find birds' eggs, fossils, and insects as well as plants, and the arranging and displaying of specimens, became favourite pastimes. Detailed drawings were often made to record specific examples. This was especially true with plants, as dried or pressed specimens lost their colour and their three-dimensional quality. This closeness to nature often stimulated an enthusiasm for pursuing further knowledge of the sciences.

Developments in chemistry and physics produced new fields of study in which the findings were applied to botanical phenomena. Scientists sought explanations for their observations, developing theories that were applied to agriculture and horticulture. Various experiments were carried out in the attempt to understand plant behaviour. The analysis of habitats led to the study of plant requirements in terms of temperature, moisture, and nutrients. Soils were examined to determine their influence on plant growth: it had been observed that the colour of the bloom of some plants, such as the hydrangea, changed when the plant was grown in different soils. Trials were carried out to assess the effects of light, for it had been noticed that all plants tend to lean towards the source of light – blooms of some genera, sunflowers for example, actually turned on their stems as the source of light moved. Most plants bloomed during the day, many closing as the daylight decreased, but others, such as species of oenothera and the night-blooming cereus, blossomed only in the dark. As the technology for chemical analysis was improved, the contents of plant compounds were revealed; these discoveries were particularly important in plants used for medicinal purposes. Science was beginning to develop methods of extracting and purifying drug substances. The first isolation of a plant alkaloid was announced in Germany in 1816: this was morphia, derived from opium, the secretion of immature poppy seed pods. The role of birds and insects in plant pollination was recognized and led eventually to greater understanding of plant breeding. (The concept of plant sexuality was not fully accepted in the early nineteenth century – many chose to deny it.)

These and other mysteries of plant growth and habit were probed by scientists throughout the nineteenth century. But in the days before science could offer satisfactory explanations, many believed the natural world was governed by religious and/or magical relationships. Plants were awarded symbolic meanings based on their habitat or the shape and colour of their blossoms. In classical times, the shapes and colours of leaves and flowers were regarded as indicators of their use in medicine, a philosophy later known as the "Doctrine of Signatures." This theory hypothesized that plants used in relieving human suffering demonstrated their purpose by resembling parts of the human body. A few examples of this old belief associated cordate leaves with heart ailments, reniform leaves with the kidneys, and the colour red with blood. This method of identifying medicinal plants persisted in folk medicine well into the 1800s, although it had been abandoned by physicians, as had the astrological associations expounded by seventeenth-century herbalists such as Nicholas Culpepper.

In the early nineteenth century plants and medicine were closely related: physicians studied botany as a mandatory requirement for their degree, as plants supplied many of the drugs in use at the time. The scientific men who took part in or stimulated plant collecting were usually doctors. Training for this profession was offered by universities, and the two outstanding schools in Europe were at Leyden and Edinburgh. Many of the first doctors in Upper Canada were graduates of Edinburgh University. In the early eighteenth century this school published the authoritative textbook *The Pharmacopoeia of the Royal College of Physicians of Edinburgh* by a Dr Lewis, routinely updating it at intervals. It classed medicines in three categories: "Chemical Preparations of Vegetables ... of animals ... [and] of minerals" (Lewis 1748: table of contents).

An updated edition of Dr Lewis's pharmacopoeia was printed in 1796 in Philadelphia, the cultural centre in the American colonies during the eighteenth century. Here the sciences could be studied, and the first comprehensive libraries in America were assembled. The city attracted scientists, and some of the early botanists in America lived in the vicinity, including John Bartram, who established the first American botanical garden. David Landreth began his nursery and seed business there in 1784 and Bernard M'Mahon shortly after in 1802. Both were patronized by President Thomas Jefferson, who was intensely interested in gardening and sought to improve American gardens with newly introduced species. Benjamin Franklin, another Philadelphian, was also a student of horticulture; his contributions were primarily of an economic nature, as he was particularly interested in reducing the colony's reliance on imported plant material. Like growers in Britain, he tried to introduce the elusive medicinal variety of rhubarb. In 1752 he published an American edition of the *Medica Britannica* with an appendix of American plants, compiled by Bartram.

Medicine was one of the sciences for which Philadelphia had a deserved reputation. The hospital had its own physic garden under the supervision of Professor Barton; he was later hired by Harvard University in Massachusetts in 1806 to establish a physic garden there. The Academy of Natural Sciences was founded in Philadelphia in 1812. It became the repository of many herbariums and maintained one of the most complete botanical libraries in the country.

In New York City similar developments in botanical knowledge were taking place. Dr Hosack established the Elgin Botanical Garden in 1801 as a teaching aid for his medical students, stocking it with plant species from London, Copenhagen, Paris, Florence, and the West Indies. A few years before, in 1793, the Prince Nursery had opened the Linnaean Botanical Garden on Long Island.

Many of the plants brought to gardens in America were extensively used for medical purposes. In Britain medical practitioners were not permitted to supply drugs; this was the prerogative of pharmacists. In America there was no such limiting of professional practices, and doctors often had their own gardens from which they could gather appropriate plant material for their prescriptions. Medicinal plants were also grown by many households to supply ingredients for traditional remedies for common illnesses. Women were expected to know how to handle plants as part of their duties associated with food preparation and general housekeeping. This included the management of the still-room where the extracts and oils from plants were distilled for use in various medicinal and household formulas.

The housewife also filled the role of caretaker when members of the household took ill. Her skill and knowledge of plants was important in all handling of food and medicinal preparations, whether she carried on these duties personally or supervised their execution by household staff. Mrs Simcoe, the wife of the first lieutenant-governor of Upper Canada, carefully noted in her diary the use of plants that were new to her, recording those that were edible and those that were reputed to have healing properties. She also observed the use of plants by the native Indians, noting several that were used for snakebite. For most women this knowledge was passed from generation to generation. The oral aspect was important, not only because many were illiterate but because the teaching of these skills demanded a "hands-on" experience. A mistake in the identification of a plant or in the preparation of a medicine could have disastrous results for the patient.

Folk medicine was important to colonists in America as settlements were sparse and travel was slow and difficult. There were many drawbacks to living in rural areas, but "the greatest handicap the settlers experienced was the difficulty of getting medical attention" (Reaman 1970:63). The few printed cookbooks and household directories available usually included formulas to be used for healing. Among these recipes there was almost always one for treating the bite of a "mad dog," a reminder that the outcome of rabies was certain death in those times. Early journals and travel accounts contain many references to illness, especially digestive complaints resulting from a poor diet and unclean water. Outbreaks of contagious diseases such as cholera, smallpox, and venereal disease often devastated small communities. Fevers, catarrh (the inflammation of nasal and throat passages), ague (which could have been malaria or tuberculosis), and pulmonary problems were the most frequently mentioned ailments. Wrote Catharine Parr Traill, "Ague is the disease most dreaded by new settlers and to many persons it has proved a great drawback, especially to such who go to uncleared land … remedies are as plentiful as blackberries" (Traill 1855/1969:205). Both Mrs Simcoe and Mrs Jameson reported having ague during their stay in Upper Canada.

In isolated areas, illness and injuries such as burns, cuts, and broken bones had to be cared for without a physician. And not only were physicians few and far between but medical practices of the time were limited. The most common procedures were bleeding, cupping, and enemas. Prescribed medication included laudanum (opium), calomel (mercury), emetics, and purgatives to cause vomiting and excretion, which were sometimes used to excess to the detriment of the patient. A number of self-professed "doctors" peddled "patented" medicines, even in remote settlements. In reaction to these conditions, there was widespread interest in herbal medicine. Observed Traill, "The old Canadian settlers are often well skilled in the use of native plants … in lonely places where the aid of a medical man is difficult to be obtained, even severe wounds are healed … by the inhabitants themselves. Some one among them who has more nerve, or more judgement than the rest is consulted upon such an occasion, and faith goes a long way with many patients in effecting a cure" (Traill 1857:200). In 1832 Samuel Thomson published his *New Guide to Health or Botanic Family Physician* in Upper Canada, first in Hamilton and later in Brockville (Godfrey 1979:20). Thomsonian doctors appeared throughout the province, as all that was required for "certification" was to read the good doctor's book. However, their herbal cures were probably less hazardous than many treatments used by accredited physicians.

Herbal remedies were also put to use in animal husbandry. The health and survival of domestic animals was a vital factor in the well-being of early farm families. Recipes for treating horses are often found inserted in farriers' day-books, calling for mixtures of "hoarhound," "cumphry," and "spicknard" to cure equine ailments. Farriers and self-styled horse-doctors were all that was available to assist the settler in animal treatment, as there were no accredited veterinarians in America until much later in the nineteenth century. The first veterinary school in the United States was founded in 1852, and the first in Canada was established in Toronto by Andrew Smith in 1862. Yet in many ways the treatment of animal diseases was better understood than the curing of human ailments. The period from the late eighteenth to the end of the nineteenth century was "the most innovative 120 years by far in the history of medicine ... so closely associated with the problems of animal disease [which were] several steps ahead in understanding infection processes" (Schwabe 1978:155).

Climatic differences also came under examination by botanists. It had been observed that fruit trees taken from Britain to Canada bloomed much too early "and had all their blossoms nipt with frost, till, after being inured to the climate, they learned to bloom later" (Rennie 1833:51). Such factors were important to gardeners learning to adapt their skills to growing conditions in an unfamiliar environment, a situation experienced by all immigrants to the Canadas.

Some plants became "inured to the climate" all too well, and settlers discovered there could be disadvantages to introducing exotic plants. By the middle of the eighteenth century some European garden plants had already escaped from North American gardens and become naturalized. A good number spread into the wilderness to become alien wildflowers, while others simply became troublesome weeds. The Swedish naturalist Peter Kalm, who visited eastern North America in 1747, "found purslane (*Portulaca oleracea*) growing plentifully in a dry sandy soil. In gardens it was one of the worst weeds" (Kalm 1770/1966 1:355). Plantain, another European introduction, was known to the Amerindians as "white man's footprints," as it could be found along all established trails.

However, many other introductions failed to thrive without special handling in the short growing season in Canada caused by long, cold winters and the late arrival of spring. Mrs Simcoe, while living at Niagara, observed, "It does not answer here to sow seeds in the Gardens till May, for tho' the weather may have been long good, when Ice comes down from the Upper Lakes late in April, it occasions the air to be so cold that Gardens near the River suffer very much" (Innes 1983:178). Gardeners had standard measures to protect young plants; cold frames, glass bells, and caps of oiled paper gave some protection but required hour-to-hour care to make sure the plants were not damaged by the heat of the sun even when the wind was cold, or by fungus infections in damp, chilly weather. Planting out was to be done after the last frost, which could take place at different times in different places and could vary from year to year. Loudon noted that to counter these difficulties, "some tribes of American Indians act upon the principle suggested by Linnaeus and plant their corn when the wild plum blooms or when the leaves of the oak are about the size of a squirrel's ear" (Loudon 1827:189). Even when gardeners learned to adapt to cold winters and hot dry summers they had to accept that Canadian weather could be capricious. The year of 1816 became known as the "year without a summer," as there were severe frosts every month, resulting in total crop failure. Many suffered during the following winter from the lack of basic food supplies.

To the newcomers, the Canadian weather appeared to go from one extreme to another. The hot, dry summers proved a real problem for those trying to raise crops. Peter Kalm described the summer heat as "excessive and without intermission" and deplored the wind that blew "mostly from the south and [brought] a great drought with it" (Kalm 1770/1966 1:58, 334). He tried to understand the life cycles – the flowering and seeding processes – of native plants in terms of their adaptation to the extremes of climate of eastern North America. Such conditions required adjustments to standard horticultural practices known to many of the new settlers. As Catherine Parr Traill observed, "It is the opinion of practical persons who have bought wisdom by some years' experience of the country that in laying out the planting of the garden the beds should not be raised as is the usual custom; and give us the reason, that the sun having such great power draws the moisture more readily from the earth where beds are elevated above the level, and, in consequence of the dryness of the ground, the plants wither away. As there appears some truth in the remark, I am inclined to adopt the plan" (Traill 1840:301).

According to the general practice of the time, the enclosed flower gardens and kitchen gardens were to be laid out in sections. Garden almanacs advised the gardener to

form a border around the whole garden from four to five feet wide ... next to the border a walk five to six feet wide; [the] centre part divided into squares, on the sides of which a border may be laid out ... in which various kinds of herbs may be raised. Also gooseberries, currants, raspberries, strawberries, etc., [the] centre planted with various kinds of vegetables. The outside borders facing east, south and west

[are] useful for the earliest fruits and vegetables; the north border, shady and cool, for raising & pricking out such young plants, herbs and cuttings as required to be screened from the intense heat of the sun. All standard trees should be excluded ... the roots take up moisture, the leaves shade and obstruct the free circulation of air and tree droppings can be injurious (Bridgeman 1829/1864:21).

Catherine Parr Traill has provided a few details outlining a layout for her garden, and these can be compared to Bridgeman's design. In the spring of 1835 she wrote, "we are having the garden, which hitherto has been nothing but a square enclosure for vegetables, laid out in a prettier form ... the fence is a sort of rude basket or hurdle work, such as you see at home, called by the country folk a wattled fence: This forms a much more picturesque fence than those usually put up of split timber. Along this little enclosure I have begun planting a sort of flowery hedge with some of the native shrubs that abound in our woods and lake-shores." Her neighbours also gardened in a fenced area: "The garden was laid out with a smooth plot of grass surrounded by borders of flowers and separated from a ripening field of wheat by a light railed fence over which a luxuriant hop vine flung its tendrils and graceful blossoms." At this home Mrs Traill admired the "stoup ... of Dutch origin," which she later copied for her own garden. She described it as "a sort of wide verandah, supported on pillars, often unbarked logs, the floor earth or plank, the roof covered with sheets of bark or shingled ... wreathed with scarlet creeper and also with the hop ... an open ante-room in which you can take your meals and enjoy the fanning breeze" (Traill 1836/1989:260, 3406).

Illustrations of Canadian gardens before the 1840s are lacking, and there are too few personal observations in the literature to demonstrate the extent to which these principles were adhered to in Upper Canada. The records left by American gardeners such as President Jefferson, the correspondence of Bartram and Collinson, the diaries of Lady Skipwith and other published works on botany, travel, medicine, and social life provide a rich resource for garden historians in the United States. In the history of Upper Canada there is little first-hand documentation of gardens or horticulture to compare with the American records. Perhaps some similar garden records will come to light now that historians are alerted to the interest in the subject. For now, we must be content with extracting titbits of information from diverse sources to construct an image of early nineteenth-century Upper Canada gardens.

One of the few prime sources available is William Claus's garden diary for the years 1818 to 1824 (NA MG19 F1). Claus was a member of the Legislative Council, an Indian Affairs official, and a commissioner of customs for the Niagara District. His home can still be seen in Niagara-on-the-Lake. While his diary does not include a graphic plan of his garden, frequent references are made to paths and "squares" in describing the location of his plants. He had a melon square and a cabbage square, a centre walk and a path in front of a flower bed. His garden was fenced, as he wrote of "two plumb [trees] left of the garden gate."

Travelling through Upper Canada with her husband, Captain Basil Hall, Mrs Hall recalled dining with Captain Fitzgibbon in a tent on his lawn in York in 1827 (NA MG24 H13). The lawn, a distinguished feature of English gardens, was a rare sight in America. A few years later, Anna Jameson described Stamford Park, the former residence of Sir Peregrine Maitland, lieutenant-governor of Upper Canada, at Niagara. It was, she said, as "the only place I saw in Upper Canada combining our ideas of an elegant, well-furnished English villa and ornamented grounds, with some of the grandest and wildest features of the forest scene ... From the lawn before the house, an open glade, commanding a park-like range of broken and undulating ground and wooded valleys, displayed beyond them the wide expanse of Lake Ontario" (Jameson 1838/1972 2:48). It may have been Maitland's garden that Susanna Moodie admired several years later when she went to Niagara Falls. Before she caught sight of the waterfall she had been "intently examining the rare shrubs and beautiful flowers that grew in an exquisite garden surrounding a very fine mansion." She was "perfectly astonished at their luxuriance" (Moodie [1854]:265). Gardens such as these may well have been supplied in the 1820s and 1830s by plantsmen like William Custead.

– 4 –

Fruits

Three and a half pages of the Toronto Nursery catalogue are devoted to listings of fruit-producing plants. Fruit-bearing species were among the first plants brought to America by the early European colonists. Once matured, they could supply crops for many years, a reliable source of familiar food for people trying to adapt to a strange new country. Tree fruits were paramount, with apples and pears frequently mentioned in early documents. Almost every home had a small orchard, and the garden held a number of smaller bush fruits. The first nurseries in the English colonies propagated fruit trees almost exclusively. Eventually large orchards were established for commercial crops to supply the growing towns and cities. Fruit formed an important part of the daily diet, eaten fresh, dried for out-of-season use, or in a variety of beverages: fresh juices, fermented wines and cider, or distilled fruit brandies. Preserved fruit, in conserves, jams, jellies, and pickles, added variety and spice to meals year around.

The North American forests that greeted the newcomers teemed with fruits. Choke-cherries, plums, raspberries, strawberries, blueberries, service berries, elderberries, and cranberries grew wild. Many of these were small and sour fruit. Native peoples made good use of them, using various cooking and drying processes which they taught the newcomers. But there were few large, sweet fruit indigenous to America, such as the apple, pear, or peach familiar to Europeans. The Dutch were the first to bring large-fruiting trees to eastern North America in the 1500s. The French brought many of the same species to their colonies in the 1600s, as did the English in the 1700s. Before the English gained control of Canada in 1760, the French had small settlements around their forts and trading posts along the St Lawrence River and the north shores of Lakes Ontario and Erie as far as Detroit. Apple and pear orchards were well established in these villages before British immigration began. The famous McIntosh apple, found in eastern Upper Canada in 1795 (but not marketed until 1835), was probably a seedling of the Fameuse variety from a previous French orchard. No named varieties came from the French pears, and most likely all have been lost. In spite of the difficulties encountered with cold winters, dry summers, and new species of insects and fungal diseases, however, the European immigrants were remarkably successful in growing fruit.

In colonial times, apples and pears were grown without much regard for their varieties. To most farmers an apple was an apple, a pear a pear, and all that mattered was the quantity of fruit gathered, for most of it was destined for the cider mill. Freshly pressed, the juices were pleasant drinks, but the bulk of the juice was made into fermented beverages like cider and perry. These were widely consumed – a pitcher of cider was on the table for all meals in most homes. Whereas tea and coffee were expensive imports, cider was cheap and good-tasting. Fermented beverages were also distilled into brandies, and these too were cheap. Cider, perry, wine, and brandy were served at all inns and taverns. William Cobbett, an English writer who lived in America from 1784 to 1800, commented that you could "drink yourself blind at the price of a sixpence" (Hedrick 1933/1966:159). Commercial production of alcoholic beverages was widespread

in New England before 1800 and soon after in Upper Canada. Juices were also fermented for vinegars, an important ingredient for preserving other foods. The pomace from the cider mill provided plenty of seeds for further plantings.

A number of fruit tree varieties brought from Europe did not fare well in the climate of Upper Canada. They tended to bloom too early to be pollinated, and the roots were often killed by deep frosts. European fruit trees taken to the New England states often adapted more easily to the milder Atlantic climate, but it was the seedling offspring of these imported trees that furnished most of the trees for orchards

Apple   *Malus* sp.

in America. Grafting was the most successful method of preserving varieties that bore abundant crops of fine-quality fruit. Seedling trees were grown for the express purpose of providing hardy root stock to which the desired scions, or cuttings, were grafted. A new variety often bore the name of the propagator who first marketed the fruit. The first evidence of large-scale production of fruit trees in the United States was Prince's Long Island nursery at Flushing, New York, in 1790 (Hedrick 1950:432).

All orchard apples fall under the scientific classification of *Malus sylvestris var. domestica* (Borkh.) Manst. of the *Rosaceae* or Rose family. The apple came originally from parts of west-central Asia and Asia Minor.

Apple trees were the first fruits listed in the Toronto Nursery catalogue and had by far the greatest number of varieties of all the fruits listed. Seventy-nine varieties, listed in order of their ripening dates, were described by the length of time apples would keep. All trees were priced at one shilling three pence, except those grafted on Paradise stock for dwarfs and espaliers which were two shillings each. The Paradise apple, *Malus pumila var. paradisia* (Mill.) Scheid., which Custead noted was "very dwarf, fruit of no estimation," was of French origin. It was the preferred root stock for grafting apple varieties. The result was a bushy, dwarf form of tree which was suitable for a home garden and lent itself well to espalier treatment.

The keeping value of apples was of great importance to early settlers. Winters were long, and there were few substitutes available once cold weather set in, freezing the ports and cutting off all imports.

Apple varieties that matured late in the season could be kept up to three or four months for use as dessert fruit, but storage, even in a cool place, was not wholly reliable. Apples emit an ethylene gas as they ripen, which hastens the ripening, and eventually the rotting, process. The first cookbook published in Upper Canada at Kingston, *The Cook Not Mad, or Rational Cookery*, gave instructions for a practical method for keeping fruit. Apples and pears "are best preserved in glazed, cylindrical, earthen vessels, large enough to contain a gallon, and closely fitted with covers … Each apple or pear should be wiped dry, then rolled in soft spongy paper, and placed carefully in the jar" (1831/1982:76). Another time-honoured technique was to slice and dry the apples, which could be reconstituted later and used for applesauce or pies in the same way as fresh fruit.

In the kitchen the apple was prepared in many ways. Applesauce was made with different seasonings and served as an accompaniment to meats and as a dessert dish. Apple pie and pudding were made from fresh or dried fruit. Apples with good keeping qualities could eaten out-of-hand during the early winter. When preserved in a sugar syrup, apples could be kept until fresh fruit appeared the following year. The old adage "an apple a day keeps the doctor away" had a factual basis; at times when a good supply of fresh vegetables and fruits were not available, preserved or dried apples furnished many of the necessary vitamins and fibre the body requires.

The rapidly growing population in Upper Canada created a market for apples, and by the early nineteenth century the benefits of growing better-quality fruit were becoming recognized. The economic returns from an orchard could be increased by supplying more and better produce from improved varieties. By 1827 fruit-growing on a commercial scale was well developed in New England and New York State. Varieties originating in these orchards were to prove exceptionally successful. Recognized varieties suitable for grafting were becoming more readily available. Their hardiness was assured, and the fruit was of a much better quality.

Many of these "new" sorts originated as seedlings of older European varieties. Custead's list included some that had been grown in Britain for over two hundred years. The Pearmain, Golden Pippin, and Genneting were described by Parkinson in 1629. The Pearmain, a soft, mealy apple with a red blush on the sunny side, was grown chiefly for cider. It was among the apples brought to America by the Pilgrims in 1653. Pearmains were also found in old French settlements around Detroit (Hedrick 1950:31,303). The Golden Pippin, a small fruit with very good flavour, maturing as late as November, was still listed as a recommended variety in the late nineteenth century. The Genneting apple, also spelled Juneting or Juneating, was a red dessert apple. There were several Gennetings; a white-fleshed, early fruiting variety was a prolific bearer, but the fruit was a poor keeper.

Pearmains and russets were preferred for the best cider. Late Yellow Vandeveres, Seek-No-Furthers, and crabs were also good cider apples. The French had an expression, "*Petites pommes, gros cidre*," showing their preference for small apples in their cider making. The Seek-No-Further apple originated near Westfield, Connecticut, in the mid-eighteenth century. This name was chosen to represent its all-round usefulness, as it was good for eating out-of-hand, for cooking, and for cider. Apple varieties were distinguished according to their uses. Dessert apples were best suited for eating fresh, having a sweet-tasting, juicy, but firm flesh, and a rich aromatic flavour; apples maturing late in the season were often best for this purpose. Cooking apples were varieties that formed a soft pulpy mass when boiled or baked; in general the early varieties were most suitable for cooking.

Nonpareils, Yellow Newtowns, and Newtown and Ribston pippins were considered dessert apples. The Nonpareil, a large, rosy-coloured fruit with a crisp texture and sweet flavour, remained a "very desirable" choice for over a century. The Yellow Newtown, a seedling variety developed in Newtown, New York, about 1730, was a yellow apple with a reddish tinge, and stored well. The Newtown Pippin, a vigorous tree and prolific bearer, was selected by Benjamin Franklin to take to London, England, in 1759. His introduction of American apples to Britain sparked the export trade of apples which continues to this day.

The term "pippin" denoted an apple variety grown from seed. Custead's list has thirteen pippin varieties. All pippins were dessert apples. Probably the best known and most successful, the Ribston Pippin, originated in Yorkshire, England, and was introduced as early as 1700. The fruit was greenish-yellow with a sweet-tart taste, suitable for use as both a dessert and cooking apple. The Ribston Pippin and Seek-No-Further are in the collection at the agricultural station at Vineland, Ontario, which is growing sixty-nine apple varieties known to have been grown in Ontario prior to 1919.

English and Winter Codlins, Nonsuches, Winesaps, Rhode Island Greenings, and Transparents were cooking apples. Codlins were sour apples of value for sauces eaten with roasted meats. Nonsuch apples were large, juicy fruit from a very hardy tree; this variety was recommended for planting in cold areas or harsh exposures. The Winesap apple with its red-coloured fruit was a late variety that originated in the more southern colonies before 1800. It is one of the few varieties on Custead's list which is still being grown commercially. The Rhode Island Greening was an extremely popular apple. Its green-yellow fruit was excellent for cooking purposes and stored well. Originating in the state of Rhode Island about 1720, it was the first really good variety of American apple and the first to be named in the United States. While it is still grown, commercial production is limited as the tender fruit do not travel well under modern shipping conditions.

Numbers 15, 16, and 17 on Custead's list were "from Mr. Cooper's famous orchard." Custead was probably referring to Joseph Cooper of Gloucester County, New Jersey. Cooper and his son were plant breeders who, from the mid-eighteenth century into the nineteenth, worked with fruiting plants to improve their quality. The "large, fair, soft and white" variety in the catalogue, yet unnamed, was probably later known as Cooper's Early White. This variety was still popular in 1876 when it was exhibited at the annual meeting of the Massachusetts Horticultural Society (Transactions 1875:116).

Apple trees are a pleasant sight in the spring when their fragrant blossoms brighten the landscape, and Custead offered one selection purely for its aesthetic quality: the Chinese Flowering Apple, *Prunus spectabilis Ait* (Hedrick 1919/1972:479). Strictly speaking, this was not an apple but a cherry. The small yellow fruit, not fit for eating, resembled a medlar.

Prince's Long Island nursery issued a catalogue in 1827, the same year as Custead's. The 171 pages contained an extensive list of fruit plants, including many also carried by Custead. Prince's had a very large stock of plants and was represented by agents in Upper Canada. Custead may have obtained his original stock from this source to propagate in his nursery. William Claus had ordered some of his fruit trees from Prince's in 1823. His diary entry for 17 March recorded that his order had been responded to, and that W. Prince would send the trees as far as Albany for fifteen dollars. On 5 June, Claus received the trees from New York and "put them out immediately" (NA MG19 FI).

Pear trees were widely grown in the early nineteenth century. In Europe, pears had been grown since the days of the Romans. By the eighteenth century the making of perry had become a commercial enterprise in France and Germany, supplying domestic and export markets. The alcoholic perry was an effervescent beverage, and much of the production in France was supplied to the makers of champagne. In England it remained a beverage for local consumption. Gerard mentions a wine made from pear juice which was "wholesome in small quantities which comforteth," but when drunk too new or by someone who was not used to it, it acted as a purgative (Gerard 1633/1975:1455).

Pear *Pyrus communis* L.

Some of the best varieties of pear originated in France, where at least three hundred varieties were known in the seventeenth century. Their popularity was partly due to the pear being a favourite fruit of Louis XIV.

The relatively new technique of espaliered trees made growing pears (and peaches) more successful, as it allowed protection from wind and cold and permitted closer attention (Grigson 1975:309). Several of better varieties of French pears were grown in England, and some reached America at an early date – among them the Bon Cretien which had been grown in France since the fifteenth century. It is said that early in the seventeenth century Peter Stuyvesant, governor of New Amsterdam (New York), imported a Summer Bon Cretien grown in a tub (Hedrick 1950:54). This pear was well known in England in Parkinson's day, and he wrote of two Bon Cretiens, the summer and the winter. The Summer Cretien he described as a long green and yellow pear sometimes with red sides; he found the Winter Cretien seldom bore fruit in the English climate unless placed against a wall for protection (Parkinson 1629/1976:592). Both of these pears were on Custead's list. In the eighteenth century the Williams' Bon Cretien was the favoured variety in England and was taken to America late in the century. In 1817 Enoch Bartlett found a Bon Cretien on his New England farm which he named the Bartlett, but was probably the English Williams' pear (Greenoak 1983:67). Today the Bartlett pear has become the fruit to which all others are compared and forms the bulk of the commercial market in North America.

Custead's catalogue listed twenty-five pear varieties, all priced at one shilling ten pence except for choice varieties grafted on quince stock, priced at two shillings sixpence. The varieties were designated "melting" (for eating pears) or "baking." Orchard pears are classified under the general nomenclature of *Pyrus communis* L. There were never as many named varieties of pears as there were of apples, for few choice varieties originated from chance seedlings. The most satisfactory methods for propagating the pear were by grafting or by division, using suckers. Quince was the preferred stock for pear scions until the twentieth century. The resultant tree was a pyramidal dwarf form suitable for the home garden. When quince stock was not available, a seedling pear tree was used instead. If grown locally the seedling tree was certain to be hardy.

The Green Chisell, Catharine, Orange, and Pound pears in Custead's catalogue all came to America in the eighteenth century and were mentioned two hundred years before in Parkinson's work. The Green Chisell was a delicate greenish-yellow pear which would "melt in the mouth." The Catharine, a yellow pear with red sides, was grown in the American colonies before 1709 (Leighton 1986:239). The Orange pear was a longtime favourite; two dozen of them were displayed at the 1874 annual meeting of the Massachusetts Horticultural Society, all from a tree that was reputed to be 235 years old. In that year the tree bore three bushels of fruit (Transactions 1874:152). The Pound pear was a good general-purpose fruit, eaten fresh or cooked.

The Seckel pear, a variety of American origin, was first found on the farm of Jacob Weiss near Philadelphia about 1760. It may have been a seedling left by the Swedish settlement that preceded the arrival of William Penn's colonists. The farm was later sold to Seckel who named the pear. It soon became the most popular variety on the Philadelphia market, and its fame spread quickly. Jefferson planted a "Sickle" pear in 1807, which he considered to be a "new" variety (Leighton 1986:240). In his 1817 book *View on Cultivated Fruit Trees*, William Coxe pronounced it to be the "finest pear" (van Ravenswaay 1977:64). The tree was slow growing, bearing small, late-ripening yellow fruit with bright red cheeks and a sweet musky scent. It became a top-ranking variety during the late nineteenth century, rivalling the Bartlett for its fine quality. The Bartlett and the Seckel varieties accounted for most of the pears grown in commercial orchards at the beginning of the twentieth century. The Seckel is less well-known today but is still grown in home gardens and is used in nurseries for hybridizing new varieties.

By the twentieth century many of the varieties in Custead's catalogue had been eliminated from nursery lists, surpassed by newer introductions. The names of several of the pears listed – the Chaumontelle, Cuisse Madame, Cresane, Veraglue, and St Germain – suggest a French origin. The remaining varieties may have been less successful in America for they do not appear to have survived the test of time or climate. Pear trees are susceptible to a number of fungal diseases, which were not well understood in the early nineteenth century. European varieties of fruit were exposed to North American fungi for which they had little resistance. A rust – its alternate host the native juniper – was particularly devastating to young pear trees. A fire-blight, for which there was no cure, swept across North America in the 1870s. The cause of this disaster was unrecognized by farmers who wrote desperate pleas to newspapers and agricultural periodicals for a way to save their orchards. The losses were irrecoverable, and it is impossible to know how many varieties were lost.

The Toronto Nursery also supplied plum, cherry, peach and nectarine trees, all fruits of the drupe, or stone, type.

There were seventeen varieties of plums for Custead's clientele to choose from. Some were labelled with the letters "L" or "S," to show they had fruit of a large size or were of superior flavour. The plum trees

cost two shillings each, except for
the New Green or Flushing Gage
and Bolmar's Washington, which
were three shillings and nine pence
each.

One of Custead's plums was
a natural species, *Prunus cerasifera*
Ehrh., the Myrobalan plum from
Asia Minor, which had been cultivated for a long time in France.
The fruit turned from green to
red to purple as it ripened and
was sweet, soft, and juicy but small,
hardly more than an inch across.
Commonly known as the Cherry
Plum, it was seldom grown for
its fruit but was more likely to be
found growing in a shrub border
or hedge. Its principal use was as
root stock for more choice varieties. One

Plum　　*Prunus cerasifera* Ehrh.

of the Myrobalan's great advantages was that it did not sucker, a troublesome
characteristic of many plums (Bailey 1902:1377). It is still the most common
stock for plum trees in modern nurseries (New York Fruit Testing 1986:13).

Custead's list included four gage-type plums: the Green Gage, New
Green Gage, Yellow Gage, and Purple Gage. The Green Gage, originally
called the Reine Claude after the wife of King Francois I in the late fifteenth
century, came from France. Several trees were taken to England in the early
eighteenth century by Sir William Gage, by whose name they were subsequently known (Greenoak 1983:83). The fruit was delicious eaten fresh and
made excellent preserves; the trees were hardy and consistently bore good
crops. The variety soon became the most popular plum on the market.
The Green Gage reached America before 1699 (New York Fruit Testing
1986:14). The Prince Nursery planted twenty-five quarts of Green Gage
seed in 1790, and from these seedlings developed a large stock of gage-type
plums. The Green Gage comes fairly true from seed, so the progeny of the
Prince plantings were variations that closely resembled their parent. Prince
gave particular attention to the growing of plums, and his 1828 catalogue
listed 140 varieties. The New Green or Flushing and the Washington were
varieties originating from Prince's experimentation, for which Custead
charged a little more than his other varieties. The Washington plum was

deep yellow marked with red, with a sweet sugary taste – a fine eating fruit. The Green Gage remains a very desirable garden variety and is still supplied by nurseries, although it is now more likely to be found under its original name, the Reine Claude.

The Red and White Magnum Bonum plums were old European cooking varieties. The fruit was very large and firm with a light bloom. The White Magnum Bonum, with a deep yellow skin, was also known as the Yellow Egg. Both these plums were grown in the mid-Atlantic states before 1788 and were still being grown in 1950 (Hedrick 1950:156).

With Cooper's Large Red Plum, we again encounter the work of Joseph Cooper of New Jersey, the nurseryman who bred three of the apples listed in Custead's catalogue. Cooper's Large Red was a plum he introduced to America from France, where it was known as La Delicieuse; the English called it Lady Lucy (Hedrick 1950:433).

The Orleans varieties of plum were medium-sized dark red or purple fruit, prized as fine cooking fruit in England. Custead offered two, the New Orleans and Smith's Orleans.

The remaining varieties in the catalogue were less frequently grown in the past and are no longer seen today. It is rather surprising there were no native plums or their hybrids on Custead's list: plums were among the first American fruit brought into cultivation by the early colonists.

William Claus recorded in his garden diary his experiments with grafting fruit in southern Upper Canada. In 1818 he grafted a Yellow Gage and an "Orleans Plumb" using cuttings from a friend's garden in Albany, New York. In the spring of 1823 he grafted two Green Gage plums, and later in the season he tried grafting an apricot on a plum root (NA MG19 FI).

Under the heading for cherries, the cata-
logue lists six varieties. The Kentish cost only one shilling three pence, and the other cherry trees were priced at two shillings six-pence. All except the Black Heart were grown in the southern American colonies before 1788 (Hedrick 1950:159). Very little information could be found for the Carnation variety.

Three of the selections were the Heart type of cherry: the White Heart, Black

Cherry   *Prunus cerasus* L.

Heart, and Ox Heart. These were sweet cherries, varieties of *Prunus avium* L. with reddish-black fruit about one inch in diameter. The sweet cherry is a tall tree growing to seventy feet with a broadly spreading crown. As at least two were required for pollination, growing sweet cherries required a good deal of space. Cherries were the first fruit tree to flower in the spring, as early as mid-April, a time when in most of the province of Upper Canada there were still killing frosts. It was also too early in the season for most natural pollinators to be active, resulting in poor crops of fruit. Custead's trees may have been too young for him to realize the limitations of these fruits in Upper Canada.

The Kentish cherry, *Prunus cerasus var. caproniana* L., was derived from a wild dwarf species that originated in Kent, England, an area well known for its cherry orchards. This very old English variety was brought to America by the early colonists of Massachusetts (Hedrick 1919/1972:459). The cherries were red with a sour or acid taste, which made them desirable for cooking purposes.

The May Duke cherry was probably a hybrid between sweet and Kentish cherries. This was the most widely grown variety in England in the nineteenth century, the fruit being much in demand. The cherries were red, turning to almost black when ripe, with a juicy, red-coloured flesh, and a slightly acid taste somewhere between sweet and sour. They were such a delectable fruit that they were mentioned by name in household recipes.

Cherry sauces were eaten with ham, tongue, poultry, duck, and wild fowl. Dark tart cherries were used in sweet dishes, pies, tarts, and puddings. Kentish cherries were pickled with juniper berries, spices and sugar. Making cherry brandy was a popular way of preserving Kentish and Duke cherries, as well as creating a rich sweet beverage for festive occasions.

Peaches came from western China or the sub-continent of Asia, and consequently were named *Prunus persica* Benth. & Hooker. Their cultivation took place very early in history – they were grown in China before 1000 B.C. Several

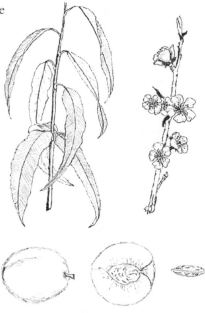

Peach
Prunus persica Benth. & Hooker

varieties were familiar to Gerard and Parkinson in seventeenth-century England. Gerard mentioned five, but Parkinson named twenty-one varieties – one of them the Newington that appeared on Custead's list.

The catalogue listed nine varieties. Four of these were in the 1790 catalogue from Prince's nursery: the Rare Ripe, Old Newington, Lemon, and Yellow or Red Cheek Malagatune (Leighton 1986:237). The Malagatune was probably the Melocoton, a variety that originated in America (Hedrick 1950:155). The similarity of the misspelling almost certainly links Custead's nursery with Prince's.

In parts of the American colonies the peach grew extremely well. The trees were short-lived, bearing crops for only four or five years before deteriorating, necessitating repeated plantings to maintain a steady production of fruit. All peach trees in early America were grown from seed, and only a few were named. Hedrick believed few peach varieties grown before 1860 could still be found in the 1950s (Hedrick 1950:155). There appeared to be a problem with "diseased" trees in Custead's time, for he included a lengthy statement in the introduction to the catalogue on how to preserve healthy trees.

An experience from the 1870s described by a subscriber to the *New England Farmer* illustrates the complexities of growing peaches from seed. The January 1871 issue printed the story of a woman who "cracked a pit which contained two kernels: desirous of noting the result she planted the kernels which in due time germinated, grew and bore, the one a large white, the other a large yellow peach; each distinct from the other in habit of growth, and appearance and flavor of fruit" (*New England Farmer* 1871:50).

The nectarine is the same species as the peach – often a single tree bore both types of fruit simultaneously. Charles Darwin was the first to record the observation that the nectarine could appear unexpectedly on a peach tree (de Candolle 1886/1964:226). The only difference is the skin of the fruit, which is soft and downy on the peach, smooth and firm on the nectarine. The two varieties offered by Custead were available from Prince's nursery in 1790. They had earlier been available from a nursery in Baltimore, Maryland (Hedrick 1950:156).

California is now the only place in North America where nectarines are grown as a commercial crop. Their culture has never been of importance in Canada.

Many attempts were made to bring the wine grape, *Vitis vinifera* L., to America. Grapes were the preferred fruit for wine-making, but they were also popular dessert fruit, and grape juice and jellies were made in the home. The fermented juice was a source of vinegar, needed for many kitchen purposes. But the European vines were tender, and the only method of growing these successfully in the North-East was in the glass-house; the first greenhouses in America were built for this purpose. However, there were several hardy native American species of grape, and efforts were made to overcome the difficulties in raising grapes by uniting the wild and culti-vated sorts. Many tried grafting im-ported cuttings to root stock of native grapes, but eventually hardy hybrids were successfully created between the imported and the native species, using the American species *Vitis aestivalis* Michx., or *V. labrusca* L. M'Mahon, in the 1806 edition of his *American Gardener*, was the first to mention the early American hybrids or to suggest grafting "of the best European kinds on our most vigorous native vines" (M'Mahon 1858/ 1976:452). One of the eight varieties of grapes listed in Custead's catalogue was the Isabella, one of these new hybrids. The Prince nursery had named this grape in 1816 after Isabella Gibbs of Brooklyn, in whose garden the first vine of this sort was found (Hedrick 1933/1966:390). The Isabella was one of few cultivated grape varieties that could be grown out-of-doors in the first half of the nineteenth century. Another such hybrid offered by Custead was Bland's Virginia. However, the practice of grafting became so successful that it became the general method of propagation and was eventually re-sponsible for saving the European grape-growing industry. An infestation of *Phylloxera*, or wood-louse, threatened to ruin European vineyards in the early twentieth century. American root stock, more resistant to this insect, was sent to Europe to replace the diseased plants, and the profitable vine-yards were revitalized.

Grape   *Vitis vinifera* L.

The interest in building an American grape industry was of prime con-cern to growers. In 1830 William Robert Prince published *A Treatise on the Vine*, which remained the most comprehensive text on the subject through the nineteenth century. The grape vine proved to be successful in southern Upper Canada, and the Niagara region of Ontario now produces many fine wines. The older varieties have been abandoned in favour of more reliable, productive varieties, and research continues in the breeding of improved grape cultivars.

Currants and gooseberries were popular fruit in
England, but have never received much attention in other European countries. The red
and white currants were *Ribes silvestre*
(Lam.) Mert. & Koch; the black
currant was the *R. nigrum L.*; the
gooseberry was the *R. grossularioides*
Maxim. All were members of *Grossulari-
aceae*, and the French had but one name,
groseille, for all three species. Unlike so many
fruits that originated in the warm climates
of Asia and the Mediterranean, currants and
gooseberries were natives of colder northern
areas of Europe, Asia, and America.

Red Currant
Ribes sylvestris (Lam.) Mert. & Koch

Cultivated varieties of red, white, and black currants were grown in
America before the end of the eighteenth century (Leighton 1986:231). Red
and white currants were more widely grown than the black. Use of these
berries was not recorded until the Middle Ages when they were first cultivated in central Europe. In the sixteenth century they were known in France
as the "*grosseillier d'outremer*," suggesting they were not native to that country
(de Candolle 1886/1964:277). During the seventeenth century they were
improved by the growers in Holland, to be known as "Dutch sorts." The
Red Dutch had very good flavour and remained one of the finest varieties
for a long time, becoming a favourite in America. A reference from 1874
suggested it might be losing ground to more recently developed varieties:
"The Red Dutch has almost entirely disappeared from our tables, which is to
be regretted, as it was considered of better quality than either the Cherry or
the Versailles, although not as large or showy" (Transactions 1874:147). In
fact, this berry did not disappear; in 1902 the "Red Dutch, though small, is
still highly prized on the Plains" (Bailey 1902:417). It was still on the table
in 1925, recommended for growing: "in most sections the Red Dutch will
be found to be the most satisfactory variety" (Bailey 1925:425).

Parkinson regarded the white currant as being "more daintie and less
common" than the red currant. The White Dutch was, like the Red Dutch,
still a valued variety in 1925, sweeter than the red, but there was little
demand for it on the American market.

Red currants were used in sauces and jellies served with venison, fowl,
ham and pork. Not only did the tart taste of the fruit relieve the fatty
consistency of these meats at the table but it could also be used as an anti-
putrefactant for their preservation. The berries had an antiseptic quality

used in folk medicine to relieve inflammations. A spoonful of red currant jelly, or a lozenge made from the berry juice, was taken to pacify a sore throat. A fine, light, often effervescent, rose-coloured wine was made from the fruit – one of Custead's varieties was called Large Champaigne Red, possibly regarded as a good variety for this purpose. Sweetened red currant juice made a refreshing beverage on a hot day. The tart berries made excellent pies and desserts.

The black currant, with a much stronger odour and taste than the red or white, never enjoyed the same popularity. It was used in France only for the manufacture of the liqueur cassis. It was seldom grown as a crop by North American gardeners, although it could be found in home gardens. An acid fruit, it makes a reasonably good wine and is a good fruit for cooking, but the scent and taste of the berries did not appeal to everyone. To some it made one of the finest jams, while others found it, as Gerard did, "to be of a stinking and somewhat loathing flavour."

Gooseberries grew wild in Britain and were brought into cultivation during the sixteenth century. The best-tasting wild gooseberries were said to come from Scotland. Dishes made from this fruit were very popular in England, a taste not shared to the same extent elsewhere in Europe. (On the European continent gooseberries were grown in Germany and the Low Countries where they were called *Kruisbezie*.) During the eighteenth century the textile workers of northern England and Scotland raised gooseberries as a hobby. They organized grower's groups, as much social organizations as horticultural ones, which held meetings and exhibitions. A song was composed by the growers with rhyming verses listing some of the favoured varieties. In 1831 no fewer than 722 varieties were grown (Greenoak 1983:41). The aim was to grow the largest berry, and, to this end, they carried out many different pruning and grooming practices. The berries were measured and weighed, but the winners did not always have the best taste – at best they were "insipid."

The gooseberry ripened early in the season, about the same time that the black elderberry was in flower – several interesting recipes in old English cookbooks combined gooseberries and elderberry blossoms. The British were very fond of gooseberry pie and made conserves of the tart fruit to be served with fish and meat. The berries made a light-coloured, effervescent alcoholic beverage that could be compared favourably with champagne.

The gooseberries brought to America did not fare well. They were subject to mildew and did not withstand the cold winters and dry summers

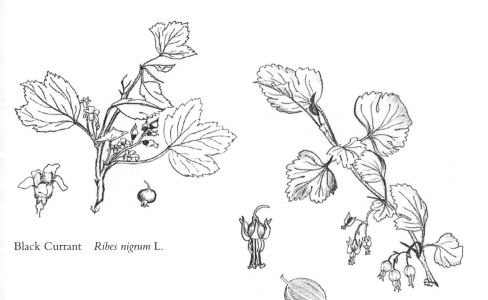

Black Currant   *Ribes nigrum* L.

Gooseberry   *Ribes grossularioides* Maxim.

Raspberry   *Rubus idaeus* L.

Strawberry   *Fragaria vesca* L.

favourably. Mildew-resistant varieties were developed in the 1830s but never gained the standing of a prized fruit (van Ravenswaay 1977:66). As very few references mention any of the varieties offered by Custead, it is not known whether they were of European or American origin.

The fungi to which the genus *Ribes* are subject include a leaf-rust, *Cronartium ribicola*, which also causes blister rust on pine trees. For this reason there are many areas in America where the growing of currants is prohibited.

Raspberries and strawberries, small fruit of the *Rosaceae* or Rose family, were both native to areas in the northern hemisphere in Europe, Asia, and America. Raspberries were found growing wild when the colonists arrived in North America. Nevertheless, immigrants brought several European varieties with them. Custead's three raspberries were of the European species *Rubus idaeus* L.: a Red, a White and a Large White Antwerp. The Red were seven and a half pence each, the White were sixpence each, and Large White Antwerps were one shilling each or seven shillings sixpence a dozen.

The Large White Antwerp was one of the most tender varieties of raspberry. The berries were very good tasting but ever so fragile. Each berry had to be picked the moment it ripened, or it would crumble into little pieces. This meant that to get the best quality of berry the bushes had to be examined daily as the fruit ripened. Custead priced this variety much higher than the other two. Perhaps this variety was more highly esteemed because of its flavour or perhaps the bushes were rare at the time.

Raspberries were eaten fresh, served with cream. Jams made from them tended to be gritty unless the pulp was strained of the seeds. The berries were sometimes used to flavour vinegars. Fresh or dried raspberry leaves were used as a tea which not only had a unique flavour but was a popular remedy for diarrhoea and dysentery.

Two of the three strawberries in Custead's catalogue were from Europe. Strawberries from the wooded mountainsides of Europe were enjoyed in Parkinson's time. The Hautbois, *Fragaria moschata* Duchesne, relatively new to England in 1629, came from Bohemia, giving it the name by which Parkinson knew it. He wrote "the Bohemia hath beene with us but of late days, but is the goodliest and greatest ... some of the berries measured to bee neere five inches about" (Parkinson 1629/1991:526).

These and the Large Hudson were offered at the price of one shilling per dozen. The Hudson was the first important variety of the native American strawberry, *Fragaria virginiana* Duchesne, which was offered by the Prince nursery in 1790. The fruit were considered "very large, very fine" (Leighton 1986:244).

The third selection was the Alpine Monthly, *Fragaria vesca* L., a small berry from Europe with excellent flavour. Moreover, as the name Monthly suggests, it bore more than once in a season. Custead charged twice as much for this variety, two shillings per dozen. The Alpine strawberry was one of the parents of our modern ever-bearing strawberries.

Most strawberries send out runners, long stems from the mother plant from which additional plants grow. The Hautbois and the Hudson were propagated from their runners, but the Alpine strawberry, which had few runners, was grown from seed.

The taste of the first spring strawberries was so enjoyable that the occasion was often celebrated. Strawberry festivals in America were regular events held by church congregations and other community organizations in which strawberry shortcake was served with gobs of rich cream. Fortunately, this tradition has continued to the present day.

5

Ornamental Trees and Flowering Shrubs

Trees and shrubs form the backbone of a garden, providing architectural interest around which other features can be displayed. Woody plants tend to live longer and grow to a greater size than herbaceous plants, so the choice of suitable species should be made with care. The Toronto Nursery catalogue offered several European species of trees and shrubs, but a good number were of American origin. Early collections of American plants taken to Europe included numerous species of woody plants that by 1827 were already grown in many European gardens. It was ironic that a number of these were re-introduced to America at a later date, although the majority of colonists were probably not aware of the plants' origins. For example, a shrub from the Carolinas, taken to England, may well not have been recognized as a native American plant when it was brought back to Upper Canada because it was not indigenous to that particular part of the continent.

It is the work of a nursery to propagate plant material in quantities sufficient to supply the current demand. Woody plants are propagated by several methods: sowing seeds, grafting, layering, or division. Growing woody plants from seed is not the most satisfactory way to maintain a species, as seeds may not always reproduce the parent. Seeds from woody plants often require specific treatment to break their dormancy; most woody plants take a considerable period of time, often counted in years, to reach a size suitable for transplanting into a garden. For successful germination, seeds require specific conditions of moisture, temperature, and temperature changes. The process is more successful when the original habitat of the plant is known and understood. However, if large numbers of plants are required, and the resultant plants do not necessarily need to be exactly like the parent, growing from seed is the cheapest way for a nursery to reproduce woody plants when time is not a major factor.

When the requirements are more stringent, grafting or layering will produce a replica of the parent. The grafting process requires compatible root stock on which to graft the scions, and a knowledge of the grafting technique best for each species. If sufficient quantities of root stock are available, grafting is the most successful way to increase a woody species. In some instances, however, a cutting can be made to grow its own root system, given the proper conditions of light, temperature, and humidity. Layering can produce rooted plants quite satisfactorily within one or two growing seasons, although this technique is not suitable for all plants; it would be difficult to layer a large tree, for example. Reproducing by division is appropriate only when the plant has several stems or grows suckers from the main stem.

Custead does not give any figures for the numbers of ornamental trees and shrubs he had in the nursery in 1827, nor is there any information on the propagation methods he used. The source of his plant material is not known for certain. It could be that not all his plants were propagated in his nursery but were obtained elsewhere and grown on in his establishment. Many of the woody plants he offered were exotic species from habitats quite different from Upper Canada.

A number of the woody plants in the catalogue had edible fruit, nuts, or berries. Some species were valuable for timber, while others had uses in dyeing or tanning processes. These applications appear to have interested Custead less than the plants' ornamental value. Species may have been selected for their appeal to the senses: for their size and shape, the colours of the blooms and foliage, and the scents of the flowers.

The catalogue listing for trees is not extensive, including only twelve selections. The species listed as "Mountain Sole" remains, unfortunately, unidentifiable. Of the remainder, six were native to North America, and the others were well-established ornamentals from Europe.

The Lombardy Poplar, *Populus nigra italica* L., was a favourite for its landscape value. The original tree, found in the Lombardy province of Italy in the 1600s, was a male clone. It was sterile, and all propagation had to be vegetative or asexual. The tree was tall-growing, to a height of ninety feet, and narrow in its outline. This habit created a striking vertical accent, much like an exclamation point. A row of Lombardy Poplars along a road or laneway made a dramatic statement and as they were fast-growing, this effect could be achieved in a relatively short time. The Lombardy Poplar was introduced to the Philadelphia area in 1784 or 1785, where it soon became the most frequently planted tree: it was not long before nearly

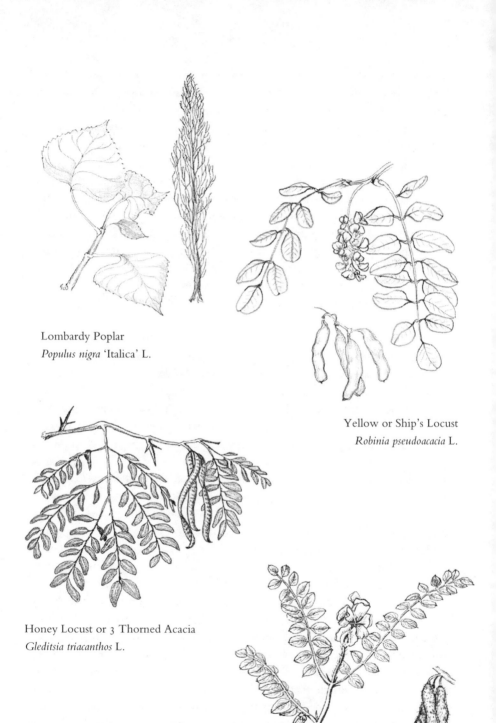

Lombardy Poplar
Populus nigra 'Italica' L.

Yellow or Ship's Locust
Robinia pseudoacacia L.

Honey Locust or 3 Thorned Acacia
Gleditsia triacanthos L.

Glutinous Acacia or Italian Locust
Robinia viscosa Vent.

every home in the region had at least one in the garden. The Lombardy Poplar was listed in the catalogue from Prince's Long Island nursery in 1790. By 1798 this nursery was known to have 10,000 of these trees, from ten to fifteen feet in height, available to its customers (Hedrick 1950:146).

The trees became popular in Canada and were planted extensively. Many old Lombardy Poplars are still standing, although few are in healthy condition, for in recent years the tree has been susceptible to a fungus, *Cryptodiaporthe populea*, which selectively attacks poplars. The canker becomes a spreading wound, destroying both the bark and the cambrium layer of the tree until it eventually encircles the trunk or the limb, killing all growth beyond the infection. As there is no known cure, the Lombardy poplar is no longer recommended for gardens, and this once-common feature of old gardens has been lost to the landscape. Few other trees can replace its dramatic architectural form.

There are three trees on Custead's list called locust: the Yellow or Ship's Locust, *Robinia pseudo-acacia* L. (now commonly called the Black Locust); the Honey Locust or Three-thorned Acacia, *Gleditsia triacanthos* L.; and the Glutinous Acacia or Italian Locust, *Robinia viscosa* Vent. All three are members of the Pea family, *Leguminosae*, and are native to North America. They have long pinnate leaves and racemes of pea-like blossoms followed by fruit pods containing a number of seeds. These trees are relatively fast growing and their leaves provide a pleasant light shade.

The white flowers of the Black Locust are heavily perfumed, adding to its desirability as an ornamental. One of the first North American trees to be taken to Europe, it was grown in Paris in the early 1600s by the herbalist to King Henri IV, Jean Robin, for whom it was named. By the early nineteenth century it had become a fashionable tree in England, and its popularity was later transferred to North America, peaking in the 1860s (Hedrick 1950:150). The wood was valued, being extremely hard and durable. It was in demand for ship's parts, such as treenails, which accounts for the common name, Ship's Locust, that Custead used. The wood was also valuable for making hard-wearing parts such as cog wheels for mill machinery and wheel hubs and axles for carriages. Another of its characteristics was its resistance to rot when in contact with the earth. This made it very useful for fence posts although the wood was seldom used for general construction. In the early seventeenth century the naturalist Catesby observed that Black Locust posts erected a century earlier at Jamestown were still in good condition (Dutton 1979:29). Although all parts of the tree are poisonous, the bark was used by the Amerindians for toothache and as a strong emetic

(Foster and Duke 1990:274), and an infusion of the flowers was used externally to treat rheumatism and headache. The flowers contain the glycoside *robinin*, which is currently being investigated for use as a diuretic.

The Honey Locust had similar features: it was an open, fine-leaved tree with pea-like blossoms followed by long seed pods. Introduced to cultivation in 1700, the Honey Locust was first illustrated by Catesby in 1731. It has been known to grow to 140 feet, much taller than the Black Locust. The leaves are both pinnate and bipinnate, which creates a lacy effect. The trunk and branches are armed with clusters of stout thorns, some simple, others trifid, accounting for the nomenclature *triacanthos*. Early colonists used the thorns for carding wool and as pins for wool and cotton sacks. The tree's bristling limbs made them useful for hedges, which, when kept well pruned, formed impenetrable barriers. Modern cultivars of the *Gleditsia triacanthos* have been bred to be virtually thornless. There is also a golden-leaved variety, which many prefer for domestic gardens.

The greenish flowers are without scent. The seed pods grow to a length of eighteen inches and are more noticeable than the flowers. The pods contain a honey-flavoured pulp which gave the tree its common name. The juice of the pods was used as an antiseptic, while a tea made from the bark helped to ease hoarseness or a sore throat. However, caution is indicated for these old remedies, as the plant contains alkaloids that are potentially toxic (Foster and Duke 1990:274).

The tree called the Glutinous or Italian Locust in the catalogue was difficult to identify. The tree now called the Clammy Locust, *Robinia viscosa* Vent., may have been the tree grown by Custead. However, there is another possibility that would seem to correspond to Custead's description of a Clammy Italian locust. A tree, once called the European Locust, was cultivated in Italy and Spain for its edible pulpy pods which contain carob. This tree, the *Ceratonia siliqua* L., now known as Carob or St John's Bread, required a warm climate similar to that of the most southerly United States. It was known to some early settlers from Europe who may have tried to establish it in the American colonies (Dutton 1979:30). In the early nineteenth century there was still a lot to be learned about the climate in North America, and gardeners tried to grow species they were familiar with in Europe. If the European Locust was the tree Custead was offering, he may be seen to be ahead of his time, for in 1854 the United States Patent Office tried to encourage cultivation of this tree by distributing free seed (Hedrick 1919/1972:157). However, it requires a Mediterranean-like climate and today is grown only in California.

The alternative suggestion is that Custead was growing the Clammy Locust, a tree listed in contemporary American nursery catalogues. The name referred to the viscid or sticky branches of the tree. *Robinia viscosa* was also called the Rose Acacia, acknowledging its attractive pendulous racemes of pinkish flowers and pinnate leaves, characteristics it shares with the European Locust. Both trees would grow to a height of thirty to forty feet at maturity.

Black Walnut, *Juglans nigra* L., is one of the North American trees introduced to Europe in the early seventeenth century. It grew in forests from present-day southern Ontario to Florida and west as far as Texas. A handsome tree with very desirable landscape features, it reaches fifty to seventy feet in height and is almost as wide in its spread. The pinnate leaves are dense and give considerable shade. The nuts are edible and good-tasting, though not as rich as the English walnut, *Juglans regia* L. The nuts were eaten fresh and pickled for out-of-season consumption to ward off scurvy. Amerindians used the nuts in various ways for food; travellers observed the nuts being pounded to a pulp, then mixed with water to form a milky fluid which was eaten as such or added to grains or beans to give them additional flavour (Erichsen-Brown 1979:69–70).

The American walnut was valued for its lumber, as the tree grows straight without branches for half its height, giving sawn boards almost flawless grain. The wood was highly prized by cabinetmakers, being hard and strong with a deep, rich colour. It was especially suited for making gunstocks, as it "absorbs more recoil than any other wood" (Dutton 1979:5). The bark gave a deep yellow dye for textiles and the leaves and hulls a brown dye that never faded; an oil pressed from the kernels was used in the manufacture of paints. Native Indians used the inner bark to relieve toothache and made a tea from the leaves that acted as a mild diuretic (Foster and Duke 1990:276). The astringent tea when applied externally also gave relief to skin problems such as eczema and herpes infections (Grieve 1931/1978:842).

Walnut trees were easily grown from the nuts, but were difficult to transplant, for even a young tree sends down a deep taproot. The roots contain *juglone*, a plant chemical that inhibits the growth of some other plants, particularly those in the Rose family and the *Solanaceae*.

The tree Custead called the New England Walnut or Hickory, *Carya ovata* (Mill.) K. Koch., is now called the Shellbark or Shagbark Hickory. Because of its similarity to the walnut, the nomenclature for this tree has changed

Black Walnut
Juglans nigra L.

New England Walnut or Hickory
Carya ovata (Mill.) K. Koch.

American Chestnut
Castanea dentata (Marshall) Borkh.

several times over the years: it was originally named *Juglans ovata* by Miller in 1768 and later changed to *Hicoria ovata* by Britton. Hickory trees, like walnuts, were introduced to Europe in the early seventeenth century. Their native habitat stretched from southern Quebec to the Carolinas. They grow to eighty feet, with a spreading crown. The smooth bark of the immature stage changes as the tree matures, becoming exfoliate, with loose strips peeling from the trunk. The fruit is a sweet white edible nut, sometimes called a white walnut. In his travels in New England during the late eighteenth century, Peter Kalm observed the bark being used for a yellow dye in the same way as that of the walnut. Dried wood chips were used in smoking meats, giving ham and bacon a sweet, rich flavour. In the spring the sap was drawn to make sugar or to ferment for a beer-like beverage. Hickory wood was tough and strong, suitable for making implement handles, barrel hoops, and spokes for wooden wheels.

Two chestnut trees, the European Horse Chestnut, *Aesculus hippocastrum* L., and the American Chestnut, *Castanea dentata* (Marshall) Borkh., were listed in the catalogue.

The Horse Chestnut was a prized ornamental in Europe. The first trees came from Constantinople in the sixteenth century. The French botanist Tradescant is said to have grown the first Horse Chestnut in England in 1633, and there are a few Horse Chestnuts still standing in Britain reputed to be over three hundred years old. The tree was widely planted as an ornamental on village streets throughout Europe, and the tradition continued in America. Longfellow's familiar poem describes the blacksmith's shop standing "under the spreading chestnut tree." It is a large tree, as high as sixty feet with a spread of fifty or more feet offering a dense shade. White flowers clustered in upright stalks appear in the spring like torches lighting up the branches. There have been various interpretations of the common name: perhaps it is because the leaf scar resembles a horseshoe, or perhaps because the hulled nuts were used to feed horses and other domesticated animals.

The Horse Chestnut has never been seriously regarded as anything but an ornamental, although children still enjoy using the nuts for their game of "knockers" or "conkers." There were no economic uses for the fruit or the wood. All parts of the tree are potentially toxic, but in the past a leaf tea was used in poultices to reduce fevers or relieve rheumatic inflammation (Foster and Duke 1990:264).

The American Chestnut was found growing from Maine to Michigan, including present-day southern Ontario. It could reach a great height, one hundred feet or more. The bur-type fruit each enclosed one to five nuts.

Although smaller than those of the European chestnut, Sturtevant claimed, they were much sweeter in taste (Hedrick 1919/1972:152). Indians made soups and breads from the beaten dark brown nutmeat and also made a beverage not unlike coffee from the roasted nuts, which had a laxative effect. The rough grey bark was used in the tanning process and provided a red dye for leather. One of the remedies for whooping cough was a decoction made from crushed leaves in alcohol; it was claimed the sedative effect controlled the violent coughing (Millspaugh 1892/1974:158).

The American Chestnut, described as "a pretty, large tree with pale yellowish flowers," is now but a memory, for the species was virtually destroyed by a blight, *Endothia parasitica*, introduced to the East Coast in 1906. The cankers produced airborne spores, quickly spread by wind, birds, and insects. No control has yet been found to counter this fungal disease. Resistant Asiatic species of chestnut are now being introduced to replace the native species in the landscape.

Two species of the Willow family, *Salicaceae*, were offered in the catalogue. One of the features of plants in this family is the typical flower cluster called a catkin.

The Yellow Willow, *Salix alba var vitellina* (L.) Stokes, is a large tree that can reach a height of over eighty feet with a trunk up to eight feet in circumference. The tree is fast-growing, up to three or four feet a year over a period of twenty years. The bark of the young branches is a golden yellow, much like the colour of an egg yolk. In Europe these trees were often pollarded – cut back to a single trunk each year – so that the tree was crowned with myriads of new yellow twigs each spring. In America the yellow branches provide added winter interest when there is little colour in the garden. The Yellow Willow was native to a large area stretching from southern Europe eastward to central Asia.

After its introduction to America, the Yellow Willow spread into the wild and is now naturalized from eastern Canada south to the Carolinas. When used as an ornamental for the colour of the bark, it must be kept pruned to encourage new growth.

The "Sleeping" or Weeping Willow was native to China. This origin was unknown when it was introduced in 1730 and received its name, *Salix babylonica* L., as it reached Europe from the Far East by way of the Euphrates River, the site of ancient Babylon. By the end of the 1700s it had been sent to America, and the Prince nursery had trees for sale in 1790. It was extremely easy to propagate as cuttings rooted readily: all that was required was to set a twig in the ground. Trees sold as Weeping Willows today are not the true species of the past but modern cultivars (Dirr 1983:634).

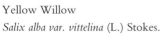

Yellow Willow
Salix alba var. vittelina (L.) Stokes.

Weeping Willow   *Salix babylonica* L.

Catalpha   *Catalpa bignonioides* Walt.

The branches of the Weeping Willow are pendulous, bending to the ground. The outline of the tree is graceful but the drooping characteristic has also linked it with sadness. In 1808 President Jefferson planted these willows around the graveyard at his home, Monticello (Dutton 1979:58–9). An image of the tree was used as a motif on nineteenth-century tombstones. The Weeping Willow was pictured on imported Chinese ceramics, which were very fashionable items in the West in the late eighteenth century. The willow pattern on tableware has never lost its appeal and is still being reproduced two hundred years after its introduction.

Since antiquity, willow trees have been used in folk medicine. The bark was fragmented or rolled into quills for sale by medieval apothecaries. Tannin and salicin are two of the ingredients found in the bark. Salicin, a precursor of the drug Aspirin, was isolated in 1825 and is now known to have anti-inflammatory properties (Stillé and Maisch 1880:1248). Preparations made from willow bark had many uses: in light doses, it acted as an aid to digestion, used particularly during convalescence from dysentery; increased doses relieved pain and reduced fevers; it could reduce the mucous discharge of nasal and throat passages; a tincture-soaked poultice or a wash served to heal corns, cuts, and rashes, and relieved discomforts of rheumatism and arthritis (Foster and Duke 1990:286). For colonists suffering from ague or intermittent fever (malaria), infusions of the bark could be used when the imported quinea or "Jesuits Bark" was not available.

The exotic-looking "Catalpha" tree listed in the catalogue, *Catalpa bigonioides* Walt., is native to the Gulf states of North America. The tree was first discovered by Catesby in the forests of Carolina, and he took it to England in 1726. It bears numerous flowers in erect panicles in the spring, followed by elongated pods in the summer. The long pods were responsible for other common names for this tree – Cigar Tree, Indian Bean, or Catawba tree. The tree grows to thirty or forty feet, with an irregular outline caused by the short crooked branching habit. The flowers are individually somewhat like foxglove, the white corolla marked with purple and yellow inside. The Catalpa grows best in the open where it can benefit from good light, but it needs to be sheltered from chilling winds.

Custead's listing of the Catalpa tree appears to be the first mention of it in Upper Canada. During the 1950s it became a favourite of nurserymen and was widely planted in Ontario. One Catalpa, placed in the middle of the front lawn, was a common sight in suburban communities.

All the trees listed by Custead as "Ornamental" were valuable in landscape design for particular characteristics of height, shape, texture, or colour.

Added features like fragrance or handsome flowers or fruit increased their value in planning a garden. Different types of foliage not only provided a variety of textures: they created various densities of shade. The Toronto Nursery may have been the first to propagate many of these trees in Upper Canada and make them available to local residents. Unfortunately, the Lombardy Poplar and the American Chestnut are no longer valid options for modern gardens.

Custead's list of "Flowering Shrubs" was extensive, and both European and North American species were included. Every selection had ornamental value, but a few were not of easy culture in the province of Upper Canada. Several of the North American species were from Atlantic coastal areas, habitats warmer and more humid than could be found inland. It could be that Custead grew these plants in greenhouses and intended them for clients with similar facilities. Perhaps he was unaware of their sensitivity to severe frosts that could damage young growth or even kill the roots. In spite of these shortcomings, his list contained some of the most valuable garden shrubs available to gardeners in the 1820s.

The list began with European Syrango, *Philadelphus coronarius* L., a shrub now known as the Mock Orange. In the past the Lilac and the Mock Orange were classified together in the genus *Syringa*, the name by which they were known to Custead. The shrub was native to southern Europe and southwest Asia, brought into cultivation in 1562. It is a member of the *Saxifragaceae*, a family of plants that contains many shrubs with showy flowers. The Mock Orange blooms in late spring when the white flowers perfume the air with a scent similar to orange blossoms. While it has little landscape interest after the flowering period, the Mock Orange is a very hardy plant, to be welcomed in a shrub border.

Hypericum frutex, *Hypericum prolificum* L., now called Shrubby St John's Wort, was native to eastern and central United States, and sometimes found wild in southern Upper Canada. It is one of the *Guttiferae* family, which includes many resinous shrubs. Shrubby St John's Wort has resinous dotted leaves, and its branches are two-edged, with a peeling bark. It grows from two to four feet in height, with a bushy habit. A profusion of small yellow flowers appears at the tips of new shoots in mid-summer. In the fall these become reddish fruits that provide a favourite meal for many songbirds.

Custead offered another St John's Wort, which may have been *Hypericum frondosum* Michx., a native of southeastern North America, now known as Golden St John's Wort. Similar to the Shrubby St John's Wort, it bears

Hypericum Frutex   *Hypericum prolificum* L.

European Syrango   *Philadelphus coronarius* L.

English Linden   *Tilia cordata* Mill.

Snowy Medlar   *Mespilus germanica* L.

larger and showier flowers. The branches have a reddish peeling bark; the leaves are bluish-green. Introduced to cultivation in 1747, it is still a very popular shrub in Britain, though not well known in Canada.

The Snowy Medlar, *Mespilus germanica* L., belongs to the Rose family. There is only one species in this genus but a great many varieties. The shrub, or small tree, native to southeastern Europe and Asia Minor, was grown in European gardens for its decorative appearance and small, apple-like fruit. The medlar has been known to grow a thick trunk upon maturing, up to eight inches in diameter, large for a tree that reaches a maximum height of only twenty feet. The flowers, with white or pink petals and prominent red anthers, bloom in late spring, followed by hard green fruit bearing distinctive long sepals at the base. The fruit are bitter, inedible until they have been touched by a heavy frost or stored for a while to ripen to a russet-brown colour. They were eaten when so over-ripe as to be almost rotten. The medlar was a familiar garden tree to Europeans, but it was seldom grown in Canada.

It might have been expected to find the English Linden listed under "Ornamental Trees," for the Linden, or Lime tree, was regarded as a one of the finest shade trees in Europe. Custead specifically called his selection the English species, which suggests that it was *Tilia cordata* Mill., the only linden indigenous to Britain. (The common European Linden, or Lime, *Tilia X vulgaris* Hayne, was a hybrid of two European species.) The English Linden belongs to the *Tiliaceae* and is related to the American Basswood. It can grow to a height of eighty feet or more and has glossy, heart-shaped leaves. In the late spring it bears clusters of fragrant yellowish-white flowers that appear to grow out of small leaves. The mature fruit are fuzzy nutlets. There were English Lindens growing in colonial Williamsburg in the early eighteenth century. The wood is soft, easy to carve, and was used by many craftsmen for architectural ornamentation. In Europe a medicinal linden flower water, *Aqua tille*, was prepared for administration to those suffering from indigestion, nervous disorders including headache, and inflammation of the nasal and throat passages. It was agreeably fragrant and used to cover the taste or odour of other medications.

The "Large Cole Nut" should probably read Large Cob Nut. It and the following English Filbert were hazelnut trees.

The English Filbert, *Corylus avellana* L., grows from ten to twenty feet in height. Although it can be called a tree, it generally grows with many stems, forming a thicket. The Cob Nut, *C. a. var. grandis*, is a variety that bears larger nuts than the typical species form. These nut trees were brought to America early in the seventeenth century.

The *Corylus* genus belongs to the Birch family, *Betulaceae*, a group of plants that bear both male catkins and female flowers on the same plant in separate clusters. The hard shell of the nut is roundish with a covering of leafy bracts. The nuts, good-tasting and rich in oil, are used in the making of sweet confections.

The two viburnums on the list, one an American native, the other of European origin, were very similar in habit. Both are members of *Caprifoliaceae*, the Honeysuckle or Twin-Flower family, which contains many handsome plants for garden use. The Cranberry Tree or Mountain Viburnum, *Viburnum trilobum* Marsh., grew in eastern North America from Newfoundland across the continent to present-day British Columbia. The Snow Ball or "Gilder Rose," *Viburnum opulus* L., grew wild in most of Europe north to the Arctic Circle.

Both viburnums are bushy plants with rounded tops that grow to heights between eight and twelve feet; both have rather flat flower clusters in which the centre flowers are small but fertile and the outer sterile flowers display open blooms with snow-white petals. The flower clusters are very showy, each one like a little bouquet. Later these are replaced by glossy red berries displayed in colourful clusters. The berries of the European species are edible but those of the American viburum are preferred. The Cranberry Viburnum was named for its berries, which can be made into a jelly very much like the cranberry.

The Candleberry Myrtle, *Myrica cerifera* L., known also as the Wax Myrtle, is a shrub or small tree of the *Myricaceae*, a family of plants with aromatic foliage. This broadly branching plant from the Atlantic coast will grow from eight to twenty-five feet in height. The branches, evergreen leaves, and blue-gray berries are covered with a waxy coating. The flowers are inconspicuous; male and female flowers, without sepals or petals, often occur on different plants. Colonists brought the shrub into cultivation before the end of the seventeenth century, using the wax coating from the fleshy fruit to make scented bayberry candles. By the 1750s the candles were made in sufficient quantity in the colony of Virginia to be a quality export item. The Candleberry Myrtle cannot tolerate severe frost; the foliage turns brown, then defoliates. In native stands it grows from the state of New Jersey southward to Florida.

Mountain Viburnum   *Viburnum trilobum* Marsh.

Large Cob nut   *Corylus avellana* L.

Althaea Frutex   *Hibiscus syriacus* L.

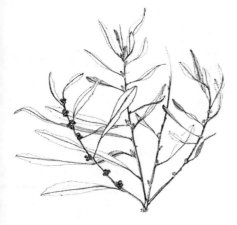

Candleberry Myrtle   *Myrica cerifera* L.

Another tender plant on Custead's list of shrubs was the red double-flowering Althea Frutex, *Hibiscus syriacus* L. Also known as the Rose of Sharon, it is one of the *Malvaceae* or Mallow family. The wide, funnel-shaped flowers are similar to hollyhocks but are short-lived. This species of hibiscus originated in eastern Asia, and was introduced to England before the end of the sixteenth century. The much-branched shrub grew to a height of eight to ten feet. By Custead's time there were several well-known varieties, and he was able to offer a double red, a single red, and a single white. The shrub was considered a hardy deciduous plant in England, but even there winter protection was advised, and growers were cautioned that the double varieties were less hardy than the singles.

Three varieties of Lilac were available: Purple and White, *Syringa vulgaris* L. and the Purple Persian Lilac, *Syringa X persica* L. These are shrubs of the *Olaceae*, or Olive family.

The Purple and White lilacs were native to the Balkan peninsula and cultivated in Turkey at a very early date. There the hollow pithy wood was used to make pipes. In 1562 the ambassador from Austria took several plants to Europe, and by the end of the century they were established in English gardens. The round-topped, many-stemmed shrub bears pyramidal spikes of flowers on the new growth in the spring. Purple forms are more common than the white. The fragrance of these flowers is quite intense and can be carried on a breeze for some distance. The fruit, a dull, greyish two-celled capsule, remains on the tree over the winter.

The Persian Lilac has been in cultivation since the early seventeenth century when it reached Europe from the Asian sub-continent. It has smaller leaves and paler blooms than the common lilac, but the short broad clusters can be so profuse as to weigh down the branches. It, too, is extremely fragrant.

Both forms of lilac were grown in the American colonies in the early 1700s and were listed in most nursery catalogues by the end of the century. Lilacs were to be found in the dooryards of most American farmhouses during the nineteenth century.

Numbers 16 and 17 in the catalogue are listed as the Brown Flowering Calycanthus and the Sweet Scented Shrub. Although they are listed as two kinds, they were more likely colour variants of the same species, *Calycanthus floridus* L., now known as Carolina Allspice or Sweetshrub. Native American shrubs from the Atlantic coastal area from Virginia to Florida, they grow to eight or ten feet, with a spread of up to twelve feet. The

Lilac   *Syringa vulgaris* L.

Sweet Scented Shrub   *Calycanthus floridus* L.

English Passion Flower   *Passiflora cerulea* L.

bloom has many dark purplish or reddish-brown sepals and petals which are similar in colour and shape. The bark, wood, leaves, and flowers of this densely hairy shrub are all very fragrant. The strong fruity scent has been likened to strawberries, pineapple, or even melon. It is said that the bark was used as a substitute for cinnamon by the early settlers.

One plant that certainly was intended for the "stove" house or hothouse was the English Passion Flower, *Passiflora cerulea* L. This flowering vine had been found in Brazil and introduced to cultivation in 1699. The flowers are intricate and intriguing, certain to interest the curious gardener. In the centre of the bloom is a circular formation like a crown, around which rows of filaments, petals, and sepals are arranged. The patterns created were likened to symbols of the Crucifixion, or the Passion of Christ. The fragrant flowers are short-lived, followed by a small yellow fruit.

The Bladder Senna, *Colutea arborescens* L., is a small shrub, a member of the Pea family, *Leguminoseae*, with typical features of pinnate leaves, and pea-like blossoms and seed pods. The flowers are yellow, emerging in racemes or clusters from leaf axils. The pods, which are responsible for the plant's common name, are inflated like bladders. Each pod contains thirty to forty easily propagated seeds. However, the Bladder Senna is hardy only in warm climates as it suffers major damage by severe frosts. It is native to the Mediterranean region, growing well in the same conditions as wine vineyards. The leaves of the plant were widely used as an emetic, in the same manner as the true senna.

"Mezerion," the *Daphne mezereum* L., is one of the first shrubs to bloom in the garden. In Europe this is as early as February; in Canada the rosy purple flowers cover the small bush about the same time as crocuses bloom. The flowers appear before the leaves, which makes them more visible, as they are stemless and emerge from the leaf axils in groups of three. The shrub bears bright red berries in early summer, but these are hidden by the foliage. Mezereon is now a favourite small shrub for rock gardens. As few plants bloom this early in spring, it should be planted where it can easily be seen, and close enough to a passage or entrance where the perfume can be enjoyed. The bark of Mezereon was used in the eighteenth century in the treatment of syphilis, but its value in this respect is unfounded.

"Cletha" [sic] or Clethra is now known as the Sweet Pepperbush. *Clethra alnifolia* L., the Clethra with alder-like leaves, is a member of *Ericaceae*, the

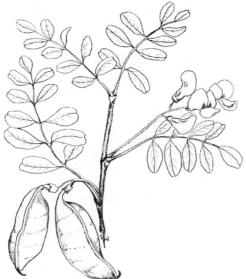

Bladder Senna   *Colutea arborescens* L.

Mezerion   *Daphne mezereum* L.

Clethra   *Clethra alnifolia* L.

Heath family, plants of the north temperate zone. This species was discovered in eastern North America and identified in 1731, one of the plants
Catesby introduced to England. It is a bushy shrub, growing from four to
nine feet in height. The flowers are fragrant, creamy-white bell-shaped
blooms held in erect spire-like clusters. The Sweet Pepperbush flowers in
mid-summer when few other shrubs are in bloom. Though very hardy, it
requires a very acid soil to perform well.

Barberry appears on Custead's list, but it is not numbered or priced.
Berberis vulgaris L. was a widely grown plant in the early nineteenth century, having arrived in America with settlers two hundred years earlier.
The plant grows from three to six feet, its thorny branches, bent at the tips,
arching gracefully outward. Barberry was a popular hedge plant; in the
spring it bears yellow flowers followed by red berries in the fall when the
foliage turns from a bluish-green to a bronzy red.

   Barberry was also a useful plant: its berries were made into jelly, its roots
could be used to make a yellow dye, and its bark, which contains anti-
bacterial chemicals, was used medicinally. However, the plant is a host for
the fungus *Puccinia graminis*, a wheat rust, and has been outlawed in many
areas where grain crops are grown.

The Strawberry Tree derives its name from its fruit, which truly resembles
the strawberry. The curious feature of this plant is that it blooms in the fall
at the same time the berries from the previous year are mature. This shrub,
Arbutus unedo L., a native of southern Europe, was grown as an evergreen
ornamental in the warmer regions for many centuries. The creamy-white
flowers appear in clusters at the end of sticky, hairy branches. The remarkable fruit is edible but quite tasteless. The Strawberry Tree is a member of
the Heath family and requires an acid soil to flourish.

The Scarlet Flowering Trumpet Creeper, *Campsis radiscans* (L.) Seem., was
a popular garden vine native to eastern North America. It was brought to
Europe in 1640, one of the early introductions of North American plants.
The vine has compound leaves, with clusters of bright orange-red flowers
occurring at the tips of branches. It grows to a length of thirty feet, making it very effective for covering arches, trellises, and the like. It belongs to
the *Bignoniaceae*, the same family as the Catalpa. Like the Catalpa, the
Trumpet Vine has long seed pods that split lengthwise to release many
winged seeds. Catesby painted the Trumpet Vine in the early eighteenth
century, representing it with a hummingbird attracted to the funnel-
shaped red flowers.

Barberry   *Berberis vulgaris* L.

Strawberry Tree   *Arbutus unedo* L.

Scarlet trumpet flowering creeper
Campsis radicans (L.) Seem

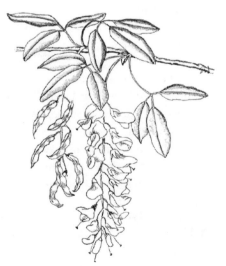

Laburnam   *Laburnum anagroides* Medic.

"Laburam," or Laburnum, was a shrub or small tree about fifteen feet high belonging to the Pea family, *Leguminosae*. Originally a native of southern Europe, *Laburnum anagyroides* Medic. was introduced to gardens in the sixteenth century for its decorative character. Bright yellow pea-like flowers hanging in clusters up to ten inches long gave it the common name Golden Chain Tree. Long, curved pods appear on the tree later in the season. Garden records kept in Virginia show that it was grown there in the late eighteenth century. While all parts of the tree are poisonous, the seed pods are particularly toxic and should not be left on the ground or the tree where they may inadvertently be consumed.

The Red Berried Spindle Tree was likely *Euonymus atropurpureus* Jacq., a shrubby, smooth-barked species growing from six to eighteen feet. The flowers are purple, inconspicuously displayed. The angular four-valved fruit capsules have a red outer layer that opens to show a fleshy red berry. In the fall, as the fruit ripen, the leaves turn to a yellowish-red. The fruit remain on the shrub after the leaves have fallen, providing interest in the garden during the winter months.

In the early seventeenth century the Pyracantha or Evergreen Thorn was introduced to European gardens from the eastern Mediterranean area. *Pyracantha coccinea Roem* was ably described by Parkinson, who considered it a fine ornamental. Now more commonly called Firethorn, it is still regarded as a desirable shrub. A member of the Rose family, it has thorny stems and white flowers very like those of the Hawthorn. In the fall its clusters of bright red berries, dramatically displayed against the glossy dark green foliage, last for several months. It is marginally hardy in the warmest parts of southern Ontario but even there needs winter protection.

The Double Flowering Almond in gardens today is either *Prunus glandulosa* Thun. or *Prunus triloba* Lindl. All references consulted referred the dates of introduction to be later than 1827, the date of Custead's catalogue. Both species originated in China and were identified after 1850. Custead's Flowering Almond, classified as *Amygdalus nana* in a 1791 issue of the *Botanical Magazine*, is now known as the Dwarf Russian Almond, *Prunus tenella* Batsch. Its native habitat stretched from central Europe east to Siberia, and therefore it was likely to do well in Upper Canada. This hardy, low, deciduous shrub has narrow, deep-green glossy leaves. In the double form the clusters of rose-red flowers look much like small roses. The fruit are greyish-yellow with a velvety surface.

Red berried Spindle Tree
Euonymus atropurpureus Jacq.

Pyracantha or Ever Green Thorn
Pyracantha coccinea Roem.

Double flowering Almond
Prunus tenella Batsch.

Venetian Sumack   *Cotinus coggygria* Scop.

"Venitian Sumack" [sic] is better known today as the Smoke Tree, a striking ornamental that has been cultivated since 1656. The *Cotinus coggyria* Scop. belongs to the Sumac family, *Anacardiaceae*. The shrub is many-stemmed, reaching a height of fifteen feet. In the fall the leaves turn to shades of yellow, orange, and red. But the fame of the plant does not rest on the leaf colour: the yellow flowers, which are very small but profuse, are borne on many-branched terminal clusters. The purplish-green stalks of the sterile flowers are long silky plumes that turn to reddish-brown or a brown smoky colour in the fall. The twigs are aromatic when crushed. In southern Europe the Smoke Bush was cultivated for use in the tanning process.

Hawthorn bushes are now so common in open fields and old pastures in Ontario that it is difficult to realize that they are an introduced species. The English Hawthorn, *Crataegus laevigata* (Poir.) DC, was widely grown in the British Isles, where they were used to form dense hedges surrounding farm fields. The shrub or small tree can be pruned or shaped to almost any form. By pinning down, or layering, overlapping branches, an impenetrable thorny barrier can be created.

The hawthorn was native to a widespread area from Europe and North Africa eastward to India. Formerly classified as *C. oxyacantha*, the English Hawthorn had many varieties and hybridized readily with other species of the same genus, resulting in a confusing number of hybrids and varieties. In general they are round-topped shrubs from ten to twenty feet in height, blooming in the spring with small clusters of five-petalled white flowers, followed by red berries. The berries, or haws, are small, apple-like fruit containing two stones, very tart in taste but agreeable to small mammals, game birds, and songbirds. This accounts for the naturalization of the shrub, as the seeds, which germinate readily, were widely distributed.

For unusual texture in the garden, the French Tamarisk is one of the best choices. *Tamarix gallica* L. is a shrub with long flexible stems which arch outwardly, covered with extremely small leaves no more than one-sixteenth of an inch long, appearing as small bluish scales on the branches. The flowers are pinkish-white, small, but densely clustered on the ends of the branches. The whole plant appears as a pink cloud when in bloom, its feathery branches moving easily in the wind. The tamarisk is a member of the *Tamaricaceae*, native to Asia Minor. In southeastern Europe it was called the manna plant, for the seeds were shaken out of the tree for use in baking a sweet cake with honey and almonds. This very desirable garden ornamental is severely damaged when touched by frost, but in some areas of the northern United States it has been treated as a herbaceous perennial.

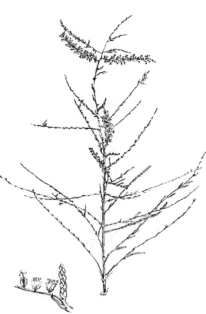

European Hawthorn   *Crataegus* sp.

French Tamarisk   *Tamarix gallica* L.

Southern Wood
Artemesia abrotanum L.

English Nightshade
Solanum dulcamara L.

"Southern Wood," *Artemisia abrotanum* L., a woody sub-shrub of the *Compositae*, was grown for its aromatic greyish-green foliage. Native to southern Europe where it has been known since time immemorial and grown in herb gardens, it has become naturalized over most of central, southern and western Europe. It grows to a height of three feet, with many stems. The finely dissected leaves are a grey-green colour. The flowers are inconspicuous, borne in terminal clusters. Southernwood was a favourite for the herb garden as the aromatic leaves have insecticidal properties and were used in the home as a moth deterrent; the plant was known in France as *garde-robe* for its protection of linens and clothing. Bath water and wash basins were pleasantly scented with the dried or fresh leaves. The stems provided a yellow dye.

The plant called English Nightshade, *Solanum dulcamara* L., was a straggly vine from Europe related to the eggplant, the tomato, and the potato. The vine grows, in a bushy fashion, from four to eight feet. The flowers are drooping, appearing to be pointing downward, the purple petals wide open or recurved. The bright red fruit hang in bunches. All parts of the plant are poisonous. The leaves and the fruit have been used medicinally in the past, but they contain steroids and toxic alkaloids that can cause convulsions and paralysis and may weaken the action of the heart. The English or Woody Nightshade has become naturalized in America and can be found growing wild in most waste places.

Periwinkle or "ever Green Myrtle," *Vinca minor* L., is an attractive, low-growing sub-shrub that makes a handsome ground cover. A trailing woody-stemmed plant, it only reaches a height of ten inches. The stems can root at every joint, creating a ground-hugging mass. Blue flowers appear in leaf axils from spring into summer, just peeking above the shining green foliage. Periwinkle belongs to the *Apocynaceae* or Dogbane family, whose plants have a milky juice. It is a hardy plant, native to Europe and grown in gardens since the Middle Ages.

Another shrub in Custead's collection from the southeastern United States was the Rose Acacia, *Robinia hispida* L. Identified and introduced into cultivation in the mid-eighteenth century, it grows from six to ten feet with a spreading, irregular habit. Gardeners found it did well when trained against a wall or trellis. The branches and leaf stems are covered with red bristles. The shrub belongs to the *Leguminosae*, a plant family with compound leaves and pea-like flowers. Also called the Bristly Locust, it blooms

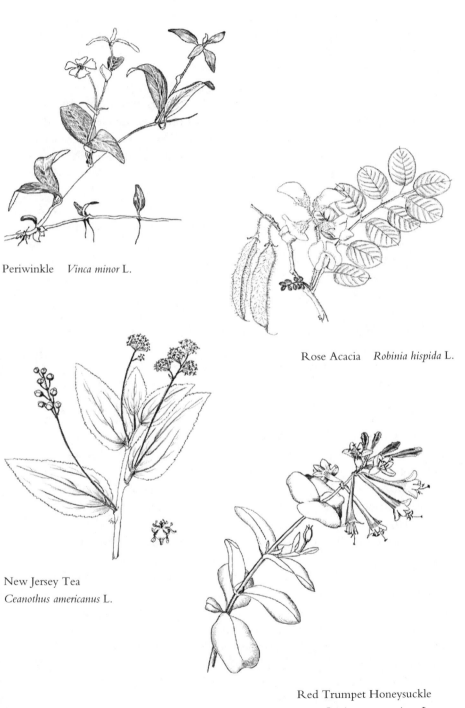

Periwinkle   *Vinca minor* L.

Rose Acacia   *Robinia hispida* L.

New Jersey Tea
Ceanothus americanus L.

Red Trumpet Honeysuckle
Lonicera sempervirens L.

profusely in the summer months with rose-pink flowers. Although the fruit of the genus *Robinia* are long, flat seed pods, the Rose Acacia species seldom sets seed. Nineteenth-century gardeners claimed it was not hardy north of Pennsylvania.

New Jersey Tea was so-named because early colonists on the Atlantic shores learned from the Amerindians to use the leaves of this native plant as a beverage. The tea was also used as a multi-purpose medication for colds, fevers, stomach-ache, and respiratory problems. New Jersey Tea, *Ceanothus americanus* L., identified in 1713, belongs to the Buckthorn family. It is a dwarf shrub, growing to a height of three or four feet. The flowers are individually small but are grouped into showy, flat-topped clusters. The flowers contain saponin and were used as a soap. The fruit are capsules, each containing three seeds. Roots of the plant, red in colour and growing up to six inches in diameter, were used to make dyes, ranging from buff to cinnamon colours, depending on the mordant used.

Following the list of shrubs in the catalogue was a section for honeysuckles. Unlike the rest of the list, these were not priced. Six varieties were offered: Early Sweet Italian, *Lonicera caprifolium* L.; English White, *L. xylosteum* L.; Scarlet Monthly Trumpet, *L. sempervirens* L.; English Woodbine, *L. periclymenum* L.; and a Striped Monthly and a Variegated Leaved, both probably varieties of *L. periclymenum*.

Honeysuckles, the genus *Lonicera* in the *Caprifoliaceae*, are woody plants with opposite leaves and flowers borne in the leaf axils, in pairs or sometimes as whorls of bloom. There are close to two hundred species in this genus, and the varieties number many, many more. Honeysuckles are native to the northern hemisphere and both Eurasian and American species were grown in early nineteenth-century gardens. One of Custead's species was a shrub, and the remainder were climbers. One was a native of North America; the rest were Eurasian species.

Early Sweet Italian Honeysuckle, one of the climbers, could grow to eighteen feet. It had large, very fragrant flowers, from cream to yellowish-white, sometimes with a tinge of pink, occurring in whorls in the leaf axils. It bloomed in late spring or early summer. The fruit were round, orange-red berries.

The one shrub-type honeysuckle included in Custead's list was the English White Honeysuckle. It grew to a height between six and ten feet, much branched, with small axillary cream-coloured flowers. This species was native to England where it was called Fly Honeysuckle and was cultivated over a long period.

Scarlet Flowering Trumpet Honeysuckle was discovered in North America in the mid-seventeenth century. A woody vine extending to lengths of twenty feet or more, it bore richly coloured flowers, red on the outside and yellow inside and particularly attractive to hummingbirds. Many nineteenth-century garden writers thought this species was the finest honeysuckle, even though it lacked fragrance. In its native habitat of south-east North America it was an evergreen, and growers in England often treated it as a greenhouse plant. It was very hardy but acted as a deciduous plant in the north.

English Woodbine was a common vine in Europe and western Asia, brought into cultivation for its handsome red and yellow-white flowers in terminal clusters. Blooming throughout the season, it later bore bitter red berries. There were many varieties of this well-known vine, and the last two selections on Custead's list were probably examples of these variations. The name Striped Monthly described a vine that bloomed "monthly" or repeatedly, with variegated flowers; for example, the modern variety "Belgica" has white flowers flushed with purple. The Variegated Leaved Honeysuckle was possibly another variety of the Common Woodbine. The variety "Aurea" had leaves variegated with yellow; "Quercina," an oak-leaved variety, sometimes had leaves variegated white. In American catalogues of the early nineteenth century all these variations were treated as separate species. Without coloured illustrations an explicit nomenclature is difficult, but all the species mentioned here were known in Custead's day and available in the United States where he appears to have obtained a good deal of his plant material.

6

Biennials and Perennials

Biennial and perennial plants are herbaceous – fleshy, often green stems, not woody as in trees or shrubs – and live for two or more years. Many are grown for their usefulness as foods, medicines, or in other domestic applications. But the decorative qualities of some of these "useful" plants should not be overlooked. Kitchen gardens in the eighteenth and early nineteenth century contained both annual and perennial plants, serviceable and ornamental. The fern-like foliage of asparagus or the large leaves and tall flower spikes of rhubarb added visual interest to the garden. The dense, dark foliage of hop vines shaded verandah and covered fences.

Biennials and perennials were offered by nurseries as living plants. In the Toronto Nursery catalogue several of the same species were listed twice, as plants under "Biennials and Perennials," and again as seeds under the headings for vegetables, herbs, and annuals. (Where such duplication occurred, they are here treated where they appeared first as biennials and perennials and omitted in later chapters.)

A few of the plants in Custead's catalogue would not have proven hardy in most areas of Upper Canada, while others would show such adaptability that in time they would escape from gardens to become common wildflowers. Many European species, whether they were brought intentionally or arrived inadvertently, took so well to their new environment they had spread to the wild as early as the mid-eighteenth century. Kalm noted several such straying plants as early as the 1740s. He frequently saw asparagus growing near fences in "uncultivated sandy fields" (Kalm 1770/1966:89).

Several plants in this section had the potential for becoming commercial crops, being of value for domestic use as foods, dyes, insect controls, or medicinal remedies. The Toronto Nursery may have been the source of plants later grown as income-producing crops on established farms. In the early nineteenth century, farmers in Upper Canada needed diversity in their crops to secure markets and provide income for further improvements. Yet in this list there was no lack of herbaceous plants that were to be appreciated purely for their distinctive ornamental characteristics.

Custead's list began with the Peony, *Paeonia officinalis* L., in the *Paeoniaceae* family. (All plants designated *officinalis* were once cultivated for their use as pharmaceuticals.) The peony was grown for many centuries in both physic and ornamental gardens. In classical times it was so respected that it was named to commemorate Paeon, physician to the Greek gods. Until the late eighteenth century folk medicine treated epilepsy, the "falling sickness," with a piece of peony root hung about the neck to prevent and cure attacks. The shiny, black, pea-like seeds were used in both ancient and medieval times to treat women's problems in childbirth and menstruation to "cleanse the womb." Modern medical science has determined that the plant contains some harmful poisons, and its use is no longer recommended, although it remained in pharmacopoeias until the late nineteenth century. A nauseous milky juice extracted from the root was used in treating whooping cough, diarrhoea, and epilepsy; however, even then its effectiveness was "neither confirmed or condemned" (Stillé and Maisch 1880:1053).

Peony, double crimson
Paeonia officinalis L.

The peony was also endowed with magical properties, said to keep devils and evil spirits away. Such superstitions may have arisen from the observation that seeds from some species glow mysteriously in the dark (Gerard 1633/ 1975:983). The plant's use in rituals to protect the applicant from storms or relieve melancholy or nightmares was probably more in the domain of witches and sorcerers than medical practitioners.

The double form of *Paeonia officinalis var. rubra plena* appeared in the middle of the sixteenth century, probably introduced to England from the Low Countries. By 1629 Parkinson wrote that it "is so frequent in every Garden of note, through every Countrey, that it is almost labour in vaine to describe it." In the early 1800s the double peony was among the most admired garden plants, prized for planting in large borders and shrubberies.

The brightly coloured full-blown flowers, up to five inches in diameter, were impressive, although their weight often dragged the flower stalks to the ground unless staked. The blooms were much in demand as cut flowers, considered "very ornamental in Basons or Flower pots when placed in Rooms" (Miller 1754/1969:1004). When the flowering period was over, the mass of handsome deep green foliage made a good foil for other flowering plants.

Two sorts of rhubarb were available: the Tart Rhubarb, *Rheum rhaponticum* L., and Turkey Rhubarb, *Rheum palmatum* L., both of the buckwheat family, *Polgonaceae*. All species of *Rheum* were native to central and eastern Asia, where certain forms were important medicinal herbs. As far back as classical times the dried root was imported from China by western countries, but the source of medicinal rhubarb was jealously guarded by growers and international dealers. It was delivered to Europe through Russia and India, which accounted for its being known as Russian or Indian rhubarb in the trade. The search for the "true" rhubarb, which supplied the most effective and dependable cathartic in common use, began two thousand years ago and even now has been only partially solved.

The first rhubarb in Europe, *Rheum rhaponticum*, was grown in the botanical garden in Padua in 1608. When its medicinal value proved disappointing, the plant made its way from the physic garden into the kitchen garden. There it gained a reputation as the "pie plant," used for "the making of Tarts in the Spring of the Year as these may be had before Gooseberries are large enough for that purpose ... the pulpy part will bake very tender, and almost as clear as the Apricot" (Miller 1754/1969:741). This is the rhubarb that was brought to Canada in the eighteenth century, which Catharine Parr Traill advised "should always find a place in your garden" (Traill 1855/1969:49). One of the first fresh crops from the spring garden, most welcome after months of dried fruits and root vegetables, rhubarb was also used in conserves, made into wine, and administered as a mild purgative. When Mrs Simcoe visited Montreal on her way back to England in 1795, she was shown a plant in Mrs Frobisher's garden called "strawberry spinach," which was probably rhubarb. When her hostess declared that it was very pretty but poisonous, Mrs Simcoe replied that she had often eaten it in Upper Canada with no ill effects (Innis 1983:194). The leaf stalks were safe for consumption, though the leaves could be very toxic, causing serious illness, even death, if cooked "as spinach." Cases of oxalic poisoning resulting from using rhubarb leaves as a vegetable were reported in Great Britain during World War II when food shortages encouraged people to make the most of their garden produce.

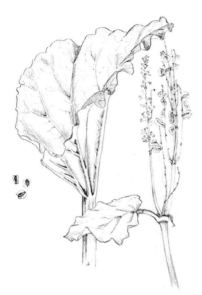

Tart Rhubarb   *Rheum rhaponticum* L.

Turkey Rhubarb   *Rheum palmatum* L.

Leeks   *Allium porrum* L.

Shallots   *Allium cepa aggregatum* L.

& Scives   *Allium schoenoprasum* L.

An Englishman who had served as physician to the Russian Czar took seeds of *Rheum palmatum* to Britain in 1762 in hopes that this would be the elusive medicinal plant. A large plant with wide palmate leaves, it had seed stalks up to six feet in height. Within two years several plants were grown successfully in the Edinburgh Botanical Garden, and seeds from the plants were made available to the public by 1770. At this time the value of imported dried rhubarb root from Russia amounted to 200,000 British pounds annually. This situation prompted the Society for the Encouragement of Arts, Manufacturing and Commerce to offer a gold medal to those raising "not less than 100 plants" in an attempt to relieve the dependence on imports. The medal was won by a Dr William Fordyce in 1791 for raising more than three hundred "true" rhubarb plants and transplanting them in "a thriving condition" (Henery 1975: 2:33). But this species of rhubarb, like all others, failed to be the "true" one. It was then proposed that it was not the particular species but the climate and growing conditions in China that produced the best-quality drug. Efforts to isolate the effective components have successively resulted in failure.

The prized root was long and thick, its fleshy yellow interior, when dried and ground, yielding a bright yellow powder. There were many complaints that unscrupulous merchants were adultering the true rhubarb root with other species of rhubarb and colouring it with turmeric. However, there was no dispute over the effectiveness of rhubarb root in relieving constipation and the discomfort of haemorrhoids and in treating dysentery and diarrhoea, as well as its safety of application even when administered to children. Different treatments were a matter of dosage and associated medication. While the search for the "true" medicinal rhubarb continues to this day, the most satisfactory solution appears to be adjusting the dosage to the illness and the patient.

Three members of the *Allium* genus, all of the Lily family, *Liliaceae*, were grown for sale as plants: leeks, *Allium porrum* L., shallots, *Allium cepa* L., *aggregatum group*, and chives, *Allium schoenoprasum* L. All three have been grown in southern Europe and the Near East for culinary use since antiquity. Only chives have been found growing in the wild; the original sources for the others have long since been lost.

The leek is a biennial plant, harvested in the first year as a vegetable and left for the formation of seeds in the second year. Leeks were known in ancient Egypt for both culinary and medicinal purposes. The medicinal application was similar to that of the related *Allium sativum* L., the garlic plant. Gerard referred to using the juice to treat snakebite, as ear drops to relieve pain and noise, and boiled with barley to clear the chest, even though consuming the plant would produce "wind" and cause terrible dreams (Gerard 1633/1975:175). In the nineteenth century the leek was eaten to stimulate the appetite and relieve lung congestion, and as a gentle diuretic stimulant. While leeks were never featured in English cooking, they were highly regarded on the continent and widely cultivated by the French in their homeland and in Lower Canada. They were also familiar to the Scots, many of whom came to settle in Upper Canada. Loudon wrote: "Leeks formerly constituted an ingredient in the dish called *porridge*, which some suppose it to be derived from the Latin *porrum*" (Loudon 1827:641). Leeks were used primarily as an ingredient for soups but were also lightly braised and served as a vegetable.

Shallots were first described in Europe in the mid-sixteenth century. They were probably one of the many plants introduced to Europe from the Near East after the Crusades. Shallots are milder-tasting than other onions of the *Allum cepa* species and were preferred for certain recipes. When grown from seed they require two years for the bulbs to reach an adequate size, so they were usually planted in a permanent position and left to form clumps, which could be divided and harvested and the smaller bulbs replanted. The plant flowered in the second season but rarely set seed in a northern climate: "Some old authors denominate it the Barren Onion ... as it seldom sends up a flower-stalk" (Loudon 1827:642).

Scives, cives, or chives have leaves and flowers similar in appearance to shallots but do not form bulbs. The plant is perennial, tending to form clumps that can be divided to increase the number of plants. Chives were used for flavouring soups, sauces, and salads, or wherever a mild onion taste was desired; only the leaves were consumed. The plant contained a volatile oil that dissipated during drying so that the leaves lost their potency soon after cutting. The profuse flowering habit made them useful as a low-growing ornamental border plant. When they were dead-headed after the first early summer blooming, a second flowering was forced for the early fall.

Asparagus, *Asparagus officinalis* L., is another member of the Lily family, *Liliaceae*. As the name indicates, it was another edible plant also used for medicinal purposes. The young shoots were employed as a diuretic for dropsy and gout, and the high fibre content of the stems contributed a mild laxative effect. Old medical texts refer to the "offensive odour" of urine after the young plant was eaten. Though the seeds have not been used extensively, they have been found to have antibiotic properties.

Asparagus was indigenous to Europe, cultivated in the Mediterranean region for over two thousand years. The plant came to America with some of the earliest settlers, for it had already escaped to the wild in the 1740s

Asparagus   *Asparagus officinalis* L.

Italian Spiderwort
Paradisia liliastrum Bertol.

Hops   *Humulus lupulus* L.

when Peter Kalm travelled through the United States and Canada (Kalm 1770/1966 1:89). Once planted, an asparagus plant can persist for many years even when completely neglected. Many old asparagus clumps found around Ontario homesteads have been there for generations. It was one of the earliest vegetables in the spring garden; fresh asparagus sprouts on the dinner table were a gastronomical treat for colonists after winter meals limited to stored root vegetables.

Italian Spiderwort, another member of the Lily family, was grown only for its ornamental value. *Paradisia liliastrum* Bertol. was also called St Bruno's Lily and has a history of name changes over the centuries. Native to the mountains of southern Europe, it was thought to be the plant called *Phalangium allobrogicum* by the ancient writers and by Clusius in the sixteenth century. Gerard (1633/1975) and Parkinson (1629/1991) called it the "Great Italian Spiderwort," a *Phalangium*, but Miller (1754) placed it with *Hemerocallis*, the day lilies. The nineteenth century recognized it as *Anthericum liliastrum* until 1877 when it was shown to be a monotypic genus – the one species in the genus *Paradisia* (Bailey 1902:1210). The plant had defied efforts in classification as it produced white lily-like blooms with six petals, superficially like those of the *Anthericum* genus, but grew from rhizomes with thick clustered roots, not a bulb. The difference between *Paradisia* and other genera lies in the relationships of the stamens to the ovary – a very subtle distinction, but such are the criteria dear to taxonomists. While the name *Paradisia* has been interpreted as indicating that this flower is worthy of growing in Paradise, it was more likely chosen to recognize the work of Giovanni Paradisi, a botanist of Modena, Italy.

Garden guides recommended that these lilies "deserve a place in the open Border of every curious Flower-garden … for their long continuance in Flower"; placed in "an eastern Aspect, where they may be protected from the Sun in the Heat of the Day, they will continue in Beauty longer than when they are more exposed" (Miller 1754/1969:1059). St Bruno's Lily is hardy in southern Ontario and other mild areas in Canada but may not survive the winter in many parts of the country. In the early twentieth century it was recommended for planting in "lawn vases," a practice that may be worth reviving now that container gardening is popular (Bailey 1902:71).

Hops, *Humulus lupulus* L., a member of the hemp family or *Cannabidaceae*, was a popular plant in early Upper Canada. Hop vines have been cultivated since the times of the Romans, who ate the new young shoots as a spring vegetable, prepared as a salad and eaten raw or cooked, much like asparagus.

When the vine had grown, the flowers were harvested for medicinal purposes. The plant produces both male and female flowers. The female flowers, or strobiles, are leafy cone-like catkins with a fine yellow resinous powder containing the chemical lupulin. Whole flowers, or just the powder, were used as a blood purifier and to treat venereal diseases and intestinal worms. As the use of lupulin induced a sleepy condition, it was long considered to be a narcotic, a premise that has recently been rejected. It is now classified as a sedative and is still used in herbal pillows to treat insomnia and headaches.

Today hops are associated almost exclusively with the brewing of beer. This practice began in Germany and the Low Countries and spread to England sometime during the sixteenth century. Hops revolutionized the brewing industry in Britain, for in replacing the bitter herbs previously used, they added a peculiar aroma and flavour while acting as a preservative. Beer brewed with hops kept better and could therefore be marketed over greater distances, affecting distribution patterns and the location of manufacturing plants. Dutch settlers in New Amsterdam are credited with bringing hops to America in the sixteenth century, but hop growing was not common until 1800. By the 1840s numerous hops fields could be found in Vermont and New York.

Hops were grown on a small scale in Upper Canada, perhaps only a plant or two for family use or as an ornamental. The rapid, dense growth of the vine made its "graceful drapery" useful for screening verandahs to filter the hot summer sun. Catharine Parr Traill considered hops to be another plant no settler's home could be without, as it was a principal ingredient in making yeast for raising bread (Traill 1855/1969:88). "Hop-rising" was judged to be superior to brewer's yeast because it had no bitter taste and gave better keeping quality to the bread. American recipe books, among them the popular *American Frugal Housewife* (Child 1833/1965), gave instructions for yeast-making from hops. Traill, ever mindful of the settler's well-being, added that the "hops will always sell well if carefully harvested." Hops were never an important agricultural crop in Canada until World War II when imports were restricted. Eastern Ontario farmers turned many of their fields into hops yards, transforming the landscape from grain fields into a forest of hop poles.

Three perennial herbs in the Mint family, *Labiatae*, are included here: Sage, *Salvia officinalis* L.; Hyssop, *Hyssopus officinalis* L.; and Monarda, *Monarda didyma* L., aromatic herbs with a history of both culinary and medicinal applications.

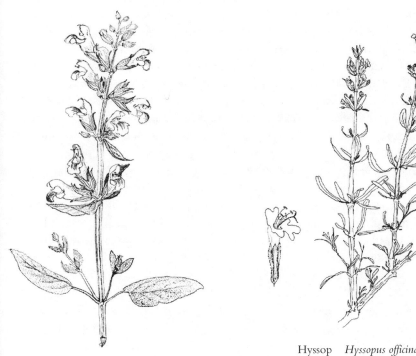

Hyssop   *Hyssopus officinalis* L.

Sage   *Salvia officinalis* L.

Crimson Menardi   *Monarda didyma* L.

A much-quoted medieval adage, *"Cur moriatur homo cui salvia cresit inn horto?"* ("Why should a man die who has sage in his garden?") demonstrated the degree of faith once placed on this plant. Sage has been known and used since time immemorial, one of the first plants of the Mediterranean region to be introduced to cultivation. Its assets were indispensible and undisputed, its very name meaning "to heal." The Romans called it the Holy Herb, *herba sancta*. Medical uses date to Hippocrates in the fourth century B.C. and persisted until the late nineteenth century. The plant contains several natural chemicals which are strong preservatives, with antibacterial and antifungal properties. The fresh leaves were used in poultices for wounds and skin eruptions, to soothe insect bites, and to clean and whiten teeth and promote strong gums. An infusion of dried leaves sweetened with honey served as a gargle for sore throats and to heal mouth infections. Claims were made for sage's effectiveness in cases of liver and chronic lung diseases and in the prevention of natural abortion.

The most common use of sage was as a tea; a hot infusion was said to break a fever, and a cold infusion in water or wine was used to treat night sweating associated with tuberculosis. Well persons drank it as a healthful beverage, as it was "singular good for the head and braine; it quicketh the sences and memory" (Gerard 1633/1975:766). In America a sage tea with milk was given children at bedtime. Sage tea was so highly prized by the Chinese in the eighteenth century that they traded three pounds of China tea for one pound of dried sage leaves. Modern medicine has recognized sage's validity in easing the discomfort and pain of flatulence, but the herb no longer enjoys the reputation as a cure-all.

The culinary uses of sage were important in European cuisine, and in England it was the most commonly used herb. The red form, offered by the Toronto Nursery, was preferred. Sage was well suited for use with rich and fatty meats such as pork, goose and duck. It is still one of the major seasonings in poultry stuffings, sausage, and sage cheese.

Hyssop, *Hyssopus officinalis* L., believed to be the only species in its genus, came originally from central Asia and the Mediterranean area of southern Europe. Known to the ancient Greeks and Romans, it has a long history of medicinal applications using the dried leaf and flower parts and oil extracted from the seeds. Until the twentieth century hyssop was used as an expectorant to relieve coughs and lung ailments and the symptoms of the common cold. Mixed with sage to make a tea, it eased the discomfort of sore throats. Fresh leaves were used externally as poultices for skin irritations, bruises, sore muscles, and rheumatism. Recent analysis has shown the oil to have anti-viral properties which have been used to control infections caused by the herpes virus.

Hyssop was also at home in the kitchen, where it flavoured soups and meat dishes. In recent years commercial preparations of pickles, meat sauces, and candy have included hyssop as an ingredient. The oil has been used in liqueurs (bitters and chartreuse) and as a fragrance for soaps and perfumes.

The compact bushy plant was an Elizabethan favourite for the low decorative edgings used in knot gardens. During succeeding centuries its place was in the herb or physic garden, until the twentieth century when it was again recognized as an ornamental for the border.

Custead's "Crimson Monardi" [sic] was also known as Bee Balm, Oswego Tea, or Bergamot. *Monarda didyma* L. was native to eastern North America, named appropriately for the first European to describe plants from the Americas – the Spanish physician Nicolas Monardes, who published his work in Seville in 1565. The English translation in 1577 was titled *Joyfull Newes out of the Newe Founde Worlde*. Monarda was among the plants sent to England by Bartram in the mid-eighteenth century, and by 1760 it was in great demand in the Covent Garden market. The plant blooms rather late in the season, a characteristic appreciated by British gardeners who had few European plants to add colour to the late summer garden.

There are several species in the genus *Monarda*, a group of plants generally referred to as the "horsemints," all native to North America. The red-flowered species, *Monarda didyma*, gained the attention of early travellers such as Peter Kalm, who admired its bright colour along with that of the Cardinal Flower, calling them some of the finest red flowers known. Kalm also noticed that hummingbirds, "the most admirable of all the rare birds in North America ... fluttered chiefly about the Monarda with crimson flowers" (Kalm 1770/1966 1:112).

Early settlers learned to make a tea from the dried leaves of monarda from the Oswego tribe of Amerindians. The beverage, called Oswego tea, became popular in the eighteenth century in the British colonies to the south protesting the British taxes on China tea. The other common name, Bergamot, referred to the taste, which was likened to that of the bergamot orange. The tea also relieved digestive problems, flatulence, and nausea. An instructional text, *Partridge on Dyeing*, published in New York in 1834, found red monarda to be a reliable source of a pink dye. Settlers were advised to grow this plant "plentifully" in their kitchen gardens, but its decorative qualities alone frequently assured it of a place.

Six plants on the list of biennials and perennials belonged to the Daisy family, *Compositae*. Wormwood, Tarragon, and Chamomile were well-known herbs; the Caledonian Thistle, Dahlia, and English Daisy were grown for their ornamental value.

Wormwood   *Artemisia absinthum* L.

Tarragon   *Artemisia dracunculus* L.

Chamomile   *Chamaemelum nobile* (L.) All.

Wormwood, *Artemisia absinthium* L., was associated with the goddess Artemis in ancient Greece. Legends of this goddess reveal the dichotomy of good and evil in a single deity, and the same two-edged properties may also be assigned to the characteristics of the plant. Wormwood is one of the most bitter herbs, with a persistent lingering taste, but it also has many beneficial attributes. For hundreds of years a wormwood tea was administered as a stimulant, tonic, and vermifuge. The leaves had an antiseptic content that resisted decay, and they were used for treating wounds and infections that could lead to gangrene. Dried leaves were placed in closets and chests to repel moths and vermin. As a strewing herb it freshened the air in a room and acted as a mild disinfectant. Many alcoholic beverages, including wine and vermouth, were flavoured with wormwood, and at one time it was used instead of hops in making beer.

In the early nineteenth century wormwood was considered a valuable medicinal plant, an ingredient of many home remedies. It was used in commercial preparations such as "Portland Powder," sold as a cure for gout. Its adverse side was the toxic effect produced when it was used internally, either in excessive dosages or continual usage, as it contains chemicals that act upon the human nervous system, causing violent convulsions, delirium, hallucinations, and even death. When reactions of chronic degenerating intoxication and insanity were observed in persons habitually ingesting alcoholic beverages made with wormwood, such as wine and absinthe, many countries prohibited its use in their manufacture. Because of its association with adverse effects, wormwood is no longer recommended for medicinal use, although its antiseptic properties are still acknowledged. The plant is used in a small way as a household insect repellant, but today it is grown primarily for the ornamental value of its deeply cut silvery foliage.

Tarragon, *Artemisia dracunculus* L., has been grown throughout garden history as a culinary herb. Even Gerard could find little else to say about its use: "neither doe we know what other use this herbe hath" (Gerard 1633/1975:249). The plant is often called French Tarragon, a perennial that does not set seed and therefore must be propagated by division. It is sometimes confused with a sub-species that does flower but has little flavour, called Russian or Siberian Tarragon (see chapter 11).

The taste of tarragon is similar to anise or licorice, with an added spicy tang. This intensifies as it is chewed and acts to stimulate the digestive juices. It is indispensible in continental French cuisine with fish, shellfish, lobster, and chicken and is included in recipes for salads, sauces, preserves, and herb butters. It is also one of the herbs that give a distinct flavour to Dubonnet. In America tarragon is not as well known, for it does not acquire the same intense flavour in cultivation as in the warm and dry Mediterranean climate. In southern France it is grown commercially for its oil, which is extracted by distillation and used in the manufacture of prepared foods. The scented oil is volatile, evaporating at room temperature, and is lost as the herb is dried.

The herb and its oil were used in folk medicine as a diuretic, to relieve chronic bronchitis and to promote menstruation, but modern research has not confirmed the validity of these applications.

Chamomile, *Chamaemelum nobile* (L.) All., has been in continuous cultivation for thousands of years and is still grown commercially in Europe for the many medicinal virtues of its small daisy-like flowers. The species form had single white or yellow flower rays, while garden varieties had larger white-rayed, often double forms. The single flowering varieties were preferred for medicinal uses. A beverage made from the dried flowers had many soothing and healing properties as a tonic, a sedative, or a cure for migraine headaches, stomach disorders, or attacks of *delirium tremens*. The dried flowers were applied externally in warm compresses on sprains, swellings, abscesses, earache, and rheumatic joints. In the nineteenth century the flowers were known to every housekeeper for "their valuable medicinal qualities." While modern medicine no longer prescribes chamomile in treatment, the herb is not harmful and makes a pleasant, relaxing tea. Continuous use or heavy dosages should be avoided, however, as these may cause nausea, vomiting, or drowsy disorientation.

Chamomile flowers were also used for cosmetic purposes, as a rinse for blond hair and, mixed with honey, for a facial mask. The fragrant stems and foliage were used as a strewing herb to freshen the house or stored with linens and clothing. The pleasant scent added fragrance to bath water or finger bowls for the table.

In the garden chamomile was used wherever a low, mat-forming plant was required. It was sometimes used instead of grass, giving off its refreshing scent when walked upon; a non-flowering variety was best suited for lawns. Enclosed medieval gardens used it to make seats to rest on, the spongy fragrant foliage cushioning low stone walls. In the small urban gardens of the twentieth century, chamomile can be used to advantage by reviving either of these old practices.

The Caledonian or Scotch Thistle, *Onopordum acanthium* L., was native to the British Isles. The purple flower has long been recognized as the floral emblem of the Scottish people, and nurseries often sold it under the name "Robert Bruce." In the eighteenth century it was found as a wayside plant that grew "upon the Sides of dry Banks and other uncultivated places" (Miller 1754/1969:257). It came into favour with gardeners in the nineteenth century when its remarkable colouring, texture, and size were

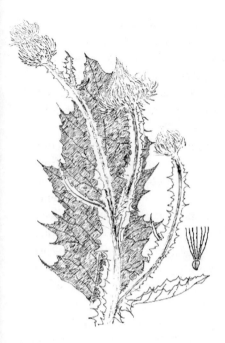

Caledonian Thistle
Onopordum acanthium L.

Dahlies   *Dahlia var.*

English Daisy   *Bellis perennis* L.

recognized for their ornamental value in landscaping. Planted against the shady background of shrubbery, its silvery appearance effected a dramatic contrast. Its "bold habit" made it handsome enough to be used as a prominent feature in a specimen planting, and Victorian gardeners incorporated it into ornate bedding schemes. By the twentieth century, however, it had lost its appeal and was seen in private gardens only as a remembrance of the "Old Country."

The thistle had several domestic applications, but there is no record of it being grown as a crop. The tender young stalks and flower buds (which resemble the globe artichoke) were eaten after being peeled and boiled. In the seventeenth century the cottony fibres of the seed pods were mixed with feathers and down for use in furnishings such as pillows. The seeds were rich in oil used for lamp fuel and cooking; three pounds of oil could be pressed from twelve pounds of seed. Custead's clientele may have wanted these thistles for their landscaped grounds, for their domestic uses, or simply for the symbolism and nostalgia they represented to Scots settlers in Canada.

"Dahlies" or Dahlias, another of the *Compositae*, were among the most expensive plants offered by the Toronto Nursery. This is not surprising as they had only been introduced to America in the 1820s, as *Dahlia variabilis*. Custead advised his customers that his stock would not be ready until the following year; apparently he had only begun to propagate these plants. Dahlias grow from a tuberous root; it is not known whether Custead had acquired tubers or was growing them from seed.

All dahlias came originally from Mexico, where they were regarded as a vegetable and a medicinal plant. An Aztec herbal of 1582 recommended their use for urinary problems. The plant was described and illustrated by Spanish botanists in the seventeenth century, but the first tubers did not reach Europe until 1789 or 1790, when they were introduced as an edible plant. The new delicacy did not appeal to European palates, but the plant intrigued botanists. In 1804, the German explorer Von Humboldt sent "Georgine" (dahlia) seed to England where the plants became known as Georgians. In Leipzig, where the most advanced botanical work was taking place, seeds from the wild plants readily produced varieties. Two years later in 1806 there were fifty-five varieties, including one double. This began a fanatical fashion for the plant. The Royal Horticultural Society in England recognized sixty-two sorts in 1826, and by 1841 a grower offered as many as 1,200 kinds. The craze subsided somewhat by the 1860s, as did the inflated prices, but the flower did not lose its popularity. In the 1858 edition of M'Mahon's *American Gardener*, the dahlia had been "brought to perfection in all shades of color except pure blue" (M'Mahon 1858/1976: n., 406). In Boston, seedsman-grower Joseph Breck did not have much success with dahlias, however: after paying from one to ten guineas each for tubers he received from England, he found them "small and weak [and] they proved a perfect failure, and not a single blossom from the whole rewarded me for the expense, trouble and vexation which I experienced" (Breck 1866:180).

The genus was officially recognized as *Dahlia* in 1791, yet it continued to be known as the Georgian until well into the 1800s. There are now at least 14,000 named cultivars available, all derived from two Mexican species, the *Dahlia pinnata* Cav. and *Dahlia coccinea* Cav. So many variations in the flower form and colour exist that botanists now recognize ten different categories for dahlia cultivars.

The tiny English Daisy, *Bellis perennis* L., was also of the *Compositae* family, with rayed petals and central florets. It grew wild in Great Britain, spreading through fields and pastures. Unlike many such prolific plants which have been relegated to the category of weeds, gardeners welcomed the English Daisy into their gardens and cultivated it with care. It offered everything a gardener could ask for in a garden plant: easy cultivation and propagation with delightful flowers that bloomed in pretty colours throughout the summer months. In the late eighteenth century English flower growers could hardly keep up with the demand for the plant in London markets. At that time there were twelve kinds listed by the growers, including several doubles and a quilled variety.

After acknowledging these positive attributes, it is disappointing to relate that the English daisy is not particularly hardy in most of Canada. It was grown on the coast of New England in the early nineteenth century but only with the protection of hotbeds and frames. In most of America it succeeds best as a hardy annual sown from seed. Varieties from seed are unpredictable: "If seed from double flowers is sown, the product will be single, semi-double and a few double sorts, with a variety of colors and shades" (Breck 1866:137).

The name of the genus, *Bellis*, has had several interpretations, with some believing it came from the Latin for beautiful (*bellus*), and others thinking the Latin word for war (*bellum*) was more likely. Proponents of the latter view are supported by the plant's medicinal uses: poultices of the leaves and flowers reduced the inflammation of wounds, abcesses, and the swelling of sprains, as they might have done on early battlefields where the English Daisy grew. Infusions of the plant aided unsettled stomachs and inflammation in the upper respiratory tract. These applications were folk remedies

by the end of the eighteenth century when the English Daisy was grown
for its horticultural value alone. It has also been used as a pot plant, but a
modern gardener has commented that when potted they look like plastic
plants. Such is the fate of a plant with such perfection.

Custead listed a Purple Perennial "Convolvolus," a plant that has been hard
to identify with certainty. The *Convolvulus* genus is confusing, as it formerly
included plants now classified as *Ipomoea* or as *Calystegia*. Attempts to find a
perennial species with a purple flower narrowed the selection, and the pos-
sibilities were further limited by eliminating those not known in the 1820s.
None of the contemporary nursery catalogues examined listed such a plant.
After much speculation, three species were selected, any one of which
could have been grown by Custead: *Convolvulus canariensis* L., *C. lineatus* L.,
or *C. humilis* Jacq.

The most likely candidate for the catalogue entry was *Convolvulus canariensis*, known as Canary Bindweed, a native of the Canary Islands brought
into cultivation in Europe at the end of the seventeenth century. In its
native habitat it is a half-hardy evergreen, but in England it was necessary to
protect it in winter, or to grow it in a greenhouse, and it would not have
been a dependable perennial in Canada. The flowers, borne in axillary clusters, could vary from a pale blue to a violet-purple. The stem grew "to considerable Height and must be supported with strong Stakes" (Miller 1754/
1969:365). From his experience Miller also noted that the plant bloomed
freely but seldom bore seeds. Canary Bindweed was illustrated in Curtis's
Botanical Magazine in 1809.

Convolvulus lineatus, a low-growing plant with erect stems only eight or
ten inches high, was native to southern Europe and taken into gardens
around 1770. It spread rapidly by underground root and was quite hardy in
Britain. The flowers of this species were light reddish-purple. Several eighteenth and nineteenth century gardening books described this plant as
bindweed, but it was seldom mentioned in twentieth century horticultural
dictionaries. Perhaps the invasive creeping rootstalks were responsible for
its decline as a garden plant.

Another plant meeting the requisite characteristics, but not as well
known, was *Convolvulus humilis*, a small plant from the eastern Mediterranean area. It was a tender, short-lived perennial about fifteen inches high,
with tiny half-inch blue or violet flowers occurring singly in leaf axils.

The convolvulus that Custead grew could have been given to him by
one of his patrons, and while he was able to determine the family to which
it belonged, he may not have known the species.

A plant often found in early herb gardens was Dyer's Madder, *Rubia tinctoria* L., grown for the bright red dye provided by the roots. Most of the plants in the family *Rubiaceae* were of tropical origin. Several related species were brought into cultivation for commercial crops rather than as garden ornamentals, such as coffee and cinchona (the plant that supplied quinine). Madder was native to southeast Europe and Asia, its use for dyes recorded in ancient times. The plant was cultivated in Asia Minor, and the dye product exported to Europe. The intense colour became known as Turkey red. To produce the dye, the roots of the plant were first dried, then subjected to treatment with both alkaline and acid solutions and partial fermentation. The final product was an orange-red crystalline substance that could be dissolved in alcohol. The crystals produced colours ranging from bright red to purple, depending on the acidity or alkalinity of the dye bath. Eventually several European countries involved in the textile trade, notably Holland, France, and Germany, cultivated their own supply of this valuable plant. Several attempts to grow madder in southern England were unsuccessful in fulfilling the needs of the British textile industry. Madder remained the principal source of red dye until synthetic alizarin was formulated in 1868.

Madder also had medicinal uses and is still grown for these properties in eastern Europe and Asia. Again it is the root that supplies the effective ingredients. Crushed roots were applied to wounds to help the healing process, and preparations taken internally were recommended for dissolving stones in the urinary tract, to relieve suppressed menstruation, and as a diuretic. The alizarin contained in these preparations coloured urine, bones, and mothers' milk a startling red (Wood 1858:653).

Two Foxgloves, a Purple and a White, *Digitalis purpurea* L. and *D. p. var alba*, were members of the Snapdragon family, *Scrophulariaceae*. The foxglove grew wild in southern and western Europe, springing up spontaneously in rough sandy ground. In England it was given local names such as Witch's Thimble, or Bluidy-Man's Finger, as people associated it with ancient Druid rites carried out in mid-summer when the plant was in bloom. In the species form probably offered in the catalogue, the flowers were either purple or white. Other colours were known: Parkinson had pink and white forms in 1629, and a yellow and a creamy-white were added to the colour range in the eighteenth century. When Peter Kalm visited Philadelphia in the 1740s he was shown a pink foxglove, the earliest record of this plant on this side of the Atlantic. Garden forms derived from the wild species were treated as biennials. A rosette of leaves formed in the first year sent up a flower spike two to four feet high in the second season.

Dyer's Madder   *Rubia tinctoria* L.

Purple Foxglove   *Digitalis purpurea* L.

Snapdragon   *Antirrhinum majus* L.

The drug digitalis originally extracted from the leaves is used in modern medicine as one of the principal drugs for the treatment of cardiac conditions, but its historical use in folk medicine was minimal. Even Gerard, who was quick to report any interesting use for the plants he described, dismissed the foxglove as "of no use, neither have they any place amongst medicines" (Gerard 1975/1633:791). Beyond several external applications like poultices and salves for treating wounds and skin eruptions, little else was recorded. The first disciplined medical treatment using foxglove was published in the late eighteenth century in England by Dr William Withering, who used it successfully with dropsy (oedema) patients. By 1880 many tests were carried out to analyse the complex drug, experimenting with various dosages and observing reactions. Only in the twentieth century has digitalis become a reliable and indispensible drug for treating heart conditions.

The "Snap Dragon," *Antirrhinum majus L.*, was related to the foxglove. Today it is cultivated as an annual, but in its native habitat around the Mediterranean it was perennial. It had become a garden plant by the sixteenth century, prized for its tall spikes of colourful and interesting flowers. The common name refers to the shape of the flower: the corolla is a pouch-like tube, divided into two lobed lips, an upper and a lower, and when the sides of the pouch are pressed together, the lips open like the mouth of a toad or "dragon" – as every child knows. The botanical name *Antirrhinum* means "like a nose, or snout." This described the seed pod, "a fruit resembling a Calf's Head, which is divided in the middle by a partition into two Cells, in which are contained many seeds" (Miller 1754/1969:102).

According to Gerard the plant had no practical purpose and was "good for nothing in the use of Physicke." Some magical properties were assigned to it, suggesting that a woman would be more seductive if she wore the plant in her shoes, or that a man could avoid becoming bewitched if he carried it on his person. In the eighteenth and nineteenth centuries it was a popular florists' flower, grown both in the open and in cool greenhouses for the trade in cut flowers.

The original species of snapdragon had deep reddish-purple flowers with yellow throats. In time, by process of selection, the flower colours were increased to include white, yellow, mauve, red, or pink blooms. These variations were not stable and did not come true from seed. Some of the colours received individual names, but in the later nineteenth century it was "unnecessary to enumerate the varieties as an equal amount of variation can be obtained spontaneously from seed" (Nicholson 1887 1:89). The colour-range of the flowers can be predetermined to some extent before flowering by examining the colour of the stem: light coloured stems will produce pale hues, and dark or reddish stems will bear deeply coloured flowers.

There were several members of the *Caryophyllaceae* on the list: Rose Campion, Scarlet Lychnis, and several species of Pinks. Rose Campion, *Lychnis coronaria* (L.) Desr., and Scarlet Lychnis, *Lychnis chalcedonia* L., are both showy plants with long histories as garden plants.

The flamboyant Rose Campion was in gardens of the early civilizations in India and the Mediterranean region. The plant was described by several Roman writers, and the name given it, *Lychnis*, derived from the Latin for "lamp." This may have been in reference to the clear, bright colour of the flowers, or to the ancient practice of making lamp wicks from the soft leaves. The plant was found in European gardens throughout the Middle Ages and was grown "plentifully" in Elizabethan England. When Linnaeus studied it in the eighteenth century he reclassified it as *Agrostemma coronaria*, the name by which it was known in the early 1800s. The name *Lychnis* was restored later in the nineteenth century, but there is still some confusion surrounding the genus. The five-petalled flower was a brilliant rose colour, almost magenta, emphasized by its strong contrast with the velvety silvery-grey leaves. Variations were known in the eighteenth century, including double forms and flowers graded in colour from white to pink, but these varieties are now rare. Rose Campion was brought to New England in the early years of settlement and grown so widely that it has become a roadside wildflower in some American states. It would have been a familiar garden plant to Custead's clientele and a welcome addition to their flower beds.

In antiquity Rose Campion was used for garlands and perhaps as a medicinal herb for snakebite, but little value has been ascribed to its use as a remedial herb. An early nineteenth century reference revealed that this "very ornamental [plant] is eaten by horses, goats and sheep" (Perthensis 1807 1:328).

Scarlet Lychnis, a close relative, also had a five-petalled flower, but its appearance suggested the design of a Maltese Cross, another of its popular names. *Lychnis chalcedonia* originally came from eastern Asia, Siberia, and possibly Japan and has been so long in cultivation that how it reached Europe is unknown. Some believe that the story is revealed in another of the common names, Jerusalem Cross, an indication that the plant arrived in Europe as a result of the Crusades to the Holy Land. Scarlet Lychnis is one of the oldest and most common border perennials, which has escaped from gardens and self-sown itself in the wild in both Europe and parts of North America.

Scarlet Lychnis   *Lychnis chalcedonia* L.

Rose Campion
Lychnis coronaria (L.) Desr.

Chinese Pink
Dianthus chinensis L.

Clove Pinks   *Dianthus caryophyllus* L.

Individually the flowers are very small, only an inch across, but they are borne in dense, flat-topped clusters at the ends of branches. In bright shades of red ranging from brick to a brilliant scarlet, the plant gained the immediate attention of an observer. The colour was sometimes so strident that care was taken to place the plant among others that would complement it or provide a suitable background.

The group of flowers known as Pinks include a number of species in the genus *Dianthus*, five of which were offered by the Toronto Nursery. Garden pinks were so named for the "pinked" (i.e. fringed or toothed) edges of their petals. Greatly admired and universally grown, these flowers have in turn given their name to the English language to describe a colour and a condition, "in the pink." Not only were the flowers appealingly attractive but most species were highly scented, with a spicy fragrance resembling that of cloves (*Caryophyllus aromaticus*). Species of the *Dianthus* genus native to the Mediterranean found their way into gardens before the Middle Ages. They were among the flowers depicted in the *millefleurs* tapestries of the late fifteenth century. *Dianthus plumaris* and *D. caryophyllus* were both well established in English gardens by the sixteenth century, taken there by either the Normans or Crusaders returning from North Africa. There were so many variations within the genus that Gerard remarked that "a great and large volume would not suffice to write of every one [as] every yeare every clymate and countrey bringeth forth new sorts" (Gerard 1633/1975:589).

Trade with the Far East in the early eighteenth-century brought the Chinese or Indian Pink, *Dianthus chinensis*, to Europe and America. The plants were treated as annuals, for although they were perennial in their native habitat, they proved tender in the European climate. Their erect, stiff stems bore clusters of flowers in such variety that "in a bed where there may be one hundred plants, scarcely two will be found alike" (Breck 1866:197). This species was one of the parents of *Dianthus latifolius*, the Broadleaved Pink. This garden hybrid was very popular as a border plant in the nineteenth century. The large double crimson and red flowers appeared throughout the season in multiple clusters.

The common pinks, which Custead offered in fine double varieties in various colours, were of garden origin, *Dianthus hortensis*. These were favourite florists' flowers and had many variations usually featuring more than one colour in the individual petals. By the 1820s there were over three hundred sorts (Loudon 1827:860). Fine examples, especially doubles, were frequently given the name of their grower, such as "Bat's Double Red," one of the few early nineteenth century varieties still extant (Brickell 1986:96).

About 1770 a seedling plant with a red margin on white petals began a craze for "laced pinks," blooms in which the colour in the eye of the flower was repeated on the edges of the petals.

The Clove Pink, *Dianthus caryophyllus*, was also called the Border Carnation or Clove Gilliflower. This species was indigenous to southern Europe and North Africa and had been cultivated by the Moors for use as flavouring and scent in sherbets and beverages. In spite of its Mediterranean origins, it was quite hardy in colder climates. The flowers were up to two inches in diameter and very fragrant with that aromatic clove-like scent that distinguishes this genus. The fringed petals ranged from white to red through shades of rose and lilac. The red variety became the symbol of true love, seen in wedding portraits from the Low Countries. It was the emblem of Napoleon's Legion of Honour and later that of the political socialists. Variations in the petals and the colour included those called flakes, bizarres, and picotees. By the 1820s it was so widely grown that it lost its place as a fashionable plant and was neglected by growers, although it remained a favourite in the cottage garden. In the 1950s interest in old varieties was stimulated anew in Britain, and specimens were sought out in old gardens to record and propagate. (These were not the carnations we find today as cut flowers and buttonholes, which are hothouse plants developed in the twentieth century.)

Custead's Pheasant Eyed Pink, *Dianthus plumarius*, also known as the Scotch Pink or the Grass Pink, was one of the parents of the common garden pink. The leaves of this species were a pale blue-green and very narrow. The fragrant flowers varied in colour from white to pink or purple, occasionally variegated. The petals of the species were deeply fringed, or feathered, with a well-defined eye of a different hue.

All the pinks were wonderful choices for the flower border for their colour, texture, and fragrance. They were easily propagated in the nursery by seed or by layering. Because of the seemingly endless differences possible, it would be hard to determine the exact colour or petal variations that Custead offered at a time when the popularity of these flowers was at its peak.

Hollyhocks were another all-time garden favourite. Members of the Mallow family, the genus *Alcea* has several species of the tall, showy plants introduced to Europe from China in the mid-sixteenth century. The Chinese had cultivated hollyhocks for upwards of a thousand years as an economic crop grown for its hemp-like fibre. The source of the original species is unknown, as even the oldest species identified are now believed to be hybrids. The Antwerp Hollyhock, now classified as *Alcea ficifolia* L., generally had

Hollyhock   *Alcea rosea var. nigra* L.

Double Columbine
Aquilegia vulgaris L.

Virginian Virgin's Bower
Clematis virginiana L.

yellow or orange flowers. Custead's Black Antwerp Hollyhock was more likely the variety *Alcea rosea var. nigra* which has such deep maroon flowers as to appear almost black. There were a number of so-called Antwerp Holly-hocks, as growers in Belgium specialized in the genus in the early nine-teenth century, creating a great many novel named varieties.

The Yellow and Chinese Hollyhocks listed were both doubles. It was characteristic of this period in garden history for double flowers to be pre-ferred. When nursery grown from seed, the plants that produced single blooms were quickly weeded out to prevent them from breeding with the more desirable doubles.

Popular in eighteenth-century gardens in the American colonies, holly-hocks remained fashionable until the mid-nineteenth century. However, they were later devastated by a fungal disease, *Puccinia malvacearum*, first noticed in Europe in 1869; and many named varieties were lost. This disease, also known as hollyhock rust, remains a threat to the plant that can only be overcome by repeated fungicidal spraying and destruction of all affected parts (Pirone 1978:128). Present-day hollyhocks are seldom named as they were in the past, except for being either single or double.

The word for the genus, *Alcea*, was derived from the Greek verb "to heal." Hollyhocks were once much-used medicinal plants, the flowers made into various preparations for healing throat and lung ailments, coughs, and colds. When dried, hollyhock flowers turn a deep purple-black, and these were used as a dye and as a colouring for wine.

Columbines and Clematis are members of the Ranunculus family, which is known to contain toxic substances. The seeds of the columbine could be life-threatening if ingested, particularly by children, and species of clematis can cause skin inflammation and blistering when handled. Nonetheless, this family has given the garden some of its prettiest and best-loved plants.

The Toronto nursery had five varieties of Double Columbine. *Aquilegia vulgaris* L. was a native of Europe and central Asia. The attractive and fan-ciful spurred blooms of this species endeared it to many generations who endowed the flowers with symbolic meanings. The flower, which many thought resembled a dove (*columba* in Latin), was used in Renaissance paintings as the Christian symbol of the Holy Ghost. A stalk bearing seven flowers was likened to the seven gifts of the Spirit referred to in Isaiah 2:2. In secular references the columbine and the dianthus pictured together represented a perfect marriage, and artists used this symbolism in wedding portraits.

Double columbines such as Custead offered were introduced in the eigh-teenth century. These did not usually have spurred flowers, the doubling of the five petals alternating with sepals creating a full but crowded bloom. Columbines were found in a range of colours from white through pinks and blues to a dark purple. They attracted bees and butterflies and were easily cross-pollinated unless the different colours were kept well apart. As a result columbine seed often produced many variants, five of which were represented in the Toronto Nursery. To maintain a specific colour or a double, the parent plants had to be separated from other columbines or carefully hand-pollinated.

Columbines are short-lived perennials but self-seed so readily that, once established, they remain in the garden for years. After several generations self-seeded plants revert to the single purple form.

Custead had three species of *Clematis* in the catalogue: the Sweet Scented Virgin's Bower, *Clematis viticella* L., Virginian Bower, *Clematis virginiana* L., and Traveller's Joy, *Clematis vitalba* L. All three plants were vines that climbed by twisting their leaf stalks around a support. In English and American gardens of the late eighteenth and early nineteenth centuries, they were used to cover the arbours, pergolas, and trellises that were intrinsic to garden design of the period. Less elaborate home gardens used the "most ornamental" clematis as a shade plant for the veranda (Traill 1855/1969:15). The vines grew quickly, flowered prettily, and had interesting feathery seed heads. These became quite conspicuous in the late summer and were responsible for the fanciful common names: Old Man's Beard, Grandfather's Whiskers, Devil's Hair, Hedge Feathers, Father Time. All three species had trifoliate leaves and flowers with coloured sepals but no petals. Some species were monoecious: that is, there were male and female plants.

Clematis viticella, the Sweet Scented Virgin's Bower, was grown in England by the physician to Queen Elizabeth I, the Virgin Queen. It was a woody vine with small red or blue flowers. Parkinson recorded a double variety in 1629. By the late eighteenth century there was a choice of four sorts: red, blue, and purple single-flowered varieties, and a purple double. The blooms were fragrant, with a faint touch of almond. This species was one of the parents of the *Clematis* "Jackmanni," now the most common garden sort, introduced in 1862. During the peak of its popularity in the nineteenth century, many plants of this species were destroyed by a disease, possibly a fungal infection.

Clematis virginiana, Virginian Bower, was native to North America, found wild from Nova Scotia to Manitoba. This vigorous-growing species climbed over shrubs and river banks in places where the soil was somewhat alkaline. The American clematis was introduced to Europe in 1767, one of

the plants exchanged between the two continents by enthusiastic collectors. The flowers were off-white, the seed heads very prominent fluffy,
silky clusters.

Clematis vitalba, Traveller's Joy, was native to Europe. It had a longer
cultural history than the other two described here. In folklore the plant was
related to thunderstorms. Early Romans believed that vines grown on the
walls of the home would protect it from storms; on the north side of the
Alps the belief was that the vine attracted thunder and lightning (Pizetti and
Cocker 1975 1:255). The vine grew rampantly along roadsides in Europe, a
pretty sight enjoyed by travellers when the plant was in flower and after it
had gone to seed. Gypsies travelling the roads used the irritating leaves to
induce inflammation and blistering on their children's limbs to arouse sym-
pathy when begging. The exceedingly vigorous vine grew to forty feet or
more, often strangling other growth. The small ivory-white flowers with a
vanilla-like scent were less spectacular than the large greyish-white, feathery seed heads.

The catalogue listed two very different plants belonging to the Bellflower
family, *Campanulaceae*: Canterbury Bells with blue, white, or purple flowers,
Campanula medium L., and the Scarlet Cardinal Flower, *Lobelia cardinalis* L.

The bell-shaped flowers of Campanulas have assured plants in this family
of a place in the garden for many centuries. "All these Bell-flowers do
grow in our Gardens, where they are cherished for the beautie of their
flowers," wrote Parkinson in 1629 (Parkinson 1629/1991:357). Canterbury
Bells, *Campanula medium*, had the largest blooms of all the species in the
genus, and was probably the best known and longest in cultivation. The
plant was native to southwestern Europe, but the first mention of it was in
the writings of Dodoens, physician to Maximilian II, sixteenth-century
emperor of Rome. The English herbalist Gerard, who borrowed a translation from the Latin of Dodoens work for his own *Herbal*, first described the
plant in English in 1597. The flowers were called Coventry or Canterbury
Bells as they were found growing in the "low woods and hedge-rowes"
near these towns (Gerard 1633/1975:450).

Canterbury Bells were popular with American gardeners in the late
eighteenth century. Seeds were sent from Europe in 1760 in one of the
many exchanges between botany enthusiasts. President Jefferson grew them
in a flower bed combined with white poppies and African marigolds – an
interesting and richly coloured mixture of white, blues, and purples con-
trasted with brilliant golden-yellow (Leighton 1986:402). Canterbury Bells
were biennial plants, producing a basal rosette of leaves in the first year and

Blue Canterbury Bell *Campanula medium* L.

Cardinal Flower
Lobelia cardinalis L.

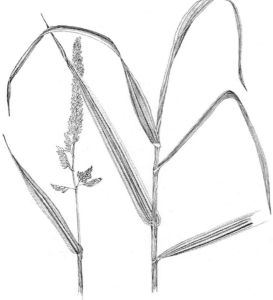

Ribband Grass *Phalaris arundinacea var. picta* L.

sending up profusely blooming stalks of large bell-shaped flowers in the second season. There were double forms of the plant, but in the early nineteenth century these were not as highly regarded and were "cultivated only for their oddity" (Breck 1866:137). At present a popular variety is a semi-double form, called the Cup and Saucer, but this form was not widely grown until late in the nineteenth century.

The roots of the plant had a pleasantly sweet taste and were used as a vegetable in a similar manner to rampion, a related species. In the past the plant was prescribed in folk medicine to treat mouth and throat infections, but neither of these uses has persisted.

The vivid, intense red of the Cardinal Flower was unrivalled in the flower world. The *Lobelia cardinalis* L. was native to North America, growing "neere the river of Canada, where the French plantation in America is seated" (Parkinson 1629/1991:357). No one could forget the first encounter with this plant in shady woods where it appears to glow like a flame. Early travellers to America were truly impressed by it: the eighteenth century botanist Peter Kalm was so enthusiastic about the Cardinal Flower he claimed this land was "adorned with the finest red imaginable" (Kalm 1770/1966 1:323). Later Mrs Simcoe admired the Cardinal Flower "which grows in the wettest and most shady places [and] is a beautiful colour" (Innis 1983:82). She was told the Indians used the root of the plant as a medicine. There were other historic references to medicinal uses of this plant by the Amerindians, particularly for the treatment of syphilis. Most members in the Lobelia genus, including the Cardinal Flower, are quite poisonous. Modern analysis has shown the plant to contain several alkaloids that affect the body's nervous system by first exciting, then paralysing nerve cells.

The Cardinal Flower was introduced to Europe from New France in the sixteenth century but was first described in English by Parkinson (1629/1991), who got his plants from Paris. By the mid-eighteenth century it was "greatly prized by the Curious for the Beauty of its rich crimson Flowers, which exceed all the Flowers I have yet seen, in the Deepness of its Colour ... These Plants are natives of Virginia and Carolina ... from whence the Seeds are often sent back to England [to] arrive here in the spring" (Miller 1754/1969:1194). Europeans often had difficulty in raising the plant from seed. Seeds were best sown as soon as they ripened, and the overseas voyage reduced their viability. Curiously, the Cardinal Flower was so-called not because of its colour but because the first plant to flower in Europe was in the garden of Cardinal Barberini in Rome (Pizetti & Cocker 2:784).

"Ribband" or Ribbon Grass was the only member of the Grass family, *Gramineae*, to be offered as a nursery plant. Ribbon Grass, *Phalaris arundi-naceae var picta* L., was a favourite with British landscape gardeners in the eighteenth and early nineteenth century. This school of garden design favoured long vistas towards a river or pond over lawns spotted with natu-ralistic clumps of trees or shrubs. This required plants with distinctive char-acteristics to serve as accents. Ribbon Grass grew to a height from three to five feet. The bright green leaves were longitudinally marked with creamy-white or yellow stripes, and the feathery seed heads moved gracefully in a breeze. The size, foliage markings, and habit provided the gardener with a distinctive element for such large-scale vistas. A body of water – a lake or stream – figured prominently in this school of landscape design. As Ribbon Grass grew particularly well on damp stream-sides and in swampy areas, it could transform a difficult location into an asset. The dried seed heads made plumes for use in arrangements for winter bouquets.

American gardeners followed the example of their British counterparts, using Ribbon Grass as an ornamental. It became quite popular in the nine-teenth century and can still be found in old gardens or around abandoned home sites. The only drawback to this decorative plant was its tendency to become invasive, spreading rapidly by underground stolons. When left uncontrolled, or placed where it could not be confined, it could easily become a nuisance and difficult to eradicate once established. It was not a plant for the flower bed or a small garden.

Two garden plants belonging to the Mustard family, *Cruciferae*, bear little resemblance to the cabbages and kale to which they were related save for their flowers, four petals in the form of a cross. Wall Flower, *Erysimum cheiri* (L.) Crantz, and Sweet Rocket, *Hesperis matronalis* L., have stalks of pretty and colourful flowers deserving of a place in the garden border.

Wallflower was given its common name because it was found growing wild on old walls in England. Many thought this plant arrived in Britain inadvertently with the stone the Normans imported for their buildings. Wallflower was indigenous to the eastern Mediterranean area, introduced to European gardens many centuries ago. Its most admired feature was the fragrance of the flowers, which smelled like violets. In the seventeenth century it was treated as an indoor plant, and the blooms were used in nosegays.

In the Middle Ages the wallflower was regarded as a symbol of good fortune and often worn by travellers to assure successful journeys. The yellow flowers were sought after for their medicinal values as their colour

Wallflower
Erysimum cheiri (L.) Crantz.

Sweet Rocket   *Hesperis matronalis* L.

French Honeysuckle
Hedysarum coronarium L.

recommended them for the treatment of jaundice, according to the Doctrine of Signatures. The oil distilled from the flowers was used for female disorders, for fertility and difficult labour; however, all medical applications were discontinued in the nineteenth century when the oil was found to contain toxins that affected muscles and acted on the central nervous system.

Where winters were mild and the air moist, the wallflower flourished, even in the most desolate ground. It was never as popular in America as it was in Europe, much to the regret of many gardeners. It survived the winters in Pennsylvania and Virginia, but New England gardeners found it necessary to take the plant into the greenhouse for protection. Perennial in hospitable environments, in cooler climates it was treated as a biennial, seeded in the greenhouse the first year and placed out in the border the following season.

Sweet Rocket also had scented blooms, most pronounced in the evenings. In the eighteenth century it was a favourite of ladies, who enjoyed bouquets in their bedchambers, dressing rooms, and apartments. It was said that Marie-Antoinette had the flowers sent to her while she was imprisoned during the French Revolution. The plant was most appreciated for the attractive flowers and their perfume, but it also had culinary and medicinal uses: the young leaves were eaten as a salad vegetable, and infusions of the leaves were used to treat fevers and as a mild emetic.

In parts of eastern Canada in late spring the clouds of pale purple and white flowers seen along roadsides and in old pastures are Sweet Rocket that has escaped from old gardens. It is often called "wild phlox," which is a misnomer: Sweet Rocket has four petals, while the phloxes have five.

There were both single and double forms of Sweet Rocket in the eighteenth century. The double form was a mutant which had to be propagated by division or cuttings. There is no record of the double form reaching America: in the early 1800s M'Mahon of Philadelphia declared the double "extremely beautiful and fragrant; I have not yet had the pleasure of seeing one of them in this country" (M'Mahon 1858/1976:413). They are no longer in general cultivation, even in England. The double white was especially admired but is now extremely rare, although it was exhibited as late as 1972 in Britain (Brickell 1986:129).

French Honeysuckle is neither from France nor related to the Honeysuckle (*Lonicera*) genus. How it got its name is unknown. It is a member of the Pea family, *Leguminosae*, classified as *Hedysarum coronarium* L. Other members of the Pea family named in the catalogue list of biennials and perennials were Everlasting Pea, White and Blue Sophora, White and Yellow Broom, and Maryland Cassia.

The plant known as French Honeysuckle truly was an old-fashioned garden favourite, even in 1827. It can be traced back to the ancient Greek Dioscorides, who named it *Hedysarum* for its "sweet smell." In 1629 Parkinson regretted its common English name; he called it the "red Sattin flower although some foolishly call it, the Red or French Honeysuckle" (Parkinson 1629/1976:340). Regardless of his criticism, the name stuck, and it continued to be known as the French Honeysuckle after it was brought to America. President Washington had it "planted at each column of the covered ways" in his late eighteenth-century garden (Leighton 1986:427).

In England this plant was grown by gardeners near London to supply city markets with fragrant cut blooms in the spring. Miller recommended putting the plants in the large border of the "Pleasure Garden," as they had a fine appearance when the "very handsome flowers" were blossoming (Miller 1754/1969:606). Other plants in the genus *Hedysarum* were grown as forage crops, and French Honeysuckle was occasionally used for this purpose too as it was considered an excellent fodder for horses. While it was never included in pharmacopoeias, it was used in folk medicine: Gerard referred to the use of new leaves being "good for the stomacke when taken in drink [and] it is thought to hinder conception, if it be applied with honie before the act" (Gerard 1633/1975:1236).

There were two European species of the Everlasting Pea, *Lathyrus latifolia L.* and *Lathyrus grandiflorus* Sibth. & Sm. Perennial flowering peas would have been familiar to the settlers in Upper Canada, and there were also native species with purple flowers that grew wild in moist environments along the shores of the Great Lakes. Mrs Simcoe reported "everlasting Peas creeping in abundance of a purple colour" on the Toronto Peninsula in 1793 (Innis 1983:102). However, it was probably the European species that were listed in Custead's catalogue. These were widely planted in early gardens and have since escaped to be considered alien wildflowers.

Both European species had rose-purple flowers, very similar to the well-known Sweet Pea but without its lovely fragrance. Perennial peas were among the most easily cultivated garden plants and have been grown in cottage gardens since the sixteenth century. The flower clusters made good cut blooms, regarded as "very ornamental in Basons or Pots of Flowers to place in Chimneys or other parts of Large Rooms" (Miller 1754/1969:753). The decorative, rambling growth of these vining plants made them popular for training over trellises, arbours, and fences. Their habit also allowed them to be useful in other ways; Miller suggested "these plants are very proper to

Everlasting Pea   *Lathyrus latifolia* L.

Blue Sophora   *Baptisia australis* (L.) R. Br.

Yellow Broom
Cytisus scoparius (L.) Link.

Maryland Cassia   *Senna marilandica* (L.) Link.

plant against a dead Hedge, where they will run over it" – presumably a solution for disguising a less successful feature of a garden.

Sophora, White and Blue, were also members of the Pea family. The name is now outdated, and these plants are today known as *Baptisia alba* (L.) Vent. and *Baptisia australis* (L.) R. Br. They were illustrated in *Curtis' Botanical Magazine* in 1801 under the name *Sophora*. The genus was renamed in 1811, but the old nomenclature remained in use for many years. The word "Baptisia" comes from the Greek meaning "to dye," as several plants in this genus were used for a blue dye. Though likened to indigo, the colour was weak in comparison with that from the tropical plant *Indigofera tinctoria*.

Both white and blue species of *Baptisia* were native to North America and had found their way into European gardens by the middle of the eighteenth century. The flowers were like those of the Sweet Pea, borne on upright spikes rising above the foliage. *Baptisia* was a handsome plant for the border as the bluish-green foliage acted as an interesting background foil for other flowers after the blooming period was over. Its native habitat was from Pennsylvania south to Florida and west to the Mississippi, but by the end of the nineteenth century, having escaped from gardens, it could be found growing wild as far north as Vermont.

White and Yellow Broom were species of *Cytisus*. White Broom, *Cytisus multiflorus* (L'Herit. ex Ait) Sweet, was also known as Spanish Broom. Yellow Broom, *Cytisus scoparius* (L.) Link., was the Common or Scotch Broom. The name "broom" was a confusing term as it was used for several species in separate but closely related genera. To add to the confusion, one of the *Cytisus* species was called *Genista* in the florist trade.

White Broom was the only species of this extensive and complex group of plants to have white flowers. The first plants were introduced to English gardens from their native habitat in the Iberian Peninsula in 1752. Marginally hardy in more northerly gardens, and presumably in Upper Canada, White Broom grew to a height of six to eight feet. It could be grown successfully as a potted plant by severe pruning after flowering to a height of eighteen inches.

Yellow Broom was native to Europe and Great Britain, creating brilliant masses of yellow colour in the spring. The pea-like flowers completely covered the foliage, as they were larger than the tiny leaves. The plant owes its common name to the use of its twigs for making brooms. It grew well even in sandy, gravelly soils and was used for shrubberies where little else would succeed.

Common or Yellow Broom was introduced to official medical practice in the seventeenth century by a Dr Mead, who had noted its use in folk medicine and used it to treat patients suffering from dropsy. His example was followed successfully by other practitioners: "No other medicine is entitled to more credit than broom for removing dropsical effusions" (Stillé and Maisch 1880:1281). The plant had other medicinal applications, both internal and external. Shepherds were in the practice of using fresh tops from twigs to treat ailing sheep. It had diuretic and cathartic properties, and was still much in use for these purposes in the late nineteenth century. In America it was used as fodder for pigs, one of the steps in the production of the succulent hams for which Virginia was famous.

Maryland Cassia, as its name suggests, was native to the eastern states of the American colonies. Seeds were sent to Europe in the early eighteenth century where the plant was first classified as *Cassia marilandica* L. but is now named *Senna marilandica* (L.) Link. It closely resembled Alexandrian Senna, and the dried and macerated leaves had a similar purgative action. The American species of senna was not as potent as the African plant, and it was regarded as a poor medicinal substitute. To overcome this, it was prescribed in larger doses. The dried leaves had a very unpleasant odour, and when used unadulterated could cause severe cramps and vomiting. The medication was usually prepared and administered in combination with other ingredients. The Shaker herb industry made small pressed cakes of senna leaves mixed with cloves, cinnamon, ginger, and other herbs to lessen the nauseous effect. Today many alternatives to these purgative drugs are available, and senna is now rarely used in western medicine.

Moss Pinks were members of the Phlox genus in the family *Polemoniaceae*. All species of phlox were native to North America, and their discovery in the eighteenth century added a great deal of colour and interest to European gardens. Moss Pinks, *Phlox subulata* L., were originally found in an area bounded by southern Ontario and the state of Michigan on the north, and on the south by the mountains of North Carolina. They were first described by the botanist-collector John Bartram in his correspondence with Peter Collinson in London. On 10 December 1745, Bartram sent Collinson "one sod of fine creeping spring Lychnis." The British horticulturist Reginald Farrer suggested that this date be celebrated annually as a horticultural holiday, for the little plant has proven to be one of the most successful American plants introduced to gardens.

When in bloom, masses of flowers in rosy shades of lilac through light to dark pink or white cover the cushion of leaves. It was much used in rockeries, a garden fancy that became increasingly popular in the

Moss Pink   *Phlox subulata* L.

Iris or Flower de Luce   *Iris germanica* L.

Blackberry Lily   *Belamcanda chinensis* (L.) DC.

nineteenth century. The American botanical encyclopedist Liberty Hyde Bailey wrote of the Moss Pink: "It is a much prized old garden plant, useful for colonizing where it is desired to cover the earth with a mat. It is much used in cemeteries. It blooms profusely in the spring" (Bailey 1902: 3:1308).

Two irises, the Large Purple German and a Dwarf Purple, and their relative, the Blackberry Lily, listed in the catalogue were all members of the Iris family, *Iridaceae*. So popular was this family in the early nineteenth century that the French botanical artist Pierre-Joseph Redouté devoted a whole volume of 468 water-colour paintings to *Les Liliacees*. (His other major work was a volume of roses, done principally for Napoleon's Josephine.)

The Large Purple German Iris, *Iris germanica* L., was a tall bearded species, an old hybrid. The name Flower de Luce or Fleur de Luce associated the iris with the fleur-de-lys on the French coat of arms used by Louis VIII at the beginning of the thirteenth century. The Dwarf Purple Iris was probably also a hybrid, a cross between *Iris germanica, Iris pumila*, and *Iris chamaeiris* (Pizetti and Cocker: 1975 1:677).

Irises were in cultivation in ancient Egypt, where they were used in rituals at the Temple of the Sphinx. Over two hundred species have been identified, and modern botanists have divided the complex genus into several groups for more accurate identification. Both kinds offered in Custead's catalogue belonged to the bearded iris group, which have thick "beards" on the three reflexed outer petals, known as falls. This flower was popular with German florists, who supplied much of the nursery stock on the market. Consequently, bearded irises were given the name German Iris. The Purple German Iris was scented, and the large blooms lasted well as a cut flower, filling a room with their fragrance. Hybridization of this group of iris began in Germany in the 1830s, eventually resulting in many new forms of colour and habit now seen in modern nurseries. As a garden plant the old Purple German Iris has survived the test of time. The tall stately stalks with a striking show of colour stand well above the spiky foliage, and when the flowers are over, the light blue-green of the stiff leaves add an accent and a texture to the flower border.

Early Mediterranean societies used the iris plant medicinally. The rhizomes were dried and powdered for use as an emetic and in formulas for treating bronchitis and asthma. The juice of the root had a strong purgative effect. Irises were grown commercially for use in the perfume industry: after a period of time the dried roots acquired a violet-like scent and also

acted as a fixative. For this purpose, the roots of a white variety was preferred – *Iris germanica var florentina*, known in the trade as orris root. In medieval times petals of the deep purple iris were ground with alum to make a
clear green pigment for manuscript illustrators.

The Blackberry Lily, *Belamcanda chinensis* (L.) DC, is not as well known as
perhaps it should be in modern gardens. Seeds of this plant were first sent
from China to the Jardin des Plantes in Paris and to Peter Collinson in
England by the French Jesuit priest Pierre Nicholas d'Incarville. Father
d'Incarville was a missionary in Peking from 1740 to 1757, and his interest
in botany enriched the gardens of Europe with many introductions from
the Far East. The plant was already known, for it was discussed in botanical
literature as early as 1632 and had been named *Ixia chinensis* (Nicholson
1887: 3:23). The common name was given in recognition of the seeds,
clusters of many small round black berries that appeared as the pods broke
open. The orange-yellow flowers, spotted with dark red-purple markings,
accounted for an alternate name, the Leopard Flower. The flowers last only
a day, but are profusely produced so the plant remains in bloom over a
fairly long period.

Several enthusiastic gardeners in the United States grew blackberry lilies
in the eighteenth century as an ornamental in the pleasure garden. Since
that time it has spread to become a roadside wildflower in parts of the
southern states. In China, where the Blackberry Lily is indigenous, it has
been used for centuries as a medicinal plant in remedies for throat ailments.

The Primrose family, *Primulaceae*, was represented in Custead's nursery
by three natives of Europe: the Polyanthus, *Primula X polyantha* Mill., the
Cowslip, *Primula veris* L., and the English Primrose, *Primula vulgaris* Huds.,
all well known and loved by gardeners. The bright colours of these flowers
in early spring were keenly appreciated in Europe and Britain. However,
the mild winters there, ending early in February or March, provided growing conditions very different from those in Upper Canada.

The Polyanthus was probably the hardiest of the three Primulas. Custead
offered "many varieties," and indeed, there were innumerable choices in
1827. These hybrid plants emerged in the seventeenth century and quickly
became garden favourites, cherished for their brightly coloured flowers.
During the eighteenth century they became the darlings of the florist trade
and a speciality of Dutch growers. A century later they were taken up
by the artisan gardeners in Britain, who surpassed even the Dutch in the

Cowslip   *Primula veris* L.

Polyanthus   *Primula X polyantha* Mill.

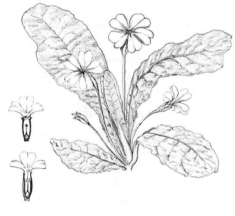

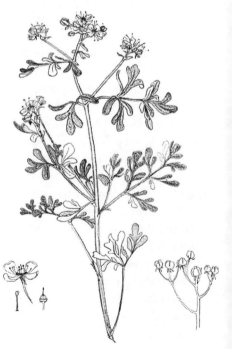

English Primrose   *Primula vulgaris* Huds.

Rue   *Ruta graveolens* L.

production of exquisite blooms. The competition among growers at exhibitions was fierce. Strict criteria were established for judging the qualities of a plant. For the Gold Lace, one of the most popular varieties, it was required:

The tube of the corolla should be short ... The eye should be round, of a bright clear yellow and distinct from the ground colour ... The ground-colour is most admired when shaded with a light and dark rich crimson, resembling velvet, with one mark or stripe from the edging down to the eye, where it should terminate in a fine point. The edging should resemble a bright gold lace, bold, clear and distinct, and so nearly of the same colour as the eye and stripes are scarcely to be distinguished; in short, the polyanthus should possess a graceful elegance of form, a richness of colouring, and symmetry of parts, not to be found in any other flower (Loudon 1827:853).

These were demanding specifications. Plants that did not meet show standards were to be destroyed or planted in the wilderness portion of the garden where they would provide interest even though they were "not very valuable Flowers" (Miller 1754/1969:1120).

Cowslip, a native of Europe and western Asia, was transplanted into gardens hundreds of years ago, for, as its name *Primula veris* implies, it was the first flower of spring. In Britain this small plant grew in woodlands, moist pastures, and meadowlands. One of the common names was Keys of Heaven, as the pendulous flower cluster resembled a bunch of keys, said to have been dropped by St Peter, causing the flower to grow where they fell. In the garden the cowslip was a natural for planting under hedges and along shady walks where they were enjoyed before other plants bloomed. The subtle fragrance of the flowers had a sweetness likened to anise or apricots. As cowslip was used for a number of household remedies, it was convenient to have it close by in the home garden.

In the past the plant was thought to have narcotic properties and was used to relieve toothache and control convulsions. The dried root, known in the pharmaceutical trade as *radix arthriticus*, was believed to cure gout, rheumatism, and paralysis. Common household preparations included a syrup for bronchial and respiratory conditions and an infusion used as a sedative for insomnia and anxiety. Cowslip wine, made from the fermented petals, enjoyed a long history of use in treating debilitating illnesses including consumption. Mrs Glasse gave a recipe for the wine in her cookery book of 1770. Few medications had "as favorable a record of their virtues as this humble plant enjoys" (Stillé and Maisch 1880:1176). Blemishes and wrinkles were removed from the complexion using a flower-water, which "improved beauty." The "humble" cowslip is still in use in folk medicine, and modern analysis has shown that it contains no harmful or narcotic ingredients. Care should be taken in handling the plant, however, as contact can cause a violent rash in sensitive persons.

The English Primrose, *Primula vulgaris*, was another wildflower of Europe and Great Britain that bloomed very early in spring. If the weather was mild, the primrose bloomed in February. As the long winter in central Canada could continue well into March or even April, many British immigrants yearned for the sight of these they had known "back home." Catharine Parr Traill wrote with nostalgia of "the pale primroses, the cowslip and the bluebell ... what would [the immigrant's wife] not give for one, just one, of those old familiar flowers" (Traill 1855/1969:13). No doubt many immigrants tried to bring the familiar primrose into their gardens, and William Custead's nursery tried to meet this demand. However, the natural conditions of this part of the country did not meet the plant's environmental requirements. The cold wet spring, the dry summer, and the limestone soil were all factors to be avoided if the plant were to grow well. Primroses, and their relative the cowslip, were sometimes treated as pot plants, but this could never replace the memory of the lush and colourful carpet of primroses in their native woodlands.

In the early nineteenth century several varieties of primrose were available. The common yellow, creamy white, and white-flowered primroses were popular in Shakespeare's day. The French botanist Tradescant introduced a purple sub-species from Turkey in the seventeenth century which added pinks and reds to the colour range when cross-bred. Some varieties were natural hybrids, such as the double-flowered variety that had the appearance of a tube within a tube, called Hose-in-Hose, or Jack-in-the-Green. In the 1830s a British nursery listed six sorts, including sulphur yellow, pink, lilac, purple, crimson, and a double white (Brickell 1986:190).

In literature the primrose was used to symbolize sterility. Although nature provided the flower with two different sexual arrangements to accommodate a variety of natural pollinators, the plant did not set seed readily as very few insects were active in the early spring when the flowers were in bloom. Unless pollinated artificially, the plant was best increased by division.

Primroses were more than a pretty flower, for they were grown as a salad green in Europe in the sixteenth century. The flowers and dried roots provided medications for dressing wounds, curing headaches, and easing the pain of rheumatism. These applications are no longer in use, and the common wild yellow primrose is now seldom seen in gardens, displaced by its more colourful progeny and the many *Primula* hybrids.

Rue, a plant with strongly aromatic foliage, was near the end of Custead's list of nursery plants. For centuries rue, *Ruta graveolens* L., was an important medicinal plant; ironically, present-day medicine considers it extremely toxic. Some persons may be so sensitive to the plant that merely touching it will arouse an allergic response, raising skin blisters. But in the past it was regarded almost as a miracle drug, used for colic, inducing abortion, and relieving bronchitis distress and pains in the chest, and as a cure for epilepsy. In the Middle Ages the bitter leaves were used in salads and egg and fish dishes and as a flavouring in wines and liqueurs.

It was during this period that the herb was given several common names. The name Herb of Grace resulted from the use of sprigs of the plant to sprinkle holy water during Mass in the Catholic Church. The name Herb of Repentance came from the nosegays carried by judges and juries and spread on the floors of courtrooms in fear of exposure to jail-fever, or typhus. The strong scent and the many curative properties assigned to rue made it appear to be magical. Medieval folklore included using rue to ward off the curses of witches and for an antidote to poisons.

Rue does have disinfectant properties, effective against vermin and fleas, which made some of the above uses plausible. It helped to rid linens of bedbugs and was hung in windows as a fly repellant. It had lost none of its early reputation by the middle of the eighteenth century, for Miller felt the "ragged and stumpy" plant was grown "chiefly for its medicinal use, or to furnish the Balconies for the Citizens in the Spring" (Miller 1754/1969:1234). Many did use rue for decorative purposes, particularly as dwarf hedges along pathways and as dense, dark-coloured edgings for formal beds.

"Capus" or Caper Spurge, *Euphorbia lathyris* L., was so-called because the seeds of this plant were once used as a substitute for expensive imported capers, the seeds of a Mediterranean shrub. This practice was not recommended for regular use, for the seeds could have a violently purgative action. Caper Spurge belongs to the Spurge family, *Euphorbiaceae*. All plants in this family have succulent stems containing a milky juice which can cause a blistering rash. The juice was used, as was the sap from plants in the Ranunculus family,

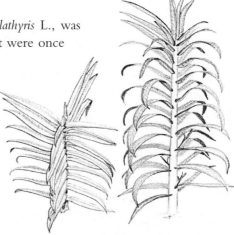

Caper Spurge   *Euphorbia lathyris* L.

by beggars to evoke pity when seeking alms, a practice that continues to the present.

Another name for Caper Spurge was Mole Plant, as gardeners put faith in growing the plant to prevent damage from burrowing rodents. The milky juice in the roots was supposed to act as a repellant. Treatises have been written on this subject, estimating the number of plants to be used and their placement for the greatest effect, but the true value of this procedure has never been proven. Originally from southern Europe, Caper Spurge was grown in America from the eighteenth century and has become naturalized in several southeastern states and California. It is only marginally hardy in the northeast but can be carried from year to year by removing the plant to a frost-free place over the winter.

7

Roses

Although roses are woody plants, they were not included under "Flowering Shrubs" in the Toronto Nursery catalogue. Instead they were given a separate section, for roses were regarded as candidates for the flower garden, not the typical nineteenth-century shrubbery. Among Custead's long list of roses were many old varieties which are now rare or unavailable. These tended to be large, widely branching hardy bushes that bloomed for only a few weeks in early summer with richly fragrant flowers. In 1827 the hybridization that took place after the introduction of Chinese roses was in its infancy. When new hybrids entered the market, offering more choices in the colour of the blooms and longer-lasting flowering periods, many older roses fell out of favour and have since become quite rare. Recent interest in reviving old species and varieties has created a demand to which specialized nurseries have responded, making several old favourites once again available to the modern gardener.

The thirty-two named roses named in the catalogue reflect the keen public interest in roses at that time. Few conscientious gardeners would have been without this popular garden plant, and "curious" gardeners would certainly have had more than one sort.

The rose can claim to be the most loved of all flowers throughout history, celebrated in story and song. Studies of its history, care, and culture have filled many volumes. Roses were cherished for their beauty, valued for their perfume, admired for their colour, and respected for their medicinal virtues. They have been in continuous cultivation since the earliest of civilized times in the Mediterranean region and the Near East. The visual concept of the Garden of Eden in medieval manuscripts was derived from the small enclosed rose gardens of the ancient Near East. In Christian times the rose became a symbol for the fall of man, the thorns a reminder of his sins and the flowers representing the lost glory of Paradise. (The very word "paradise" was adapted from the Arabic for garden.)

Red roses had a special symbolic significance – in Greek legend associated with the blood of Aphrodite, streaming from her wounded feet as she ran through the forest mourning the death of Adonis. In the Christian tradition, the red rose represented the life or blood of Christ. The red *Rosa gallica var. officinalis* L., the Apothecary Rose, was listed in pharmacopoeias, and in America the Shakers sold it among their medicinal herbs. Its astringent quality made it useful in healing wounds and relieving inflammation. Fresh rose petals, gathered in the morning when the flower was in full bloom and the oil content at its highest, were used for the manufacture of rose oil, extracted by distillation. The oils were made into ointments to clear the complexion; rose water was used to bathe sores in the eyes. Syrups of "rose and honey" were given to the sick, the feeble, and the melancholy.

The fragrance was thought to "comfort the brain and the heart and quickeneth the spirit." Dried rose petals lent their scent to household linens stored in closets and chests, pot-pourris perfumed the room, and sachets were tucked into clothing. The perfume and cosmetic industries use attar of roses, which has been produced in the Near East and Mediterranean region since ancient times. Made from the *Rosa damascena*, the Damask Rose, the valuable attar requires one hundred pounds of petals to produce half an ounce of the fragrance. In eastern countries diluted rose water is an ingredient of many food dishes and beverages; at wedding ceremonies it is sprinkled from beautifully crafted containers made expressly for the purpose. In the West the rose has become the favourite gift flower to express love and caring.

Early immigrants to Canada often brought cuttings with them and were very proud of the roses grown in their gardens. They are one of the few flowers travellers mentioned by name in their journeys through Canada. Anna Jameson was obviously pleased when Colonel Talbot offered her a bouquet of the "most beautiful buds" from his garden roses (Jameson 1838/1972 2:197), raised from cuttings he had brought from Britain. That American nurseries were able to supply numerous species and varieties by the end of the eighteenth century is confirmed by a glance at the Prince Nursery catalogue from 1790.

Roses almost defy classification, as there are so many natural and cultivated hybrids. However, the old hybrid roses in Custead's catalogue can be grouped into major classes of garden types: Gallicas, Centifolias, Albas and

Damasks. In addition, there were several species roses: the Sweet Brier, *Rosa rubiginosa* L., the Copper Coloured, *Rosa foetida X bicolor* Herrm., and the Michigan Rose, *Rosa setigera* Michx.

The *Rosa gallica*, originally a native of Europe, was one of the first to be brought into cultivation. It had a tendency to hybridize freely and was used to parent innumerable hybrids, making the Gallicas the largest class of old roses. Gallica roses in the Toronto Nursery catalogue included the Double Velvet, the Large Provence, the Unique White Provence, the Frankfort, and the Rosa Mundi. (The Crimson Dwarf and the Large Crimson Rose may also have been Gallicas.) The Double Velvet had a deep, dark red richly scented flower with velvet-textured petals. The blooms of the Provence (or Provins) rose were usually double, either white or red. They had solitary, highly fragrant flowers and were among the commonest sorts in England in the late eighteenth

Sweet Briar
Rosa rubiginosa L.

century. The Frankfort Rose had scentless and insignificant blooms but was a vigorous and hardy plant, making it a favourite rootstock for the grafting of more tender roses. The Rosa Mundi, *Rosa gallica* "Versicolor," was a natural sport or mutant, with fragrant semi-double blooms, the red petals gaily striped with white. The scent of the blooms of Gallica roses improved when dried. An infusion of the petals was used as an astringent and tonic as well as a vehicle for other medicines.

Centifolia roses, originally from the Caucasus, were known in antiquity and described by ancient writers. As so many varieties have been derived from this ancient rose, it is believed that the original Centifolia was a natural hybrid, of unknown origin. Centifolias were favourites of Dutch breeders who produced over two thousand varieties during the eighteenth century (Pizetti and Cocker 1975: 2:1133).

The blooms of Centifolias were generally clusters of red or pink flowers, some with a bluish or purplish tint. An oil was extracted from the petals by distillation for *Aqua Rosea* (rose water), which was slightly laxative. As it had a pleasant odour and taste, it was often used to make a syrup to mix with other less pleasant-tasting cathartics.

The double forms of Centifolia roses had in-curved petals, which were responsible for its common names, such as Cabbage Rose and Hundred-Leaved Rose. These and the Moss Rose were the Centifolias listed in the 1827 catalogue. The Moss Rose, a genetic mutant, was distinguished by the curious "mossy" covering on the leaf stalks and sepals. This "moss" was actually composed of many minute resin-scented glands.

The Single and Double White Roses and Maiden's Blush were roses of the Alba type, especially popular during the reign of Elizabeth I. It is believed that these are ancient, natural hybrids between *Rosa canina* L. and *Rosa gallica* L. They have been grown commercially in southern Europe for many centuries for the oil extracted from their intensely scented blooms. The plants are hardy and of vigorous growth with distinctive grey-green leaves. The Double White had a delicate pinkish touch on the petals which was more intense in the Maiden's Blush, *Rosa X alba* "Incarnata," a full double sort.

The Damask roses, represented in the catalogue by the Red Damask, the White Monthly, and the York and Lancaster, were large spiny shrubs. The Red Damask could grow to seven feet in height, bearing clusters of double

Maidens' Blush
Rosa X alba 'Incarnata'

blooms. The White Monthly had large fragrant recurrent blooms, the summer flowers followed by a second blooming in the fall. The York and Lancaster, *Rosa X damascena var. semperflorens* "Versicolor," was a fall blooming rose, a semi-double with petals striped in two tones of pink, or red and white.

All naturally occurring or species roses were native to the northern hemisphere. The Sweet Brier or Eglantine was native to Europe and had a long history of cultivation. It was noted for its fragrant foliage, particularly pronounced after a rain. The Sweet Brier was grown in Upper Canada at least as early as 1795, for Mrs Simcoe mentioned it in her diary. On a visit to a dairy she observed that the leaves of the Sweet Brier, steeped in boiling water and "put into Jars or Milk pans or anything that is to be washed out purifies them sooner & better than anything else" (Innis 1983:166).

The Copper Coloured Rose owes its coppery appearance to the unusual colouring of its petals, orange-red on the upper surfaces and golden yellow on the undersides. The colour yellow was rarely found in species roses, and so this rose was used to parent some of the earliest yellow-flowering hybrids. The *Rosa foetida* "Bicolor" was a natural hybrid from Asia which had been sent to the Holy Roman Emperor in Austria by the Sultan of Turkey. It is better known today as the Austrian Copper.

The Michigan Rose, or Prairie Rose, *Rosa setigera* Michx., a native of North America, was sent to Europe around 1800 by the French botanist Andre Michaux. A rambler type, blooming late in the season with clusters of dark pink flowers, it was one of the few North American species in Empress Josephine's collection at Malmaison.

The Multifloral Rose, or Garland Rose, *Rosa multiflora* Thunb. ex Murray, came from Japan and China. First described in Europe in 1822, it may have arrived in America at this time or perhaps even earlier, carried by ships trading with the Orient, as it had reached Custead's Canadian nursery only five years later. This species took only too well to the American climate, readily escaping from gardens to the wild. Its vigorous growth has made it a nuisance in many Atlantic states as it tangles with other growth, often strangling native shrubs and trees. The Thornless Rose, *Rosa pendulina* L., was also a vigorous grower with large single flowers of dark pink or light red. It was first cultivated in Europe in the late seventeenth century and listed among the roses in the 1790 catalogue of the Prince Nursery.

In the late eighteenth and early nineteenth centuries, new species of roses arrived from the Far East, adding fresh genetic material. "Old" species were cross-bred with the imported species to create exciting new hybrids. The China Rose, *Rosa chinensis* Jacq., was known to Philip Miller in 1752 but was not in distribution until the 1780s. The first tea rose, *Rosa X odorata* (Andrews) Sweet, was introduced to England in 1808. The continuous flowering habit of the oriental roses intrigued and delighted Europeans, and

Copper Coloured Rose
Rosa foetida 'Bicolor'

this new characteristic was kept in many hybrids. Custead offered these two new oriental species as tender plants for the greenhouse: the "Rosa Indica Rubra" (*Rosa chinensis*) and the "Rosa Semperflorens palida Odorata" (*Rosa odorata*), at three shillings nine pence each. For the garden there was the Portland Rose, one of the new China hybrids introduced about 1809. Several roses on Custead's "to be increased" list are unknown today and may well have been early China hybrids that have not survived. Their comparatively high prices, over seven shillings, suggest their rarity or novelty.

Hybrid perpetuals, noisettes, and hybrid teas were unknown in 1827, but that is not to say there was not a diverse and attractive repertoire to choose from for the rose garden. Napoleon's Josephine made roses very fashionable among the elite as she attempted to collect every known variety for her garden at Malmaison. Her collection was illustrated by the artist Redouté and set a standard envied and emulated by other collectors. England and France shared a mutual interest in roses even during the bitter Napoleonic wars; English gardeners were permitted special passports to enter France to advise Josephine on the selection and care of her roses.

Roses are still among the most prized garden plants, often grown in beds separated from the rest of the garden. There are now over one hundred recognized rose species and over a thousand named varieties from which to choose. Modern hybridization has been extensive, as the search for longer flowering periods, more perfect blooms, or more exquisite colour continues. In England recent efforts have contributed to a series of "cottage-type" roses resembling old varieties; Canadian breeders have produced several very hardy hybrids suitable for harsher climates. In spite of their thorns, their susceptibility to many diseases, and the care they require, roses never lose their appeal.

8

Bulbous Roots

Plants that grew from bulbs, tubers, or corms featured strongly in the Toronto Nursery catalogue. While there is a botanical difference between these plant designations, all were listed under the general heading "Bulbous Rooted."

Bulbous rooted plants were popular with gardeners as most were assured of flowering. Bulbs reproduced easily by offshoots and bulbils over a relatively short period of time, making them a good investment for the nurseryman and the gardener.

Bulbs in the catalogue included many like the tulip and narcissus, suitable for planting in the garden, and others more suited to the greenhouse, hothouse, or living room. There was a range of prices for these bulbs; in general, cheaper sorts were garden species while rarer and expensive bulbs were tender sorts better grown as pot plants.

Bulbs had been shipped from Holland to North America for over a century by the time Custead opened his nursery. Shipments came by sea each spring and fall to the ports of Montreal and New York. The main problems on the long voyages were rotting caused by dampness and loss to hungry rodents.

The Mediterranean area supplied many of the bulbs grown in European gardens. The history of the cultivation of bulbous plants extends back to the Pharaohs of Egypt when lilies, anemones, and irises were grown along the Nile. During the Crusades further introductions from Turkey and the Levant enriched European gardens. In the fifteenth and sixteenth centuries, extended sea voyages to the Americas, the Orient, and South Africa greatly increased the range of exotic plants available to western horticulture.

The first recipients of exotic plant collections were usually the botanical gardens of Europe. In the seventeenth century one the most extensive collections was in Leyden, at the university famous for its school of medicine.

The Dutch soon exploited the commercial potential of these imports, becoming the greatest bulb growers and exporters in the world. Sixteenth-century Holland was under the political domination of Spain, which allowed it to share in the bounty brought back from the Spanish-controlled areas of Central and South America. In 1602 the Dutch East India Company was founded, and trade with the Far East expanded the botanical repertoire. By the eighteenth century there was no real competition for Dutch growers, and they have continued to be the prime growers and distributors of bulbous rooted plants worldwide to this day. In the early nineteenth century Holland's bulb trade had agents in America. Bulbs offered by the Toronto Nursery were primarily from New York distributors, as is evident in the catalogue's appendix, which specifically identifies the material imported from New York.

All the species and varieties offered in the catalogue were listed under common names. The bulbous rooted plants included genera from several different families of plants. The Tulip, Hyacinth, White Lily, Martagon Lily, Lily of the Valley, Day Lily, and Crown Imperials were in the *Liliaceae* or Lily family. The Narcissus, Jacobean Lily, Guernsey Lily, Atamasco Lily, and Yellow Flowering Amaryllis were in the *Amaryllidaceae* or Amaryllis family. Two genera, the Gladiolus and the Crocus, were in the Iris family, *Iridaceae*; and two more, the Ranunculus and the Anemone, were in the Ranunculus family. One selection was a genus of the *Agavaceae*. These are the present-day classifications; several of the plants have been traced through horticultural history to make the proper identification and assign the correct nomenclature.

Tulips were well represented in the Toronto Nursery catalogue with twenty-five named varieties, including doubles, Bizarres, and Biblomens. Tulips had been grown for several centuries in Turkey before their discovery by Europeans in the sixteenth century, and several of the bulbs first taken to Europe from Turkey were cultivated hybrids rather than native species. Seeds from these plants produced innumerable variations in offspring. During the seventeenth century, as the number of varieties increased, the tulip reached a peak in popularity so demanding it resulted in a craze known as "Tulipomania." The price of the bulbs soared to unbelievable heights, many buyers literally forfeiting fortunes to own a single bulb.

Wild forms of tulips from southeast Europe, Asia Minor, and China were introduced during the nineteenth century. Today the genus *Tulipa* includes at least one hundred species. When the many hybrids and cultivars are added to this, the count is into the thousands. Botanists now recognize two general classifications of *Tulipa*: the natural species and the garden hybrids. The garden hybrids are divided into fifteen groups, based on flower characteristics, the shape and number of petals, and the flowering period, i.e. early or late.

The wide choice of tulip varieties in the early nineteenth century made them one of the most popular garden flowers. A preference for blooms with variegated colouring began during the seventeenth and eighteenth centuries. The seemingly endless variations in the markings and the combinations of colour fascinated growers. Artists too were intrigued, and many Dutch and Flemish painters chose tulips as subjects for still-life paintings. The multicoloured forms were called "broken" or "rectified" tulips. These included Bizarres, with coloured streaks on a yellow ground; Biblomens, with purple markings on a white ground; and the Rose, with pink or red markings. The patterns of colouring were also categorized. When the tips of the petals bore a contrasting colour, the blooms were "feathered"; when the second colour appeared as lengthwise stripes on the petals, the flower was "flamed." Thousands upon thousands of the variegated sorts were raised by Holland growers. The first variegated form was regarded as a sport, and single-coloured plants were set among the mother-bulbs in the growing fields as "breeders." Garden books included many detailed and explicit instructions to assist growers in "breeding" these gaily hued plants. Philip Miller, a more scientific gardener, found that "there are some who pretend to have a Secret how to make any Sort of Breeders break into Stripes whenever they please; but this, I dare say, is without foundation: for from the many Experiments which I have made in the Kind, I could never find any Certainty of this Matter" (Miller 1754/1969:1420).

The true reason for the "breaking" was due not to planting methods or cultural practices but to a virus, a phenomenon not understood or diagnosed until the 1920s. The disease was carried from plant to plant by insects, particularly species of aphids. There were probably two viruses responsible for the variation of colour, one that removed colour from the bloom and another that added a deeper colour to light-coloured flowers. These viruses also caused mottled foliage. The infection eventually reduced the bulbs' vigour and longevity, and dozens of named varieties of Bizarre and Biblomen tulips of the past, the result of short-lived virus-infected bulbs, are now lost. The tulip-breaking virus, however, is still a threat to growers.

The exact coloration of the Bizarre, Biblomen, and Rose varieties offered in the Toronto Nursery catalogue may never be known. The modern Rembrandt tulips, which are broken Darwins, somewhat resemble the

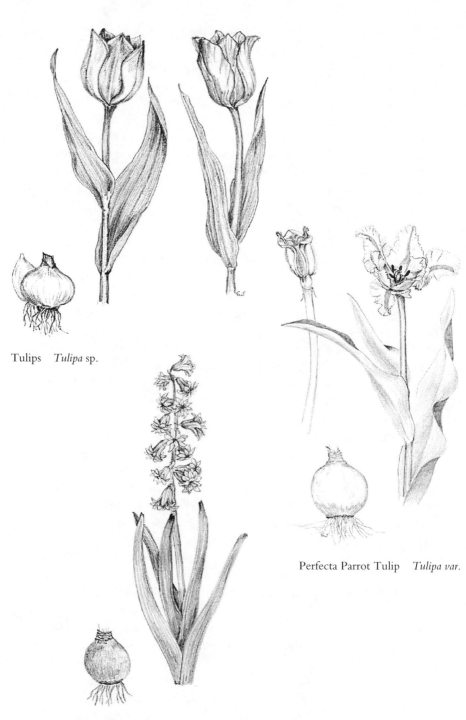

Tulips   *Tulipa* sp.

Perfecta Parrot Tulip   *Tulipa var.*

Double Hyacinth
Hyacinthus orientalis L.

colour streaking of the early Bizarres or Biblomens. Darwin tulips, introduced in 1889, have more rounded petals than early varieties, but their
colouring approximates the general appearance of old tulips. Darwins are
now the most popular bedding tulip.

Not all multicoloured tulips were short-lived. One of the seventeenth-
century favourites still available is the late-flowering Parrot tulip, which
first appeared spontaneously in Holland in 1665; all descendants were from
offsets of this original example. The flowers had twisted and fringed petals,
in shades of red or purple contrasting with yellow. Tricoloured forms
had green in the centre of the inflorescence. The "Perfecta" variety of the
Parrot offered by Custead was a tricoloured sort of unknown origin dating
to 1750.

The Duc van Toll, the Proserpine, and the Yellow Rose tulips offered
by the Toronto Nursery are also still available. The "most esteemed" Duc
van Toll varieties were early bloomers, among the first to appear in the
spring with their short-stalked blooms of single or double red or yellow
flowers (Breck 1866:377). They were mentioned in many nineteenth-
century garden books as an old species, *Tulipa suaveolens*, said to have been
introduced about 1600 (Loudon 1827:832).

Proserpine tulips were single, early-flowering sorts with very large, handsome, rosy-carmine blooms. The late-flowering Yellow Rose was a golden
yellow double. Varieties of this tulip had red markings on the yellow
ground.

Concern for the loss of early tulip varieties began over a hundred years
ago. In the 1890s a search for old varieties succeeded in preserving many
examples, which are now classified as "cottage tulips." The majority of
these were of nineteenth-century origin, but a few date to the seventeenth
and eighteenth centuries. They are not grown on a large scale by major
producers but are sometimes available from bulb specialists.

The botanical garden in Padua was the recipient of the first *Hyacinthus
orientalis* L. to reach Europe from Asia Minor in the late sixteenth century.
Hyacinths put forth such attractive and fragrant early spring blooms that
they quickly became coveted by all European gardeners. The Dutch growers excelled in the propagation of these bulbs and have to this day remained
the chief supplier of mature bulbs every autumn. Hyacinths were some of
the first bulbs brought to the English colonies, and were reported growing
in Virginia in the 1600s.

By 1750 there were at least two thousand named varieties to choose
from, including both single and double flowering plants. The doubles
appeared early in the century and were preferred over the singles. In

Custead's time double hyacinths were available in many shades of blue, red, white, and yellow. There were varieties with deeper colours in the centre of the flower, others with striped or shaded petals. The nineteenth-century florist devised specific requirements for an acceptable double hyacinth in flower shows: the stem was to be straight, strong, and tall, with at least half of it covered with blooms of an intense bright colour in a compact cluster with the top-most bell-shaped flower "perfectly erect" (Breck 1866:242). The hyacinths perfected by the florists were so desired that a single bulb of the variety *Rouge éblouissante* sold for eighty-three pounds in the early nineteenth century (Pizzeti and Cocker 1975: 1:616). Philip Miller wrote of the cost of prized sorts, "these are Varieties which have been obtained from Seeds, the number of them is continually increas'd where People constantly sow of their Seeds; and those new Flowers, which are raised, if they are large, beautiful, and very double, will always be much valued at first." He also mentioned the dedication of the Dutch growers, for there were "few other Florists thinking it worth their Trouble to wait four or five Years for the Flowers of a Plant" (Miller 1754/1969:650–1). It may be noted that the Toronto Nursery was charging as much for a hyacinth bulb with a double flower as for a rose plant.

The hyacinth was not only enjoyed in the garden: it was also a popular window-sill plant, forced in specially shaped glasses or held in a container on perforated corks. The flower pleased with its early colour and pretty bell-shaped blooms while its strong scent filled the room with perfume.

All the hyacinths in the Toronto Nursery list were doubles with specific variety names. Unfortunately, none of them are known today. Hyacinth names are "quite arbitrary, being given by the grower after himself or some public character" (Loudon 1827:828); several of Custead's tulips were named for European royalty. The popularity of hyacinths declined at the end of the nineteenth century, and today doubles are very rare, although two or three were still commercially available in 1987 in England (Stuart and Sutherland 1987:158).

Few species of the *Lilium* genus were in cultivation until the introduction of oriental species in the late nineteenth century, which led to extensive cross-breeding beginning in the twentieth century. In the early 1800s there were only three true lilies in gardens: the White Lily, *Lilium candidum* L., the Martagon Lily, *Lilium martagon* L., and the Orange Lily, *Lilium bulbiferum* L. The first two were offered by the Toronto Nursery.

Lilies were second only to roses as the most consistently favoured garden flowers in the history of horticulture. The White Lily, *Lilium candidum*, may have been one of the first flowers to be domesticated. It was grown over three thousand years ago in the eastern Mediterranean by the Minoans and Myceneans and pictured in early wall paintings. By Roman times the White Lily was forced into bloom in specially built rooms glazed with thin slices of gypsum and heated with hot water pipes. It is certainly the oldest cultivated lily and the best known and most loved of all lilies. Unfortunately it has seldom been seen in gardens in the past few decades, a victim of the fungal disease botrytis and viral infections. In order to allay the dangers of these infections, the only satisfactory solution is to destroy all affected bulbs and plants. White lilies are still available but tend to be short-lived.

Several varieties of the White Lily that were described during the eighteenth century have since become extinct. Botanical literature of the period described a double form. Unlike other species in which the doubles were avidly sought after, the double White Lily did not have the appealing simplicity of the single form. A purple-spotted variety was similarly dismissed, found to be lacking the beauty of the plain, pure white flower. However, the loss of one that had yellow-marginated leaves is regretted as it provided added garden interest when the plant was not in bloom.

Lily bulbs were once used for healing and soothing purposes as they contain a mucilaginous substance with astringent properties. The ancient Greek writer Dioscorides recommended lily bulbs as a cosmetic substance to "clear the faces and make them without wrinkles," a claim unfortunately not well founded. They were also reputed to prevent scarring in the treatment of burns and scalds. In the Far East the lily has been grown as a vegetable crop, a use dating back to ancient times.

The pure, glowing colour of the White Lily has long associated it with the concept of purity. In Greek legend the goddess Hera caused the White Lily to spring from the earth as her milk fell upon it. Venus, the Roman goddess of beauty, jealous of the lily's perfection, created a large yellow pistil in the flower's centre as a blemish. In Christian art the flower was adopted as a symbol of the Virgin's chastity, appearing in depictions of the Annunciation by medieval and Renaissance artists. By the late nineteenth century it was commonly known as the Madonna Lily, the name still in use in the trade.

Custead offered a Turk's Cap, or Martagon, Lily, *Lilium martagon* L., under "Bulbous Roots" in the catalogue, and in the appendix named five more varieties that would be available "as soon as they could be increased." All of these new varieties had been ordered from New York. Martagon lilies are a very distinct type, bearing characteristic pendulous

White Lily   *Lilium candidum* L.

Martigon or Turk's Lily
Lilium martagon L.

Yellow Day Lily
Hemerocallis lilio-asphodelus L.

flowers with reflexed petals. The original Turk's Cap introduced to gardens was found in the high alpine meadows of eastern Europe and central Asia, at altitudes up to six thousand feet. One of the hardiest of all European lilies, the native plant grew to a height of three or four feet, its leaves in whorls on a purplish-green stalk bearing up to twenty pendulous, deeply reflexed flowers in shades of purple with dark spots. The plant had a strong but disagreeable scent, which prompted gardeners to suggest they not be planted too near the house or cut for "Basins of Flowers in a Room" (Miller 1754/1969:748).

Of all lily species, the Martagon has been credited with the greatest medicinal value. Oil pressed from the bulbs was used in folk medicine for the treatment of skin eruption and burns. The bulbs of Martagon lilies have been gathered in the wild by Asian populations for food and medicine over a long period of time. In recent times this practice has severely depleted the numbers of these plants remaining in their native habitat.

In the wild state the Martagon was a hybrid, variable in its bloom and its progeny. At least a half dozen varieties had been brought into cultivation by 1827 (Loudon 1850:842), the blooms mostly in shades of purple or red, from pink to purplish-black, with dark spots, with one pure white variety. The individual blossoms were small, only one and a half inches across, but were born in a pyramidal form on the flower stalk in such profusion that the effect was very showy. Martagon bulbs are smaller than most lillies, with bright yellow scales, and they are slow to mature. Custead was being optimistic in his projection of sales from his imports, for it would have taken three or four years for bulbets to reach maturity. However, Martagon lilies were good choices for a Canadian nursery as they are very hardy, suitable for gardens in a northern climate. They also tolerate deep shade and are outstanding candidates for naturalizing in open woods and shady shrub borders.

The *Hemerocallis* genus included three species known in the early nineteenth century: the *H. lilio-asphodelus* or Yellow Day Lily, which was offered by the Toronto Nursery, and the *H. fulva* or Tawny Day Lily, which was also grown in early Canada and has now naturalized, and *H. minor,* a smaller yellow day lily. The principal appeal of these plants was their longevity with persistent and prolific flowering. The flowers last only one day, as the name suggests, but are produced so freely the plant remains in bloom over several weeks. Day lilies are very hardy, can be grown in almost any type of soil, and thrive without any particular attention. The long leaves arising from the base of the plant, arching gracefully outward, provide an architectural quality that is especially effective at the edge of a path, a stream, or a pond. The fullness of the leafy growth, crowned by showy flowers, is useful for filling corners, under shrubs, or emphasizing the ends or curves of flower beds.

The Yellow Day Lily had found a place in English gardens by the sixteenth century, coming from its native habitat in eastern Europe and Asia. In the Far East it was called the "plant of forgetfulness" as it was supposed to cure sorrow by causing loss of memory. In recent years the plant has returned to favour, as casual late twentieth-century home gardeners appreciate its ease of cultivation. This is the earliest-flowering of the common day lily species, coming into bloom in May. Its fresh delicate scent is an added bonus. After many centuries of being represented only by natural species, the day lily has recently been subjected to intense breeding programs. Today almost every colour and combinations of colours except blue or a pure white has been obtained in both singles and doubles.

The Lily of the Valley, *Convallaria majalis* L., another member of the Lily family, has been cultivated for centuries, beloved for its delicate bell-shaped flowers and its perfume. Originally a native of a widespread area including Europe and northern Asia, it has now become an endangered species in the wild, protected by law in several European countries. In the late sixteenth century, Gerard mentioned a wild red-flowered form which has since become extinct. Also lost are a broad-leaved sort and one with variegated purple-striped flowers described in the eighteenth century (Miller 1754/1969:362).

The early flowering period of the Lily of the Valley made it a symbol of the return of spring, associated with the return to life after death; it was used by Christian artists to represent the Advent of Christ. The pure white of the common form associated it with the purity of the Holy Virgin and the Immaculate Conception. This delightfully scented plant has charmed many generations, for "few plants give so much satisfaction at so little cost" (Bailey 1902:366).

Lily of the Valley has been raised commercially for the perfume industry in southern Europe. The plant also contains several chemicals with medicinal value, which were used to cure physical disorders from medieval times to the early part of this century. Extreme caution is advised in using the plant, however, as both the roots and the rhizomes contain *convallamarin*, a chemical similar to digitalis. The drug affects heart rhythm and can cause convulsions. Physicians in eastern countries have adopted its use in modern medicine, preferring it to digitalis. In the past the dried flowers and roots, steeped in alcoholic spirits, were used internally as a heart tonic, a diuretic, and an emetic. An infusion was used externally to cure blood blisters, heal sprains and bruises, and rid the skin of freckles (Stillé and Maisch 1880:458).

Lily of the Valley
Convallaria majalis L.

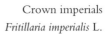

Crown imperials
Fritillaria imperialis L.

Sword Lily
Gladiolus communis L.

An unusual medieval application was to make *aqua aurea*, a potion considered "more precious than gold," by distilling an infusion of the flowers in wine. When applied to the forehead it was said to cause one to "have good common sense."

Crown Imperials, *Fritillaria imperialis* L., another genus in the Lily family, have been popular in England from the sixteenth century when they were introduced from Turkey. They had been cultivated in the Near East for hundreds of years. Their native habitat was the western Himalayas in Persia, Afghanistan, and India. A Christian legend maintained that this plant, with its curious hanging blooms, was too proud to bow its head at the passing of Christ on the eve of his crucifixion, and so has since hung its head in shame.

Toronto Nursery offered two yellow forms and three red-flowered varieties. Modern forms of the *F. imperialis* have yellow or orange blossoms; red are now uncommon. There were as many as twenty named varieties in eighteenth-century catalogues, with a wide range of colours and markings. Purple, white, red, and an unusual terra-cotta colour were offered, with some varieties having variegated, striped, or spotted flowers, or leaves striped in gold or silver. During the late nineteenth century the Crown Imperial fell out of favour, perhaps because of its unpleasant scent, and most of these varieties were lost. Earlier gardeners held them in high regard, for "of the facultie of these pleasant floures there is nothing set downe in the antient or later Writer, but are greatly esteemed for the beautifying of our gardens, and the bosoms of the beautifull" (Gerard 1633/1975:151).

Crown Imperials are not often seen in Canadian gardens today as they frequently succumb to the severity and dampness of our winters. Even the relatively mild winters of the eastern United States proved difficult for the survival of these plants in the early eighteenth century. Bulbs were sent repeatedly to America from England with little success as they require very dry conditions during their dormancy, and frequently rotted during the sea voyage. The first one to flower in America was in Williamsburg in 1739 (Dutton 1979:103).

One of the bulbs listed as a lily, the Sword Lily, was actually a member of the Iris family, *Iridaceae*. Sword Lily, the common name of the Gladiolus (the Latin word for sword), described the sturdy, upright, and sharply pointed sword-like leaves. The *Gladiolus communis* L. and the *G. italicus* Mill., both native to southern Europe, were grown in English gardens by the sixteenth century. Early in the seventeenth century the *Gladiolus byzantinus* Mill. was introduced from Turkey. The first of the South African species arrived in

England towards the middle of the eighteenth century: the *Gladiolus tristis* in 1745, the *G. blanda* in 1774, and the *G. cardinalis* in 1789. In most gladiolus species the blooms are held to one side of the flower stalk. The *G. communis* had rosy-purple or white flowers, those of the *G. italicus* were rose coloured, and the *G. byzantinus* and *G. cardinalis* had red blooms. These were the most common species of gladiolus known at the time Custead's nursery catalogue was published, but which sort he was offering is not known.

In England these species gladioli could be planted in the fall and left in the ground indefinitely. Parkinson found this practice to be regrettable, for "if it be suffered any long time in a Garden, it will rather choake and pester it, than be an ornament unto it" (Parkinson 1629/1991:189). The North American climate was less congenial to the gladiolus. In New England they were "too tender for cultivation, except in pots in the greenhouse" (Breck 1866:225). The greenhouse gardener greeted new South African species with enthusiasm for their larger, more colourful blooms. Loudon predicted that "they will become great favourites with florists ... for [their] endless variety [and] their facility of culture" (Loudon 1827:843). And so they have: the large-blossomed plants seen today in the late summer garden are the result of the hybridization that began in the 1840s with further introductions of South African species. In Canada gardeners treat them as annuals, resting the corms indoors over the winter.

Plants in the *Amaryllidaceae* or Amaryllis family were the second-largest group of bulbous plants represented in the 1827 catalogue. Custead named the narcissus and jonquils separately, but grouped the remainder under the genus Amaryllis as they were known in the Linnaen system. They have since been reclassified: the Jacobean Lily is now *Spreckalia formosissima* Herb., the Guernsey Lily is *Nerine sarniensis* Herb., the Atamasco Lily is *Zephyranthes atamasco* Herb., and the Yellow Flowering Amaryllis is *Sternbergia lutea* Ker-Gawl.

A number of species in the genus Narcissus originated in southeast Europe and neighbouring western Asia. As these bulbous plants are among the first to flower in early spring, they found a place in European gardens, even in areas where they grew wild. The ancient Greeks gave the genus its name: "narcissus" was derived from a word meaning "to grow stiff, become benumbed, or stupefied," in reference to the belief that the plant had narcotic properties (the word "narcotic" has the same Greek root). Narcotics were known to cause sleep or death, and in ancient Egypt the narcissus was used in funeral wreaths. Several Greek myths associated the plant with events that took place between the earth and the underworld. During the nineteenth century the narcissus was linked to the story of the young man who fell in love with his reflection, and so attributed the plant with the meaning of egotism or self-love in the so-called language of flowers.

The bulb and the flower have both been used in medical practices in the past. The Roman writer Pliny mentioned their use as an emetic and purgative and alluded to their narcotic powers. As late as 1876, while the plants were still being prescribed medicinally as infusions to induce vomiting in children, tests of the plant's alkaloids on dogs and frogs were producing alarming, even fatal, reactions. Modern pharmacology has isolated the very poisonous alkaloids and shown them to cause severe damage to the central nervous system and death, even in fairly small quantities.

In Parkinson's work of 1629 there were ninety-four species and varieties of narcissus known to the English gardener. French and Dutch growers were very successful in their breeding and cultivation practices, and in addition to increasing the better kinds from offsets, grew many new varieties from seed. These extensive propagation and cross-breeding programs over a long period of time have complicated the genus, which has never been fully classified to everyone's satisfaction. Only nine true species are recognized by some botanists, while others believe there are as many as fifty or sixty, with more than one hundred natural hybrids (Griffiths 1994:769, and *Reader's Digest* 1978:454). There are now over eight thousand named cultivated varieties, and the number increases every year. Modern classification is based on a system developed in 1908 by the Royal Horticultural Society in which species are individually recognized and garden varieties are placed in categories determined by their flower form. The system was revised in 1950 and again in 1977. Today narcissi are sold by their variety names which are officially recorded with the International Register.

Three narcissus varieties were available from Custead's nursery in 1827: the Double Narcissus or Daffodil, the Orange Phoenix, and the "Albo pleno oderato." The Double Narcissus or Daffodil was a double trumpet variety of *Narcissus pseudo-narcissus* L. The Orange Phoenix was the double form of *Narcissus X incomparabilis*, known as the "Great Incomparable," and acknowledged as the most handsome of all the genus. While the Holland growers knew it by this name, it was known in England as Butter and Eggs. In 1825 it was offered in New York as *Telemonious Plenus* or the Van Sion. It is now regarded as being a very old, possibly naturally occurring, hybrid of the *Narcissus pseudo-narcissus* L., the common Trumpet Daffodil, and *N. poeticus* L., the Poet's Narcissus. The single form has scentless flowers two and a half inches across, with a rich orange corona or trumpet and petals of a light yellow or milk-white colour. The trumpet and petals of the double form are hardly distinguishable from one another as the flower is so full, but the characteristic colouring remains the same. Each flower stalk is accompanied by three or four narrow bluish-green, keeled leaves about one foot long.

The *Narcissus alba pleno odorata* was the double form of another old species, the *Narcissus poeticus* L. The Poet's Narcissus, also known as the Pheasant's Eye, was one of the first narcissi to be cultivated. They were named daffodils from the ancient Greek word "asphodel," associated with lily-like flowers. When the trumpet form of narcissus was introduced, the *Narcissus pseudo-narcissus* L., they were called Bastard daffodils. The single form of the Poet's Narcissus has very fragrant flowers, a ring of petals in pure white and a very short corona of light yellow with a distinctive red edge. The double form was almost entirely white, a rarity among double narcissi. The "fragrant double white narcissus" was a sturdy plant, growing to one and a half feet, with leaves as tall as the flower stalk which bore one or occasionally two blooms. The flowers were full, wide-open, and delightfully perfumed. This was one of the first bulbous plants brought to America, so common in gardens by the mid-eighteenth century that Bartram told his English suppliers no further shipments were needed as the country was already overrun with them.

Three sorts of Jonquils were listed in the appendix to the catalogue: a Double Fragrant, a Large Single, and a Small Fragrant form. The Double Fragrant Jonquil was the double form of *Narcissus X odorus* L., a natural hybrid between *Narcissus jonquilla* L. and *N. pseudo-narcissus* L. from the Iberian peninsula. It was described and illustrated in *Curtis' Botanical Magazine* in 1806 as *Narcissus calathinus* L. The Large Single Jonquil was the *Narcissus jonquilla* L., which had a flower one and a half inches both wide and long, with leaves one and a half feet tall. The Small Fragrant Jonquil was *Narcissus assoanus Dufour*, which grew to only six inches in height. It was once called *N. juncifolius* L. because of its narrow rush-like leaves.

Jonquils acquired their name from the Spanish word for "rushes," which described the very narrow, almost cylindrical, grooved leaves. The flower stalk or scape produces two to six blossoms at a time. The bloom has a wide spreading perianth which is never reflexed. The flowers are intensely perfumed with a "strong, sweet Scent; though there are very few ladies that can bear the Smell of them: so powerful is it, that, many times, it overcomes their Spirits, especially if confin'd in a room: for which Reason they should never be planted too close to a Habitation, lest they become offensive; nor should the flowers be placed in such Rooms where Company are entertained" (Miller 1754/1969:946).

Narcissus pleno odorata
Narcissus poeticus var. L.

Narcissus Orange Phoenix
Narcissus X incomparabilis Mill.

Jonquils   *Narcissus jonquilla* L.

The first jonquil imports to America proved to be too tender for the climate. In New York, where it was regarded as only marginally hardy, it was recommended for pot culture. It became common practice to start the bulbs in the greenhouse and put out the flowering plants to brighten terraces and porches as soon as the warm spring weather arrived. A few eighteenth-century ladies may have been sensitive to their scent, but jonquils remained popular throughout the nineteenth century for their perfume and golden yellow colour.

The colour and shape of the bloom of the Jacobean Lily, *Sprekalia formossissima* Herb., was certain to arouse interest on the part of the curious gardener. The flower has six irregular petals, presenting an exotic and flamboyant appearance such as is often associated with orchids, which would excite any flower-lover. The broad central petal, rising from the centre of the flower, is flanked by two narrower recurved petals, below which the three remaining petals fall, opening to reveal six red-stemmed stamens. The flower leans to one side of the stalk, slightly drooping, almost as if the four- to five-inch bloom is too heavy for the foot-high stalk. The colour is an intense red, velvety in texture, with a sheen that appears golden in sunlight. The flower appears before the leaves, but occasionally a second stalk emerges from the opposite side of the bulb as the leaves begin to appear.

The Jacobean Lily was a native of Mexico, too tender to survive in the north temperate gardens of Canada, although Miller wrote that it had become "pretty common in the curious Garden in England" by 1754 (Miller 1754/1969:66). In European and North American gardens it was grown purely for its decorative value, but in its native Mexico the bulb had been used as an ingredient in a salve to prevent baldness (Pesman 1962:254).

The Guernsey Lily, *Nerine sarniensis* Herb., was so named for the Channel Island of Guernsey where it was extensively grown for export. How this horticultural enterprise came about is a story of serendipity. Sometime in the seventeenth century a ship on its return voyage from Japan was shipwrecked off the Isle of Guernsey. Strewn along the shore with the wreckage were flower bulbs which naturalized themselves to such an extent that they were thought to be indigenous. The local population took advantage of this situation and began to grow these "lilies" on a commercial scale. For a long time they were called *Amaryllis japonicus*, as they were suspected of being part of the original cargo from Japan. It has since been determined that the home of the Guernsey Lily was the Cape Province of South Africa. Two renowned botanists, Francis Masson and Carl Peter Thunberg, were the first to record the lily growing in the wild when they found it growing on Table Mountain in 1774. Guernsey lilies, included in a shipment of

Jacobean Lily
Sprekalia formossissima Herb.

Guernsey Lily   *Nerine sarniensis* Herb.

Atamasco Lily
Zephyranthes atamasco Herb.

Yellow Flowering Lily
Sternbergia lutea Ker-Gawl.

plants sent to John Custis (George Washington's father-in-law) in Virginia in 1740, were the first to be seen in America.

Guernsey Lily growers delivered bulbs to the English market every year in late summer, when they were immediately planted to produce their compound inflorescence a month later (Miller 1754/1969:66). The showy clusters of bloom measured up to ten inches across at the top of a flower stalk about two feet high and could remain in bloom for a month. The outstanding feature of the flowers was the length of the stamens which protruded from the corolla in a radiating pattern. Flowers of Guernsey lilies were all in the red spectrum, from a salmon-pink to a bright scarlet. The leaves followed the flowers, being produced in the winter months, which made the plant unsuitable for a northerly climate except as a greenhouse plant. The plant died back in the spring, remaining dormant for the summer months, requiring summer heat to ripen for another season of blooming.

The Atamasco Lily, *Zephyranthes atamasco* Herb., was a native of the woodlands of Virginia and the Carolinas, where it grew as "thick as the Cowslips are with us in England" (Dutton 1979:91). It can still be seen growing wild near the old capital of Williamsburg, Virginia. Parkinson was the first to describe the plant, with a flower like a lily and roots like a daffodil, and he named it the Virginian Daffodil (Parkinson 1629/1991:86–7). It was brought to the attention of a Dr Morison, a Scotsman, physician to Charles II, and the first professor of botany at Oxford University, who named it *Lilio-narcissus*. Linnaeus recognized its attributes as belonging to the Amaryllis family and renamed it the *Amaryllis atamasco* as Atamasco was the original Amerindian name for the plant.

The large tubular flowers of the Atamasco Lily appear singly on flower stalks that emerge from spathes or leaf-like bracts. The buds are tinged purple, fading to white as the flower opens wide with pointed, recurved petals. The plant adapted well to the British climate, which was not unlike its native habitat. In the northern areas of the United States and in Canada it requires the protection of a cool greenhouse.

The Yellow Flowering Amaryllis, *Sternbergia lutea* Ker-Gawl, was also known as the Autumn Daffodil as it bloomed late in the season. Few plants in English gardens bloomed in the autumn, which made these bulbs particularly desirable. Nurserymen often sold it combined with pink flowering bulbs of *Colchicum*, the Autumn Crocus, as the colours of the respective blooms made a pretty combination in the fall garden. In a mild season in Britain the two would flower continuously from September to November, each bulb being capable of producing a succession of blooms. Unfortunately, only the warmest parts of Canada are suitable for these bulbs to grow satisfactorily.

Sternbergia lutea was a native of an area stretching from the eastern Mediterranean to Iran. It is not unlike a crocus in appearance, except that it bears six stamens whereas the crocus has three. The fragrant flowers are goblet-shaped, up to two inches across, with a satin-like texture that enriches the golden-yellow colour. The flowers appear singly on each stalk, which averages about four inches in height. In areas where they are hardy, the Autumn Daffodil is an excellent candidate for the rock garden, where its diminutive size and the textures of the flowers and leaves provide a strong accent in the fall.

Two genera of *Ranunculaceae*, the Ranunculus family, were mentioned in the catalogue. "Rannunculies in sorts" were listed in the catalogue, with seven more, described by colour, added in the appendix. Similarly, "Anemones in sorts" were in the catalogue with five more, identified by colour, listed in the appendix.

The ranunculus, *Ranunculus asiaticus* L., probably reached European gardens from Asia Minor during the medieval Crusades, but their cultivation was not widespread until the seventeenth century. Gerard wrote that the "Double red Crow-foot" had been brought to Europe at "divers times and by divers persons, but they have perished by reason of their long journey and want of skill of those bringers ... when we have received them they have been as dry as ginger" (Gerard 1633/1995:960). He was referring to the small, claw-like dormant tubers which indeed look incapable of producing live plants. It was later known that the Turkish Sultan Mohammed IV (1648–1687), an avid gardener, had a number of ranunculus varieties in his collection that attracted a great deal of attention. Some of these were surreptitiously taken to Europe where Dutch growers soon discovered their value in the commercial trade.

In the hands of European growers many varieties of ranunculus were developed, several distinct classes being recognized by the end of the eighteenth century. The Turban or Turkey Ranunculus and the Persian Ranunculus were predominant. The Great Turban/Turkey Ranunculus was a hardy, coarse plant that always bore double flowers. The Persian sorts were less hardy and could bear double or single blooms. The colours of both were vibrant and included every hue except blue. There were shades of yellow, red, purple, brown, and olive, even black, and many variegated sorts as well: "yellow spotted, brown spotted, and white spotted, red and purple streaked, red and white striped, besides mottled and brindled in countless varieties" (Brickell 1969:202).

When Custead published his catalogue, the ranunculus was at its peak of popularity in England, with more named varieties than any other garden

Anemonies in sorts   *Anemone coronaria* L.

Rannunculies in sorts
Ranunculus asiaticus L.

Crocus   *Crocus vernus* Hill.

Tube Roses   *Polianthes tuberosa* L.

flower. A contemporary English catalogue offered five hundred varieties, while Dutch dealers listed up to eight hundred sorts. Only the doubles were prized. All had to be raised from offsets of the tubers, as the flowers were sterile. The florist societies in Britain set up rigid rules for the exhibition of the double ranunculus, specifying the shape, size, and colouring permitted in flower shows.

In England the tubers were planted in early spring, "never after February 10," and pampered in specially prepared beds which were sunny but cool and damp. The Boston plantsman Joseph Breck acknowledged that the *Ranunculus asiaticus* was one of the florist's "most splendid flowers in cultivation" and regretted that the North American climate was "so uncongenial for its perfection" (Breck 1866:338). Many British immigrants, nostalgic for English gardens, attempted to grow these familiar flowers in spite of the difficulties presented by the climate of Upper Canada.

Anemones, members of a related genus, were grown by florists in extravagant numbers and varieties at the beginning of the nineteenth century. A favourite of Dutch and French growers during the eighteenth century, their popularity quickly spread to Britain. A British catalogue of 1820 listed seventy-five sorts, "but few of them are named" (Loudon 1827:836).

The plants offered by Custead were possibly varieties of *Anenome coronaria* L. or those of garden origin, *A. hortensis*. The *Anemone coronaria* grew wild around the Mediterranean and was known to ancient writers but does not appear to have been introduced to European gardens until the mid-sixteenth century. The name "anemone" derived from the Greek word for wind, and its common name was Windflower. In the wild it was noted that it flourished in windy situations. The wind was responsible for their natural propagation, as "the Seed is not to be found that I could ever observe, but is carried away with the Winde" (Gerard 1633/1975:376). The red colour of the wild anemone was associated symbolically to blood, death, and sorrow. In Greek mythology the flower was thought to grow where Adonis had died, in Christian legend where Christ's blood had fallen. These beliefs were reinforced by the emergence of the plant in early spring when life returns after death in the natural world. Poppy anemones were believed to have been the biblical "lilies of the field."

The colour red is predominant in anemones, with shades of pinks and purples common; there are also white varieties. The deeply cut fern-like leaves and soft petalled flowers make them attractive garden plants. It may never be known exactly what the anemones listed in the Toronto Nursery catalogue looked like, as they were listed only by colour. Anemones fell out of favour with the Victorians, and many varieties were lost, including

some unusual infertile doubles. The modern gardener is limited to the De
Caen and St Brigid strains developed in the late nineteenth century. Today
greenhouse production of anemones for modern florist shops is a special-
ization of many growers. The plant hybridizes easily, and new strains can
be obtained readily by cross-pollination.

In Europe the curiously shaped rhizomes are planted in the fall to bloom
in the early spring. The Canadian winter is too long and harsh for this practice; for spring flowering they must be container grown. Alternatively, the
rhizomes can be planted in the spring for summer blooming and lifted in
the fall.

Species of anemone have been used medicinally, but great care must be
taken in their application, for as members of the ranunculus family, the
plant contains caustic irritants.

The bulb most commonly associated with early spring flowering in Canada
is the Crocus. In 1827 only two crocuses were recognized by botanists: the
Crocus vernus Hill. which flowered in the spring, and the *C. sativus* L.,
the fall-blooming saffron crocus (Loudon 1850:838). Both are members of
the Iris family, *Iridaceae*. Custead's crocuses included a few with trade
names and others listed simply by the colour of their bloom, which were
possibly hybrids of *C. vernus* Hill. and *C. flavus* Weston.

Crocuses are native to a widespread area that includes southern Europe,
northern Africa, Asia Minor, and western Asia. Grown in European gardens in the sixteenth century, they were taken up by Dutch growers for
mass propagation in the seventeenth. All crocus bulbs available in America
in the nineteenth century were imported from Holland and "sold at very
low prices" (Breck 1866:175). The able Dutch gardeners did a great deal of
selection and hybridizing to produce innumerable varieties, known in the
trade only by their variety names. Many of these had flowers much larger
than the *C. vernus*, from which they were derived, and these became the
most common garden crocuses. They were available in light and dark
purple, mauvish-pink, blue, and white, as well as streaked forms, but never
in yellow (Bailey 1902: 4:402). The *Crocus flavus*, with its glowing golden
colour, was probably one of the parents of crocuses in the yellow range, including the large Dutch Yellow. The Cloth of Gold Crocus (now classified
as *Crocus angustifolius* Weston), from the area north of the Black Sea in the
Crimea, may have been one of the first crocus species to be domesticated.
Its distinctive flower has reflexed outer petals, streaked with deep brown
or bronze on the outside and golden yellow inside, matching the yellow
colour of the inner petals.

In a northerly climate one of the problems in growing crocuses was "their liability to be thrown out by the frost" (Breck 1866:176). A winter mulch was recommended to help prevent frost heaves. Strangely, none of the early writers complained about the enormous appetite squirrels seem to have for these tasty treats.

The last of the bulbs offered under the heading of lilies were "Tube Roses double." Not a lily at all but a member of the Agave family, *Agavaceae*, the tuberose, *Polianthes tuberosa* L., was a native of Mexico. It had been cultivated in Europe since the sixteenth century, first described in English by Parkinson in 1629. Eighteenth-century Italian growers specialized in growing the tuberose, exporting the plants from Genoa to other parts of Europe along with shipments of orange trees. The true origin of the tuberose remained unknown for many years – for a long while it was believed to have come from India. Several American gardeners received tuberoses from England in the 1700s, and the plantsman M'Mahon had them for sale at his shop in Philadelphia in the early 1800s.

The intense perfume of the flowers accounted for the tuberose's popularity. When grown in the garden it was often potted up at flowering time to move it into the house, but to some the fragrance was overly rich and sickly sweet. The flowers open upwards along the flower-spike, assuring the plant of a long-lasting blooming period.

Custead offered a double tuberose. According to horticultural legend, the first double had been grown from seed in Leyden by a Dutch grower, M. de la Cour. He was said to be exceedingly possessive of the plant which had brought him fame. To preserve control of his prized possession he destroyed all surplus rhizomes in order "that he might have the Vanity to boast of being the only Person who was possessed of this Flower" (Miller 1754/1969:1100). By 1750 several rhizomes escaped his attention which other gardeners readily acquired for their own propagation and profitable distribution.

Unlike plants grown from bulbs which bloom repeatedly season after season, once the rhizome of the tuberose produced a flower it became exhausted and could not produce another plant. If left to grow on it would eventually reproduce itself by offsets, which took up to four years to reach blooming size. The tuberose was too tender to leave in a Canadian garden year-round and was more suitable as a container-grown plant for the greenhouse or home. By the 1860s tuberoses were grown commercially in the Carolinas for the American market. A dwarf form called the "Pearl," introduced by the New York florist Peter Henderson in 1867, is the variety most commonly offered today.

9

Greenhouse Plants

The list of greenhouse plants in Custead's 1827 catalogue is perhaps the most remarkable of all the entries. It presents an unexpected view of horticulture in early Canada, and demonstrates the wide-ranging interest in exotic plants by both professional and amateur gardeners at that time. Few other records in the early history of Upper Canada suggest there was any demand for luxury goods or any appreciation of expensive, rare plants such as those supplied by the Toronto Nursery. (Not only were tropical plants rare in the Canadas but a few listed in the catalogue were relatively new introductions to America.)

There are no physical remains of Custead's establishment, nor records to describe the buildings or facilities. To raise the stock he offered as "Greenhouse Plants" required a structure capable of admitting a good deal of sunlight, with a system of ventilation, and some means of heating the interior space. Glass for such a building would have been imported, as there were no glass-making establishments in Upper Canada in the 1820s. Imported glass was charged a duty, and customs records show boxes of glass panes were entering Upper Canada from the United States; however, no record was found associating such an import with Custead's nursery. Building details are rare for this period of history, even for major structures, and none have been found describing greenhouses. Contemporary garden literature, almanacs, and dictionaries often printed instructions for garden buildings, but there is no evidence that these were followed in this part of the country. To date there has been little investigation of this subject.

The concept of maintaining an indoor facility for tender plants goes back to the Romans. From ancient times gardeners have tried to prove they can overcome the restrictions of their environment. Various solutions have been proposed in the effort to successfully raise plants originating in a different climate. Roman hothouses were heated with hot-water pipes set in the floors. Windows were made from thin slabs of gypsum to permit light to enter and prevent heat from escaping.

By the seventeenth century European gardeners had devised temperate greenhouses for over-wintering the orange trees that decorated many large estates. This was taken a step further in the eighteenth century when heated buildings, called pineries, for the cultivation of pineapples, were common enough to be mentioned in nearly all gardeners' calendars.

Greenhouses were built in the United States as early as 1737, and drawings exist for one built in New York in 1764 (Huxley 1978:234). The greenhouse was distinct from the hothouse, also called a stove or stove house. The greenhouse was more or less an enlarged cold frame, allowing the entry of light with protection from frost, with added provision for heating on the coldest days. These buildings housed tender shrubs and plants and protected roots from deep frosts.

M'Mahon's *American Gardener* described the greenhouse as

a garden building fronted with glass, serving as a winter residence for tender plants from the warmer parts of the world, which require no more artificial heat than what is barely sufficient to keep off frost, and dispel such damps as may arise in the house, occasioned by the perspiration of the plants or a long continuance of moist weather ... [plants] not needing aid of artificial heat like stove plants ... but with the aid of a moderate fire, burned in a furnace contrived outside, within the end or back wall, communicating the heat to the flues or tunnels ranging along the inside, will be necessary not only in severe frosts, but also in moist foggy weather; a moderate fire now and then will dry up the damps, which would otherwise prove pernicious to several of the more tender kinds, especially those of succulent habit (M'Mahon 1858/1976:98).

M'Mahon originally published his work in 1806. Another contemporary reference also was concerned with dampness in the greenhouse: "Air may be given to the plants, if the weather be mild. Fire must be made if it freezes, and particularly when it begins to thaw, or if it is foggy weather, to dry the house; for dampness is as prejudicial as cold; and if there be no flue, light a few candles in frosty weather." The article continues with instructions for maintaining greenhouse plants including the American aloes, myrtles, geraniums, succulent plants, ficoides and Indian figs (Perthensis 1807:239). These were the greenhouse plants popular in the early nineteenth century, and all were included in Custead's catalogue.

The hothouse or stove, intended for tropical plants, was kept constantly at a warm temperature. Plants needing this care were designated "stove" plants. The description of the hothouse by M'Mahon included a bit of the history of its evolution. In his words, it was a building intended for the preservation of plants that were "natives of the warmer and hottest regions, as will not live in the respective countries where they are introduced, without artificial heat in winter" (M'Mahon 1858/1976:104). At first these structures were heated with open fires, but the fumes damaged the plants. The problem was eventually solved by enclosing the fire or placing the fire box outside the building with flues to carry the heat through the hothouse. To accommodate plants requiring different atmospheric conditions, various methods of providing either a dry heat or a damp heat were devised. Beds made of fermenting manure or tan-bark were successful in maintaining the moist atmosphere required by many tropical plants. Hothouse plants that were taken outdoors to decorate the garden or terrace in the summer months were acclimatized for a period in the unheated greenhouse.

M'Mahon's concept of a hothouse was an ornamental structure placed in open ground where it could be enjoyed as part of the landscaping (M'Mahon 1858/1976:98). These were the precursors of later nineteenth-century conservatories, glass-enclosed rooms added to the large homes of the well-to-do. Conservatories, however, were mainly for the display of plants rather than for their cultivation; when plants were not in bloom they were removed to the working hothouse.

A number of greenhouse and hothouse plants could be used in the living rooms of most homes. Before the advent of central heating, each room had it own heating unit. By the 1820s small wood-burning box stoves were replacing fireplaces in parlours and could adequately heat the rooms for the accommodation of tropical plants. Custead affirms that the greenhouse plants he offered "will thrive in a comfortable sitting room during winter, they are in either Pots or Boxes, and the prices are inclusive" (*Catalogue* 1827:13). Plants in the home were often placed on window-sills to take advantage of available daylight. Many homes, particularly those of log or stone, had thick walls and deep window-sills. The plants, placed close together, created their own humidity, and the cold air flowing down the glass tempered the air when the rooms were overheated. When frost did damage the foliage, the plants could be revived by dipping them in cool water.

In the home, plants with colour and scent were preferred. Fragrance of flowers was always appreciated, but it was present only when plants were in bloom. The highly perfumed carnations, gillyflowers, and wall-flowers were among the favourite houseplants, but their flowering period was limited. Plants with aromatic foliage thus became very desirable and accounted for the long-lived popularity of scented-leaved pelargoniums or "geraniums."

Desert plants were also favoured for growing indoors. These required little care, seldom needing watering, pruning, or repotting. A position with good light and adequate heat would suffice. They were objects of curiosity as well, having a variety of shapes and textures quite unlike the average herbaceous plant. When in flower some species presented a spectacular show. Custead's nursery could supply a number of these arid-loving plants. Tender sorts of shrubby plants were offered for the house, greenhouse, or conservatory, including Rosemary, Wormwood, Hydrangea, and Myrtle. The Guernsey Lily too found a place inside the home as well as in the garden.

Custead's greenhouse list began with roses, and further rose varieties were included in the appendix. He offered China Ever-blooming roses and a Multiflora Rose at two shillings sixpence each, and the "Rosa Semperflorens palida Odorata" and "Rosa Indica Rubra" at three shillings nine pence.

The China Ever-blooming Rose, *Rosa chinensis* Jacq., reached England from China in the second half of the eighteenth century but was not widely distributed until much later. Just when the first of its species appeared in America is not clear. A very tender species, it required heated conditions in cooler climates. Its foliage was evergreen, and it bloomed continuously without a dormant period. There were several forms of the China rose, from a dwarf shrub to one with a climbing stem that could grow to twenty feet. There were few, if any, thorns on the stem. These roses had blooms about two inches in diameter, varying from pale pink to bright red in singles or semi-doubles, with a light fragrance. At first these tender roses were

Chinese Everblooming Rose
Rosa chinensis Jacq.

carefully grown under bell-glasses in a sunny place for the light, but kept cool to encourage the bloom. These difficult requirements made them even more of a challenge, and gardeners who succeeded in growing them well gained not only a handsome plant but an object that was a source of pride. China roses were later crossed with European species, producing many hybrids and lending the characteristic of repeated flowering to many of the off-spring.

Custead's "Rosa Semperflorens palida Odorata" and "Rosa Indica Rubra" were varieties of *Rosa chinensis*: *R.c.* "Pallida" and *R.c.* "Semper-florens" respectively. Pallida grew to a height of three feet, bearing clusters of fragrant, blush-pink semi-double flowers. The plant gained the nick-name Tea Rose, as it was thought that its perfume resulted from growing in the proximity of tea plants in its original habitat. The first specimen of this variety reached Europe about 1810. The variety "Semperflorens" grew to a height of four to five feet, with an arching or trailing habit. The semi-double flowers were lightly scented and varied from a deep pink to a rich crimson in colour. All the China roses were considered valuable additions to the Rose family which had already given so much pleasure to their admirers. Gardeners regarded the Chinese introductions as real treasures for the challenge they offered in breeding beautiful new varieties. By the 1870s hybrid tea roses were extensively propagated in Europe and were receiving a good deal of attention from American gardeners. In time, some of these new varieties would include the hardy Noisettes and Perpetual roses; others became the mass-produced half-hardy tea roses in a wide spectrum of colours, now the most familiar of garden roses.

The Multiflora Rose, *Rosa multiflora* Thunb. ex Murray, from Korea, is also known as the Japanese Rose. How and when it first reached America is obscure. The earliest date of introduction appears to be 1822, in which case the Toronto Nursery must have had access to some of the first plants offered in America. The stems had many small thorns and could reach a length of ten to fifteen feet. The branches were sprawling, with a tendency to climb on any nearby support. The flowers, just over an inch in diameter, were borne in large clusters. The showy effect of the rambling many-branched plant covered in white flowers eventually led to over-planting of this species, to such an extent that it rapidly became naturalized in many places in the United States.

Following the China roses in the "Greenhouse Plants" list were a number of succulents. The nursery had "some varieties" of the American Aloe, *Agave americana* L., a native of South America, classified in 1640. Custead charged three shillings each for these plants. Commonly known as Cen-tury Plants, they were said to bloom once in one hundred years. This was

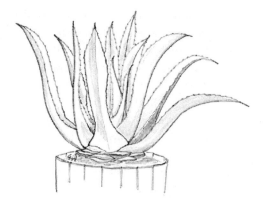

American Century Aloe   *Agave americana* L.

Indian Fig   *Opuntia ficus-indica* (L.) Mill.

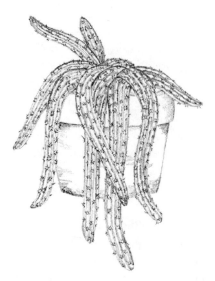

Creeping Cereus
Aporocactus flagelliformis (L.) Lem.

Rosemary   *Rosmarinus officinalis* L.

not a fact, but they were plants that seldom flowered in cultivation. A nineteenth-century description assessed their value as "noble, massive growing plants [which] form magnificent ornaments in greenhouse or conservatories; whilst, from their slow growth, they do not rapidly get too large, even for a small greenhouse" (Nicholson 1887: div.1:38). In its native environment *Agave* grew an upright flower stem from twenty-four to thirty-six feet in height. The basal leaves were nine inches broad and up to six feet in length with strong thorny margins. In South and Central America *Agave* was grown as a crop; the juices were used fresh or fermented as beverages, and the strong fibre in the leaves were used to make rope or woven into rough mats.

The Indian Fig, *Opuntia ficus-indica* (L.) Mill., better known today as the Prickly Pear, is a member of the Cactus family. It was grown as a greenhouse succulent. Native to Mexico, it was introduced to cultivation in Europe in 1731. The rounded forms of the main stems were covered with prickles. Large four-inch full yellow flowers bloomed briefly in the early summer, followed by fruit that appeared as round projections on the branched stems. There were a number of varieties of *Opuntia*, with fruit of different colours – yellow, red, or purple. The juicy red inner flesh of the fruit was edible, a major food in Mexico for several months of the year. Opuntias were grown in greenhouses more for curiosity than for their beauty or their use as a culinary dish. This plant found rapid acceptance in arid areas all around the world, from the Mediterranean to the Far East, where it was widely used for live hedges. Before the end of the nineteenth century Opuntias had already become dreaded weeds in Asian and African countries.

Creeping Cereus was another member of the Cactus family. *Aporocactus flagelliformis* (L.) Lem. was also known as Rat-Tail Cactus. It was introduced to cultivation in Europe in 1690 from Peru. This cactus was one of the first plants illustrated in the *Botanical Magazine* in 1787, which may account for the popularity of this strangely formed plant. The stems were about one inch in diameter and up to three feet long, noticeably ribbed, covered with reddish bristles. The plant crept, drooped, or climbed by means of aerial roots according to its situation. The flowers were three-inch-long curved narrow tubes. The bright purple-pink funnel-shaped flowers opened during the day and closed at night. The red fruit was edible but not particularly tasty. These cacti, popular as window plants throughout the nineteenth century, were used in conservatories to climb on architectural supports.

The Silver Leaved Wormwood offered in the catalogue may have been *Artemisia ludoviciana* Nutt. or *A. filifolia* Tort, both native to semi-tropical areas of the Americas, or *A. arborescens* L., a native of the Mediterranean area. All bore common names that included the word "silver," for example, Silver Frost, Silver Wormwood. These were short shrubby plants, three feet or less in height. The bright grey-white foliage was enhanced by the hairy textures of the leaves. All Artemisias had aromatic foliage. Some degree of rarity was attached to this particular one, as it was offered at three shillings nine pence, among the most expensive plants in the catalogue.

Rosemary, *Rosmarinus officinalis* L., was usually regarded as a herb plant. It was offered in the catalogue as a subject for the greenhouse, as this shrubby perennial was too tender to withstand a Canadian winter outdoors. Rosemary came from the Mediterranean region and had been cultivated there since ancient times when it was regarded chiefly as a medicinal plant. Chewing a leaf or two was said to improve the memory. Rosemary tea was a remedy for headache, nervous disorders, and depression. It also was taken for halitosis. Unguents and salves made from the leaves were applied externally to treat rheumatism, gout, eczema, and bruises. In the thirteenth century rosemary was used to heal a paralysis suffered by the Queen of Hungary, and a product known as Hungary Waters became a popular folk medication. The strong aromatic scent was later used in the manufacture of eau-de-Cologne. The leaves were also effective as an insect repellant. They contain a volatile oil and plant alcohols which have antiseptic properties, used in the past as gargles or medications to relieve menstrual problems, digestive ailments, and liver disfunction. The distilled oil or large doses of rosemary leaves are strong and powerful stimulants which should not be taken internally, as they have been known to cause abortion or convulsions leading to death.

Rosemary has enjoyed a reputation in folklore and literature as a symbol of fidelity between lovers. Branches of the shrub were used in marriage celebrations, funerals, and religious festivals. As a nineteenth-century house plant it probably saw use as a culinary herb for enhancing the flavour of meat and poultry or seasoning sauces.

The Chinese Chrysanthemum, *Dendranthema X grandiflorum* Kitam., was a remarkable flowering plant introduced to France from China in 1787 (Bourne 1833/1988:82). By 1833 there were forty different kinds of bloom available under this name. The chrysanthemum became a favourite flower with florists and remains to this day a popular greenhouse plant grown for

Chinese Chrysanthemum
Dendrathema X grandiflorum Kitam.

Carnation   *Dianthus caryophyllus* L.

Stock Jillyflower
Matthiola incana (L.) R. Br. & M.

Wall Flower   *Erysimum cheiri* (L.) Crantz.

show and exhibition. The flower heads were amazingly varied, some daisy-like, some globose, rounded, and full, some with quilled petals, and others yet again with long narrow petals. The different forms gained names such as "pom-pom" or "spidery" according to their appearance. The colours were in a full range from white, yellow, red, and purple, with the golden yellows the most common. The plant grew a number of stems, each with many side branches, each branchlet producing a bloom two to three inches in diameter. These plants had been in cultivation by the Chinese for many centuries, and the plants taken to Europe were evidently hybrids, their seedlings producing a multitude of varieties. It would be difficult to estimate which of the many forms Custead may have stocked, particularly if he grew his own plants from seed.

Carnations were also popular with florists. The greenhouse varieties of *Dianthus caryophyllus* L., were usually grown to supply cut flowers for bouquets. They had a distinct clove-like fragrance and were a favourite choice for nosegays, to be carried or worn by ladies on formal occasions. Custead offered several varieties, ranging in price from two shillings to three shillings nine pence. A great many varieties of carnation were available in the early nineteenth century, with prices varying according to the shape of the flower, its colouring, and its comparative rarity. During the 1820s the fashion for these flowers was at a peak, and greenhouse growers made them available year round. Their popularity led eventually to their decline: by the 1850s discriminating florists neglected them as they had become a common garden plant and were no longer considered a novelty. Many of the fancy florists' varieties were then lost. (The perpetually flowering carnation that is greenhouse-grown today for bouquets and buttonholes was created in France in the 1840s (Pizzetti and Cocker 1975: 1:395).)

"Stock Jilly-flowers," now called Autumn or Bromton Stocks, were cultivars of *Matthiola incana* (L.) R. Br. & M. cvs. These attractive, fragrant flowers from the Mediterranean region were half-hardy biennials in the garden but were grown year round in the greenhouse as cut flowers for home decoration. Stocks were members of the Mustard family, with four-petalled flowers arranged in the form of a cross. Purple flowers were most common, but white and shades of red were also known. Stocks flowered profusely, each of the many branches from the main stem producing a large terminal group of blooms. In many varieties double flowers were not uncommon. The nickname Gilly-flower was given to a number of plants that bloomed in July, including carnations.

"Wall Flowers," *Erysimum cheiri* (L.) Crantz, like stocks, were members of the Mustard family. Wallflowers were native to Europe, taken into gardens early in the sixteenth century. The original species had very fragrant, attractive flowers of a curious colour described as yellow red, or ferrous-yellow. In warm areas where the plant could be grown outdoors, it was perennial, flowering early each spring. Grown in the greenhouse, the plant required more than a year to reach the flowering stage. By the nineteenth century there were many varieties, differing mostly in the colour of the flowers, which under cultivation had developed a range from a brilliant orange through many shades of yellow to pink, red, purplish, and maroon, all with a heady perfume. These were greatly admired plants as they could remain in flower over a period of months. When propagation was repeated every few months in the greenhouse, a succession of these scented blooms could be enjoyed throughout the year.

Custead had a number of geraniums in the catalogue: Horseshoe, Silver-Edged, scented sorts with sweet, rose, balm, nutmeg and pennyroyal scents, and others with myrtle, strawberry and oak leaves. In the eighteenth century many plants were called geraniums that did not quite fit the criteria for the genus. In 1787 the French botanist L'Heritier made the botanical distinction official and created the genus *Pelargonium*. However, the old name remained the popular nomenclature for both genera, Geraniums and Pelargoniums, which has continued to the present day. By the 1800s there were many varieties of scented geraniums to choose from, some with the added attraction of colourful blooms, others with foliage of various shapes and colours.

Most species of these "Geraniums," of the genus *Pelargonium*, were from the Cape of Good Hope, South Africa. The first plants were sent to Holland by the Governor of the Cape Colony in 1609, and by the end of the century the Dutch East India Company had introduced many more geranium species and varieties to Europe. It was not until the Cape Colony came under British rule in 1806, however, that growers in England received any quantity of these imports. By this time many of the imported geraniums had already been hybridized, and the genus was quite confused.

Geraniums are shrubby or sub-shrubby plants, too tender to be grown out-of-doors as a perennial in colder climates. Because nearly all species have showy flowers and a long flowering period, they were rapidly accepted into cultivation as house plants and summer bedding plants. They did not require much space: a good sized specimen could be grown in a five- or six-inch pot. Although they could not withstand frost, geraniums grew best in a cool place with lots of sunlight and were perfect candidates for the window-sill in winter. (In well-heated modern homes with insulated window-panes the air is generally too warm for optimum conditions.) In the summer potted geraniums were placed in urns or hanging baskets where the handsome and profuse flowering was assured of gaining attention. In the late nineteenth century Victorian garden designers used the geranium extensively as a bedding plant, the red-flowered varieties in particular. It was a perfect choice in the popular red, white, and blue arrangements often found in public gardens.

Geraniums could be sorted into different categories. The Zonal, *Pelargonium X hortorum* L.H. Bail., also called Horse Shoe geraniums, had a dark horseshoe marks on the leaves and clusters of colourful flowers. The Regals, *Pelargonium X domesticum* L.H. Bail., were complex hybrids with large colourful blooms in a range of colours – pink, salmon, red, and white. The Sweet-Scented, *Pelargonium graveolens* L'Herit, had variously scented grey-green leaves and small white or pale pink flowers. Ivy-leaved geraniums, *Pelargonium peltatum* (L.) L'Herit, had bright green leaves (sometime with a circular dark zone), long trailing foliage, and small white or pale-pink flowers. Oak-leaved geraniums, *Pelargonium quercifolium* (L.) L'Herit, had wavy, deeply cut leaves. Some geraniums in the *Pelargonium fragrans* group had variegated leaves edged in white (silver) or shades of yellow (gold).

Species with scented leaves were much admired as house plants. A slight touch was all that was necessary to release a perfume into the air. Botanists and gardeners alike were astonished at the range of scents found in these plants. The different varieties were named after the fruits or spices suggested by the fragrance. The leaves were used to scent water for finger-bowls at the table and refreshing bath waters. A leaf or two added to cakes and jellies provided interesting culinary delicacies. The plants were raised commercially for their oil, which was used in the perfume industry, either with or as a substitute for the oil of roses.

The Jerusalem Cherry plant, *Solanum pseudocapsicum* L., was cultivated before 1596 in Europe. Originally from Madeira, it was related to the American pepper plants and the tomato, all members of the same family, *Solanaceae*. Unlike its edible relatives, the fruit of the Jerusalem Cherry was toxic, and the plant was grown for decorative purposes only. The small fruits changed colour as they ripened, from green to yellow to red. Set off against the dark green leaves, they made it a very handsome plant, the red and green combination an appropriate choice for Christmas decoration. Easily raised from seed, if sown in February or March in a cool but sunny

Geraniums *Pelargonium* sp.

Jerusalem Cherry *Solanum pseudocapsicum* L.

Chinese Changeable Hydrangea
Hydrangea macrophylla cvs. *hortensis*

Box leaved Myrtle *Myrtus communis* L.

greenhouse, plants would fruit in time for the Christmas season. Grown as pot plants in the home or greenhouse, they were generally fairly compact in shape, but in their native habitat they could reach a height of four feet.

Four sorts of hydrangea were listed: the Chinese Changeable, Starry, Oak Leaved, and Hortensis. These catalogue entries are particularly interesting as hydrangeas are seldom mentioned in the horticultural literature of the early nineteenth century.

Hydrangea nomenclature is a maze of taxonomists' synonyms. The Chinese Changeable and the Hortensis were two forms of *Hydrangea hortensis* Smith, now classified as *Hydrangea macrophylla* cvs. *hortensis*. The many cultivars are now divided into two groups according to the shape of their flowering heads, either Mopheads or Lace Caps. Mopheads have rounded corymbs, while Lace Caps are flatter with a margin of showy sterile flowers surrounding a compact mass of fertile flowers. Hybrid hydrangeas had been cultivated in China and Japan for a long time before Joseph Banks collected the first oriental variety to take back to England in 1790.

The incidence of colour change in the inflorescence was first noticed in 1796. This phenomenon was not well understood, except that it occurred "in consequence of the presence of some chemical constituent" (Nicholson 1887: 2:162); the colour differed when the soil chemistry was changed from alkaline to acid – the plants have blue flowers in an acidic soil and white or pinkish blooms in an alkaline soil. As many of the early oriental introductions could not withstand more than ten degrees of frost, they were grown primarily as greenhouse plants, known as "florists' hydrangeas." By the 1820s they were popular as outdoor decoration on terraces in the summer months. Placed in a frost-free place during the colder months and kept dry until spring, they were then repotted and cut back to two pairs of buds for another season's growth of handsome blooms.

The Oak Leaved Hydrangea, *Hydrangea quercifolia* Bartr., was a native of the southern United States, introduced to cultivation in 1803. The young shoots were downy red, and the leaves resembled those of the Red Oak, turning to a bronzy colour in the fall. The flower heads were pyramidal in shape, white in colour.

The plant Custead called the Starry Hydrangea was difficult to identify, as the infertile flowers of many species look star-like. It may have been the sub-species *radiata* of the *Hydrangea arborescens* L., a native of southeastern North America. The inflorescence was a flat corymb of mostly sterile white flowers, quite showy when in full bloom. (There was a *Hydrangea hortensis* ssp. *stellata*, but this plant from China was not introduced until 1868.)

The Guernsey Lily was often treated as a house plant, as the flowering period of this bulbous plant occurred in the fall before its leaves emerged. (See chapter 8 on bulbs.)

The Common Myrtle, *Myrtus communis* L., has been grown in the Mediterranean region for over two thousand years, its native origin unknown. The several forms of the species differ principally in the shape of the leaves. The plant was associated with the goddesses of love in ancient Greece and Rome, and myrtle wreaths, like those of the laurel, were awarded as crowns of distinction. It remained as a symbol of happiness, pleasure, and love in Renaissance paintings, particularly in portraiture. All parts of myrtle plants were delightfully fragrant – the twigs, leaves, flowers, and fruit. The lustrous deep green leaves had aromatic oil glands. The flowers were white or pinkish-white, the fruit a reddish or bluish-black berry. Sixteenth and seventeenth century writers Gerard and Parkinson recognized the beauty of the myrtle, but both acknowledged its need of a warm climate, as it never set fruit in the English climate. Gerard knew of a few English gardens with myrtle plants, and Parkinson had three kinds in his garden. In the nineteenth century it was treated as a pot plant, grown in greenhouses or the living room during cold weather and placed outdoors in the summer.

There were several varieties of *Myrtus communis*, differing in the shape of the leaves, including those with small narrow leaves, with broad leaves, or with leaves rounded and slightly notched at the tip like those of boxwood (*Buxus*). Custead's nursery had both the broad-leaved (*var. romana* Mill.) and the box-leaved ("Buxifolia") types. The pleasant scent of a single potted plant was sufficiently strong enough to pervade the whole house. Small branches were often used in cut flower arrangements, and it was a tradition in parts of Europe to include it in wedding bouquets. In ancient times the plant was used medicinally. Parkinson simply stated that it was an astringent, but Gerard listed many applications for its "binding" qualities both internally and externally. By the nineteenth century most of these practices were acknowledged but considered "almost obsolete" (Stillé and Maisch 1880:950).

"Pyrus Japonica or scarlet flowering Japan Apple" was listed in the catalogue appendix. This member of the Rose family, *Rosaceae*, has had many botanical names but is now known as *Chaenomeles japonica* (Thunb.) Spach. It was a dwarf plant, never more than three feet high, with brick-red flowers and yellow apple-like fruit. The fruit were much like the those of the quince, hard, aromatic, and edible only when made into preserves. They were so strongly scented that a single one placed in a bowl could perfume a room.

The botanist Carl Peter Thunberg found the first of these plants in Japan in 1784 and named it *Pyrus japonica*. About the same time Joseph Banks took another example of the genus to England from China. A specimen was sent to Kew in 1796 and named *Cydonia japonica*, resulting in inevitable confusion. A closely related species, now called *Chaenomeles speciosa* (Sweet) Nak., may also have been involved in this mixup of plants (Pizzetti and Cocker 1975: 1:216). The Boston plantsman Joseph Breck found the plant "*Cydonia japonica*, formerly *Pyrus japonica* ... valuable in the shrubbery, lawn or flower-garden" (Breck 1866:409).

Another greenhouse plant in the appendix was the Striped Rose Bay. The common name Rose Bay was used for either of two plants in the nineteenth century – the Oleander, *Nerium oleander* L. and the Great Laurel, *Rhododendron maximum* L. As there is no variety of the American laurel with variegated leaves, it was probably oleander that Custead had in his nursery. Several varieties of oleander had variegated leaves, but the "stripe" Custead referred to may have been the strong, light-coloured midrib of each leaf.

The oleander had long been in cultivation in the Mediterranean area: it was pictured in wall paint-

Striped Rose Bay   *Nerium oleander* L.

ings of ornamental gardens in Pompeii along with myrtles and viburnums. The tall dark-leaved shrubs were beautiful when in flower, the end of each branch terminating in a cluster of blooms. Oleander blossoms varied in colour from white to red; some were double; many were very fragrant. The shiny pointed leaves, in whorls of three at each leaf node, made this a handsome plant even when not in flower.

All parts of the oleander plant are poisonous. Stories from ancient times to the present tell of persons becoming ill or dying from its ingestion (Stillé and Maisch 1880:972). A recent report recorded the deaths of children who had toasted marshmallows on twigs from an oleander.

Another of the plants in the appendix was named Frost Plant. This was possibly one of the Mesembryanthemums (see also chapter 12). This genus was native to south and southwest Africa, a member of the Carpetweed family, *Aizoaceae*, a plant group commonly referred to in the early nineteenth century as Ficoides. These plants developed attributes that acclimatized them to their harsh arid environment: they grew close to the ground out of the wind and had shapes with the least surface area possible, to avoid losing moisture. Many species, such as the *Mesembryanthemum crystallinum* L., had leaves with light-reflecting pustules filled with a watery fluid. This plant had many names – Dew Plant, Ice Plant or Frost Plant, depending on its appearance. Placed on a window-sill these plants were fascinating to watch. When the flowers appeared they looked like "rubies set among diamonds" (Bourne 1833/1988:65). M'Mahon included detailed instructions for the care of plants from arid habitats in his *American Gardener*, cautioning against over-watering of succulents and advising how to gradually harden them to the outdoors when removing them from the hothouse during the summer months (M'Mahon 1858/1976:375, 416).

In the years since the Toronto Nursery published its catalogue there have been countless introductions of exotic tropical plants used today as house plants. Nevertheless, the ones offered by Custead remain some of the best choices, well worthy of seeking out for our enjoyment.

10

Seeds of Esculent Vegetables and Plants in Their Season

For most families in Upper Canada in the early nineteenth century the principal source of vegetables was the home garden. The kitchen garden, in a small enclosed area, contained vegetables grown from seed each year and a few perennial plants that would provide crops for many seasons. Vegetables required in large quantities, whether for home use or for the market, were grown as field crops. Potatoes, turnips, beans, and peas were the principal field-grown vegetables.

Immigrants from Britain were instructed to bring seeds with them. Many arrived with seeds for the foods they were familiar with, and later wrote "home" for further supplies. Published instructions to immigrants such as Catharine Parr Traill's *The Canadian Settler's Guide* offered advice on this subject, listing the seeds that were readily available in Upper Canada and those that were hard to come by. By the 1820s British seed houses and American seed growers had agents in Upper Canada. Seeds were also available from itinerant salesmen such as the travelling agents for the Shakers' seeds. The Shakers specialized in herb and vegetable seeds; the success of their enterprise was partly due to their conscientious attention to supplying viable seeds. All those not sold by the end of each season were collected and fresh seeds supplied the following year. However, Mrs Traill warned that there were many "Yankee" peddlers who sold seeds that were "little better than chaff" (Traill 1836/1989:179–80).

The section "Seeds for Esculent Vegetables" in the catalogue contains no prices or mention of the quantities available. The usual practice of retailers was simply to measure the required amount from a box or barrel of seed for the individual customer. Home gardeners likely formed the majority of customers, but there is a possibility that the Toronto Nursery might have been able to provide quantities sufficient for farm crops or a market garden.

By the end of the eighteenth century market gardens had developed around many of the larger cities in the United States. Philadelphia and New York had commercial gardens on the outskirts supplying markets and merchants with fresh produce. This concept had begun in western Europe in France and the Low Countries, where urban centres grew rapidly during the sixteenth and seventeenth centuries. Persecution of European Protestants during the sixteenth century forced many to leave their countries, and the migration of Dutch growers to England coincided with the inception of market gardens there. One consequence of this migration was the introduction of a number of vegetables familiar to immigrants from the continent but formerly rare in England.

With every wave of immigration to the New World, newcomers brought their food habits with them. This has been apparent in recent history, particularly in the period after World War II when North Americans quickly adapted to Italian pizza, Oriental dishes from Szechuan and Thailand, and piquant Latin American foods. In early Upper Canada similar adjustments took place, the diets of the English and Scots mingling with German and American traditions, enriched by foods adopted from native Indians. Ethnic origin was not the only factor in determining dietary differences; there was also a contrast between what was eaten by rich and poor.

The European diet underwent a great many changes during the seventeenth century. The dining practices of royal courts had set the fashion that was emulated by all who could afford it. The French had taken the lead, providing standards in a "nouvelle cuisine" for food preparation and service. During the next century grand homes in Britain followed suit, and their kitchens sported rows of copper pots required for cooking vegetables and sauces to accompany the dishes of roasted meats and fowl. Poorer folk were more likely to cook their entire meal in a single iron pot; a typical meal was a pudding of meat and grains wrapped in a membrane or cloth – a kind of haggis or a blood pudding – simmered in a broth that served as soup. Dried beans, brassicas, and root vegetables varied the potage.

In the Canadian colonies, for both rich and poor, the concern and preference was for vegetables that could be preserved for eating out-of-season during the long winter months. Root vegetables such as potatoes, beets, carrots, and turnips were stored in root cellars for the winter. Squash and onions would last for a number of months before deteriorating. Cucumbers and cabbages were pickled. Beans, peas, and peppers were dried for use throughout the year in stews, soups, and baked dishes.

The first extensive list of vegetable seeds available in Upper Canada appeared in an advertisement for Quetton St George's store in York, placed in the *York Gazette* in February 1808. He listed four kinds of bean, three of cabbage, two of cucumber, onions, beets, squash, turnips, melons, and parsnips, and one each of peas, carrots, celery, and lettuce. These choices would lend themselves to a simple but adequate diet of boiled dishes supplemented by salads. A number of herbs – sage, savory, burnet, caraway, and pepper grass – were included for additional seasoning and flavour.

Custead's list of 1827 included the vegetables mentioned above and added more choices. The number of varieties for some of the vegetables had increased. There were now nine kinds of beans, eight of peas, five of cabbage, lettuce, and melons, four of cucumbers, three of onions, squash, turnips, and carrots, two of beets, celery, parsley, spinach, potatoes, and radish, and one each of parsnips, salsify, sorrel, and tomatoes as well as seeds for white mustard and pepper grass. The list increased the numbers of vegetables available by adding three kinds of peppers, two of spinach, parsley, eggplant, radishes, and potatoes, as well as one each of leeks, Brussels sprouts, sorrel, nasturtiums, salsify, tomatoes, and Indian corn. Custead named the varieties for most of these choices. A few, such as the Hollow Crown parsnip, have seen little change since; they remain popular selections to this day. Other vegetables have undergone a great deal of improvement, and new varieties have replaced old ones that have disappeared from the market completely. Thanks to organized groups now trying to save old varieties, including some thought to be lost, many of these have once again been made available. While old varieties are not always the best tasting or the most prolific, they are welcomed by gene banks which exist to maintain and improve varieties of plant species.

The vegetable varieties offered by Custead were for the most part well known and widely used in Europe or the American colonies at the time. Nearly all his selections could be grown successfully in southern Ontario. A few would actually perform better in the hot dry summers of Upper Canada than they had in the cooler, damper climate of England. Contemporary American catalogues from New York and Philadelphia offered many of the same varieties; most were mentioned in M'Mahon's *American Gardener.*

The vegetable list included several perennial plants, among them those that gave the grower the first taste of fresh vegetables in the spring. Leeks and chives were ready to eat soon after the snows had gone. The Toronto Nursery offered these selections twice in the catalogue, under "Biennials and Perennials" as well as in the seed list. (In view of this duplication, those which were listed as nursery plants are treated in chapter 6.)

There were basically three categories of vegetables listed, according to their use: those in which the leaves and or stems were the edible portion, those grown for their roots, and those bearing edible fruit and/or seeds.

All but one of the plants grown for its leaves and stems were European species. The exception was the nasturtium, which came from South America. The Old World species included cabbage, Brussels sprouts, leeks, parsley, celery, asparagus, watercress, lettuce, spinach, and sorrel.

Cabbage and Brussels sprouts are members of the *Cruciferae* or Mustard family, with four-petalled flowers in the form of a cross. The food value of plants in this family had long been recognized. The medieval adage *In cruce salus* (in the cross there is health) made note of their nutritional value. It may also have been voiced to persons who were not too pleased with the taste or smell of some members of this family; a modern parallel might be "Eat your vegetables, they're good for you."

The most widely grown leafy vegetable was cabbage, *Brassica oleracea* L. It was eaten fresh, could be stored for short time, or preserved in brine or vinegar for later use.

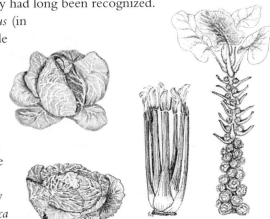

Left: Heart shaped and Savoy Cabbage   *Brassica oleracea* L.
Centre: Celery   *Apium graveolens* L.
Right: Brussels Sprouts   *Brassica oleracea* L.

Known to the early Greeks and Romans, cabbages have been in cultivation for so long that their origin remains unknown. They have not been found growing in the wild, indicating a process of selection during a lengthy period of cultivation. Cabbage had a history of use in folk medicine as a remedy for "all manner of family ills." The crushed leaves were applied externally in cases of sprained joints, arthritis, and mastitis. A syrup made from the decoction of the leaves had anti-inflammatory properties and eased coughs, asthma, and bronchitis. Present-day research has found it helpful in treating stomach ulcers and colitis (Ody 1993:42).

The cabbage varieties Custead made available were Drumhead, Early York, Early Heart Shaped, Red Dutch, and Savoy. Alphonse de Candolle described five sorts of cabbage based on the shape of the head: flat, round, egg-shaped, elliptical, and conical; variety names often reflected this characteristic. In the late eighteenth century, American gardeners President Jefferson and Lady Skipwith recorded growing all these varieties except the Early Heart Shaped. In Upper Canada William Claus had a cabbage square in his garden in 1818 in which he planted four sorts of cabbage including Drumhead and Savoy; the following year he grew Drumhead again. The Drumhead was a compact form with a flat top. The Savoy, with deep green curled leaves, was judged to be much better in flavour and the best for long keeping. Cabbages did well in most climatic conditions except the dry heat of summer, but as they took three to four months to mature, they ripened in the cooler fall weather. They were considered at their best when slightly tinged with frost. Cabbages are biennial, going to seed in the second growing year.

In almost every European country, cabbage was a major ingredient of peasant soups, best when boiled with beef stock and "much fat put among them." It was also eaten cold as a salad with a vinaigrette, or hot, boiled, or braised. It was pickled with vinegar which, in Upper Canada, was usually home-made from maple syrup or apple cider. Red cabbage was often specified in recipe books. Hannah Glasse, the authoritative eighteenth-century English cookbook author, prepared it "dressed the Dutch way" (Carson 1968:66): boiled, then "dressed" with onion, butter, and vinegar. Perhaps because of its colour, red cabbage was preferred for pickling.

Brussels sprouts were not common in the early nineteenth century. In 1821 de Candolle said that they were used on the continent, in France and Belgium, but were not grown much in English gardens until 1854 (Hedrick 1919/1972:112). They were mentioned in M'Mahon's *American Gardener*, published in Philadelphia in 1806. The Boston author Thomas G. Fessenden wrote of a "Thousand Headed" cabbage in 1828, which probably was Brussels sprouts. The New York seedsman Grant Thorburn offered only one variety in his 1828 catalogue.

To serve Brussels sprouts hot was a simple matter of boiling, draining, adding butter, and placing them in a serving dish. They were also eaten cold, dressed with a vinaigrette. Brussels sprouts were ready to pick late in the season, mid-October or after, all the more appreciated at a time when most greens and salad vegetables were over in the garden.

Vegetables cultivated for their stems included leeks and celery. (Leeks are covered in the chapter on biennials and perennials.)

Two varieties of celery – White Solid and Rose Coloured – were the choices offered. Celery, *Apium graveolens* L., was a popular vegetable throughout the nineteenth century. The earliest varieties were hollow stalked, used primarily as a seasoning. In France soups and broths were made with celery as the major ingredient. When the solid-stalked type became available, it was eaten raw, alone or mixed in a salad. When cooked it could be served separately, often with a sauce, or combined with bacon, onions, and carrots. In the later nineteenth century, specially designed glass trays and upright containers were made for presenting the stalks at the table.

Celery was usually started indoors and placed out in the spring. It took three more months to mature. To keep the stalks blanched, it was grown in a trench or earthed up to block the sunlight; there were occasional mentions in garden manuals of a technique in which each plant was wrapped in paper. After celery had been picked, it could be kept for a good part of the winter by burying it upright in soil in a frost-free place. The Rose Coloured was considered one of the best keepers. In the 1880s the American gardener Peter Henderson stated he sold far less of the red varieties than the white, and this trend has continued to the virtual exclusion of the rose or red varieties from the twentieth-century market.

In the past celery was cultivated as much for medicinal purposes as for culinary uses. It was taken as a spring tonic, for cleansing the body. Celery contains anti-toxic properties and promotes the excretion of urine; the seeds were also used as a diuretic in the treatment of gout to clear the uric acid formed in body joints. An aromatic oil distilled from the seeds was used externally for gout and arthritis as a massage or in foot baths (Ody 1993:). A chemical in the plant can cause photosensitivity, which makes the skin susceptible to severe sunburn and rashes. In recent years large-scale producers of celery have had to protect field workers and handlers from excessive exposure to the plant; now celery is usually marketed in plastic wrap.

Lettuce, spinach, sorrel, cress, and nasturtium were vegetables grown for the edible leafy parts.

Lettuce, *Lactuca sativa* L., found wild all over Europe and Asia, was cultivated by ancient civilizations from Egypt to China. Its mention in the Bible associated it with the bitter herb of the Passover ritual. It became a common plant in European gardens in the Middle Ages. It was eaten fresh – raw or wilted – in salads; it was cooked in meat

Left: Cabbage and Cos Lettuce   *Lactuca sativa* L.
Above right: Garden Sorrel   *Rumex acetosa* L.
Below right: Round leaved Spinach   *Spinachia oleracea* L.

stock, pureed for souffles, or used as an ingredient in forcemeats or stuffing. The varieties offered in the Toronto Nursery catalogue were Early, Long Leaved or Cabbage, Ice Cous, Brown Dutch, and Grand Admiral.

There are two basic forms of lettuce: the head, or cabbage lettuces, and the loose-leaved or Cos types. Head lettuces have tightly overlapping leaves forming a fairly compact mass, not unlike a cabbage. Cos lettuces grow more upright with looser leaves. Custead offered both types. The Brown Dutch was a head lettuce in which the parts of leaves exposed to sunlight turned a brown colour. It was a variety recommended throughout the nineteenth century for its hardiness. Ice Cous was a Cos type. No description of the Grand Admiral could be found. In 1818 William Claus recorded planting both types, a Cabbage Lettuce and an Imperial Cos Lettuce, in his Upper Canada garden. Lettuce is fast growing and prefers cool weather. In Canada an early spring sowing will mature before the hottest days of summer, and a later sowing will mature in the early fall. It is self-pollinating and sets seed in one season.

There are two distinct sorts of spinach, *Spinachia oleracea* L., those with prickly seeds and those with smooth seeds. Custead offered a variety of each type, the Prickly or Fall, with angular pointed leaves and prickly seed, and the Round Leaved with much broader leaves and smooth seed. Spinach probably originated in southwest Asia. The Moors found it in Persia and took it to Europe in the Middle Ages. By the seventeenth century it had become a popular vegetable on the continent but was not well known in the British Isles until much later. Parkinson wrote that "many English" had learned of it from the Dutch, and that "Gentlewomen and their Cookes" knew ways to prepare it, suggesting that it was better known by the upper classes. In America, M'Mahon of Philadelphia mentioned three sorts in 1806.

The simplest preparation of spinach was to sweat it in its own juices, press out the moisture, and season it to be served as a vegetable or used in savoury pies or tarts. It was seldom used raw in salads as is popular today. Spinach has mild laxative properties, and like all leafy vegetables, contains vitamins A, C, and E; but it also contains oxalic acid, which interferes with the body's absorption of calcium. Often considered a good source of iron, it is not as rich in either iron or oxalic acid as sorrel.

Sorrel, *Rumex acetosa* L., was a native of the North Temperate Zone and still grows wild in European meadows. In rural areas the new leaves of the wild plant were picked in early spring to use in soups or as a cooked vegetable like spinach. In Europe it was always gathered from the wild, never grown under cultivation. Its hot bitter taste, which gained it the common name "sour grass," added a nippy flavour when used raw in salads. Brought to America, it found a place in the garden but has since escaped cultivation; now naturalized, it is considered nothing more than a weed.

The plant's oxalic acid content is found mostly in the older leaves where it is so concentrated that the culinary use of sorrel must be restricted to small servings of very young leaves. Over-use can lead to serious medical problems. At one time the plant was grown in Switzerland for the commercial production of oxalic acid (Millspaugh 1892/1974:577).

Custead's "Cress or Peppergrass," *Lepidium sativum* L., is better known today as common garden cress. It is a member of the Mustard family, and its small leaves have a special taste – fresh, hot, strong, and bitter. A sturdy, much-branched annual native to Europe and most northern temperate regions, its widespread cultivation has caused it to become naturalized in many places. It was a particular favourite with the British, who ate it in salads mixed with other greens in an oil and vinegar dressing or with butter and bread, a taste learned from the Dutch (Parkinson 1629/1991:500).

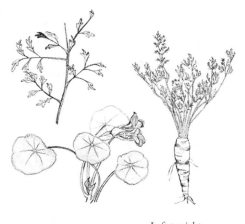

Left to right:
Pepper Grass   *Lepidium sativum* L.
Nasturtium   *Tropaeolum majus* L.
Hamburgh Parsley
Petroselinum crispum (Mill.) A.W. Hill

Cress had a well-deserved reputation as a general tonic for it was rich in vitamins and minerals, attributes that also made it useful in preventing scurvy. The hot-tasting seeds were given to children as a vermifuge.

Custead offered two varieties of parsley, *Petroselinum crispum* (Mill.) A.W. Hill, – the "Curled or double" and the "Hamburgh or large rooted." Both kinds are available today, and parsley is still in common use, although it is often seen as a garnish which is frequently left on the plate. Parsley was eaten raw or cooked, lightly sautéed in butter or deep fried. Eaten before a meal it stimulated the appetite; eaten after, its high chlorophyll content purified the breath, clearing the strong odour of foods such as garlic.

Parsley is a biennial plant, producing seeds in the second year. The plant stems provided a green dye for textiles. The leaves, root, and seeds were used medicinally as a diuretic and a carminative and in the treatment of menstruation problems.

Nasturtium, *Tropaeolum majus* L., was the only plant of this group of vegetables that originated in the New World. A native of Peru and Bolivia, it was taken to Europe as a medicinal plant. Originally called Jesuits' Cress, it had been sent to the botanist Nicolas Monardes in Spain in the sixteenth century. All parts of the plant – leaves, flowers, and seed – have antibacterial and antifungal properties useful in the treatment of urinary and respiratory infections (Stuart 1979:275).

The spicy leaves were eaten raw in salads, and the round seeds, picked while still green, were pickled in vinegar like capers. Thomas Jefferson recorded planting thirty-five little hills of "Nasturcium" in his garden in 1774. The flowers are very decorative, from shades of orange to maroon, and these are also edible.

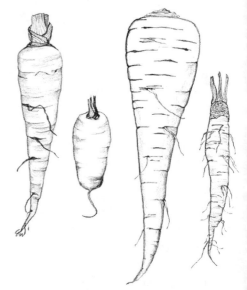

The catalogue listed several vegetables that were grown for their edible roots. Only one of these, the potato, was native to the New World; all others were well-known plants native to Europe, with a long history of cultivation. The list included beets, turnips, carrots, parsnips, radishes, rutabaga, salsify, and onions. These choices offered a variety of tastes and textures. Root vegetables were easily stored; some remained viable for many months and were simple to prepare by boiling in water. Storage was accomplished by burying the roots in sandy soil in a frost-free place over the winter season.

Left to right:
Long Orange and Horn Carrots   *Daucus carota* L.
Hollow Crowned Parsnip   *Pastinaca sativa* L.
Salsify   *Tragopodon porrifolius* L.

Three varieties of carrots were listed: Early Horn, Long Orange, and Blood Red. Carrots, *Daucus carota* L., were introduced to the North American colonies at the beginning of the seventeenth century.

There were two basic types, one with red coloured roots, the other with yellow or white. The carrot evolved from the wild umbelliferous plant known as Queen Anne's Lace, the original carrot with whitish roots. The red and orange varieties were developed in the seventeenth century by Dutch growers and were regarded as superior in flavour and texture to the earlier white or yellow forms. (All three of Custead's selections were of the red type.) The Early Horn was often mentioned in American garden literature and is still grown on heritage sites. It has a chunky, thick, cylindrical root "much esteemed" as a table carrot. The Long Orange, often grown as a field crop to supply the market, was a large tapered variety which was a good keeper (Jabs 1984:42, 194). In 1819 William Claus "sewed" a bed of carrots in his Upper Canada garden but neglected to name the variety.

Carrots contain vitamin B and carotene, essential nutrients for good health. Vitamin C is also present but is neutralized during cooking. The carrot plant is biennial, forming seeds in the second year. Decoctions of the seed were used medicinally in the past for gastric problems. Parkinson mentioned the use of the finely divided carrot leaves which "many Gentlewomen ... sticke in their hats or heads, or pin them on their armes instead of feathers" (Parkinson 1629/1991:508).

William Claus also planted a bed of parsnips, *Pastinaca sativa* L., in 1819. This vegetable, grown in Europe since the days of the Roman Empire, was brought to America in the early seventeenth century. The variety Custead offered, the Hollow Crown, has remained one of the best, still widely grown today. Parsnips are biennial plants, forming seeds in the second season. In Catholic Europe they were considered a "great nourisher especially in Lent." When they are left in the ground through the cold winter months, their starches turn to sugar, and the vegetable has a pleasant sweet taste. They can be dug out in the late winter or very early spring and enjoyed before any other root vegetable has even been planted. But when they are left for consumption later in the second season, the concentration of chemicals becomes hazardous, as in many other plants in the *Umbelliferae* or Carrot family. Several serious cases of poisoning affecting the central nervous system have been reported (Millspaugh 1892/1974:248).

Beets were a favourite vegetable of the Romans, who consumed both the root and the leaves. Two varieties of *Beta vulgaris* L. were offered in the catalogue: the Blood Red and the White or Scarcity. Blood Red was a garden variety, deep red in colour, tapered in shape. Scarcity, with a

yellow-white flesh, was a larger, coarser vegetable, but a variety that produced well even under adverse conditions. When all other crops failed,
Scarcity beets kept starvation at bay.

Beets were extraordinarily good keepers. Stored in soil or sand, the
tops carefully kept above the soil level in a frost-free place, most beets
kept until the following year's crop was ready. Though they were never
as popular at the table in England or America as they were in northern
and eastern European countries, beets were cooked and sliced, eaten hot
or cold, sometimes with sauces, pureed for soups, or pickled in sweetened
vinegar.

Three varieties of turnips followed beets on Custead's list. "Common Field,"
Brassica rapa L. and the "Swedish or rutabaga" and French *Brassica napus* L.,
are closely related to cabbage. Turnip leaves
from young plants were eaten, but they
coarsen as the plant matures; they were
grown primarily for their roots. Field
or common turnips had a thick, round,
somewhat flattened root and white,
yellow, or purplish-red flesh. As the name
implies, these were usually grown as a field
crop. Turnips do not like hot weather
conditions, and in America they were
often sown in the summer to be ready
for market in the cool fall months.

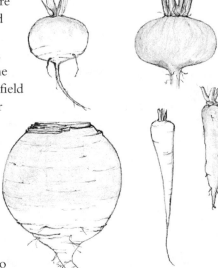

The French turnip, or navet, was
sown in the early spring to be ready
by late summer. A small bulbous
shaped root with white flesh, it was
always used fresh as it was not a good
keeper. When left in the ground too
long, navets start to form seeds
and the quality of the root de-
teriorates. It had been grown
in France for a pot vegetable
since the fifteenth century,
and Thomas Jefferson brought
some with him when he re-
turned home to America, planting them in his Virginia garden in the 1770s.

Above: French Turnip   *Brassica napus* L.
Beet   *Beta vulgaris* L.
Below: Swedish or Rutabaga   *Brassica napus* L.
Short-topt Scarlet Radish and
Black Radish   *Raphanus sativus* L.

Rutabaga or Swede turnips were introduced to England in the late
eighteenth century from Sweden and taken to America at the beginning

of the nineteenth century (Hedrick 1919/1972:106). The roots were large, the flesh a firm yellowish colour. They could remain in the ground until after fall frosts but not for the entire winter. They were excellent keepers, ready to eat all winter long. However, many found them a strong-tasting, coarse vegetable and believed that they were fit only for cattle fodder.

Radishes were another root vegetable enjoyed by the ancient Romans and continuously cultivated since that time. Originating in Asia, from Asia Minor to China, *Raphanus sativus* L. had many forms. Custead offered two: the Short Topt Scarlet and the Black Fall.

Sturtevant's Edible Plants gives six different categories of radish (Hedrick 1919/1972:484ff). The Short Topt Scarlet probably fitted into the group of Round Radishes, which came in shades of colour from white to red or purple. (This group may also have included the "turnip" radish grown by William Claus in 1819.) The Black Fall likely was the sort also known as the Black Spanish Winter, in the group of Long Black Radishes. Radishes were very fast growing, from sowing the seed to picking a matter of only four to five weeks. They were usually eaten fresh and raw, their peppery taste mellowed by the accompaniment of bread and butter. Chopped or sliced, they were a salad ingredient.

Native to the Mediterranean region, salsify or Vegetable Oyster, *Tragopodon porrifolius* L., was brought into cultivation in southern Europe in ancient times. Though seldom on the menu today, it had a long history of use in Europe where it was grown in most nineteenth-century kitchen gardens, less frequently for the market. M'Mahon mentioned it in his *American Gardener* in 1806, and William Claus sowed two rows of "salsafy" in his cucumber bed in 1818.

Salsify was grown for its long, tapered, brownish-black root, but in early spring the newly emerging stalks were prepared like asparagus. The root was boiled, fried, or used as an ingredient in fritters and baked dishes. To many, the taste was not unlike an oyster, which accounted for the common name of Vegetable Oyster.

The catalogue listed three sorts of onions: Red, White, and the Top or Tree Onion. The onion, *Allium cepa* L., is not strictly a root but a bulb that has no offshoots but sets seed for reproduction. It is believed that the bulbous form of the onion was not known in the Americas until after the arrival of Europeans and was introduced to Central and South America by the Spanish in the early sixteenth century. By the seventeenth century

onions were grown in the British and
French colonies in North America. In
1806 M'Mahon described six sorts
known to him in Philadelphia, while
Sturtevant gave descriptions of eight
different types distinguished by their
shapes (Hedrick 1919/1972:32ff).

The red and white onion seed sold by
Custead could have been any one of several of Sturtevant's types. Red onions,
with red outer skins and white inner
flesh, kept well but tended to have a
strong flavour. The most widely cultivated White Onion was the Spanish
Onion – a good keeper that would last
until the following spring. The Top or
Tree Onion belonged to the *Proliferum*
group of *Allium cepa* that does not set
seed; instead, small bulbets form at the
tops of the stalks. These were first described in the late sixteenth century.

Left: Top or Tree Onion
Above: Red Onion   *Allium cepa* L.
Below: English White Potato
Solanum tuberosum L.

Today a variety of these called Egyptian Onions are grown by curious
gardeners. The onion, in all of its forms, was a kitchen staple used in a multitude of ways. A nutritious vegetable rich in vitamins, it has antibiotic properties useful in treating throat, lung, and gastric ailments (Stuart 1979:148)
and is currently being investigated for its role in cancer prevention.

The potato was taken to Europe from its native habitat in western South
America in the early sixteenth century. There is confusion in early records
between the potato and the sweet potato, which are from very different
plant families. The English White Potato offered in the catalogue was
Solanum tuberosum L. The early history of this tuberous vegetable, destined
to become one of the most frequently planted crops in the western world,
is still not fully explained. When the Spanish originally took the potato to
Spain, it failed to gain much attention. Somehow, probably by way of the
West Indies, it reached the eastern shores of North America. In the late sixteenth century it was taken from Virginia to Ireland and England, where it
was found to grow in even the poorest soil and became the staple food of
the poorer classes, saving them from near-starvation diets. In many areas it
virtually replaced cereal crops. Later it was re-imported to North America

under the name of the English White Potato, a variety offered by Custead. He also listed "Other choice varieties" which must remain unidentified. Potatoes varied in their skin colour and the texture of their fleshy interior. Red, blue, purple, russet, and yellow skinned varieties were known in the eighteenth century. William Claus planted a variety with blue skin in his garden in 1818.

The potato belongs to the plant family *Solanaceae*, which was well known for having poisonous properties. Members of this family included Deadly Nightshade, tobacco, and Thorn-Apple, plants recognized and respected for their narcotic content. Their misuse was known to have fatal consequences. However, the family also contains eggplant, tomato, and capsicum pepper, nutritious food items. In the potato the objectionable chemicals are concentrated in the skin and the eyes of the tubers. Green-tinted skins (which occur when the tubers have been exposed to the sun during their growing period) are to be avoided (Bailey 1902:1418). Recent research in teratology, the study of birth defects, has linked the potato to congenital deformities.

Twelve species of vegetables in the catalogue were grown for their fruits or seeds. Among them were those originating in the Mediterranean region, North Africa, and Asia: mustard, melon, cucumber, eggplant, peas, and broad beans. The remainder were from the Americas: tomatoes, peppers, squash, kidney and runner beans, and Indian corn. Several of the American species were of tropical origin, perennial in their native habitat but grown as annuals in a more northerly climate.

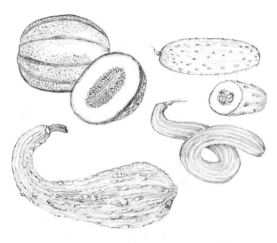

Above: Nutmeg Melon   *Cucumis melo* L.
Prickly Cucumber and Serpentine Cucumber   *Cucumis sativus* L.
Below: Early Crookneck Squash   *Cucurbita pepo* L.

Custead offered seed for five varieties of melon: Pineapple, Nutmeg, Paradise, Green Citron and Burnet. Native to tropical Africa and Asia, the melon, *Cucumis melo* L., was widely grown in the Mediterranean area; in 1629 Parkinson declared the best seed came from Spain. The plant was easily grown from seed and was widely distributed by the end of the seventeenth century. There were so many variations in this fruit that early descriptions are confusing. The Pineapple, Nutmeg, and Burnet were muskmelon types with furrowed and netted skins. The sweet smell of the ripe muskmelon gave each variety its name, according to the resemblance of the aroma. The flesh of the Nutmeg variety was a sweet-tasting green. The Pineapple was regarded as a winter melon, keeping well until the Christmas season. Green Citron, a small variety of watermelon with the seeds embedded in a solid flesh, was the preferred variety for pickling. Melons required a long growing season, which was often cut short in the northern states and Canada. When frost threatened, many nearly ripe melons were used for pickles or conserves to accompany meats.

Garden records have shown that several varieties of melons were grown in North American gardens around the beginning of the nineteenth century. President Jefferson grew Paradise and Citron melons. William Claus planted the Nutmeg, another sort of muskmelon, and a watermelon. To extend the season, he grew some of his muskmelons in a hotbed. In 1823 he recorded setting out the first on 13 July. These fruit were generally eaten raw, at the beginning of the meal as an appetizer, or at the end as a dessert. The seeds are very nutritious and were often oven dried to make a sort of nutmeat.

Cucumbers, *Cucumis sativus* L., originating in the warm climate of the Asian sub-continent, belong to the same genus as the melon. They were eaten raw, enjoyed for their refreshing cool taste but were apt to cause "wind." Cucumbers were the vegetables most commonly used for pickling; recipes differed in the herbs and spices used to give the preserves a variety of flavours ranging from sweet to sour. For pickling purposes the fruit was picked when very small. After excess moisture had been removed by immersion in a brine, they were preserved in vinegar. The fruit were produced in groups of three on trailing plants, the vine often trained over a trellis or fence-like structure to allow the fruit to fall free. In England cucumbers were grown year-round in greenhouses designed specifically for their culture.

Several varieties of cucumbers were grown in America in the eighteenth century. Custead listed four in his catalogue: Early Frame, Long Prickly, Short Prickly, and Serpentine. Some cucumbers were grown in hot-beds or cold frames to extend the growing period and for protection early in the season; the one called Early Frame suggests that it was intended for such treatment. This variety produced small chunky fruit, barely twice as long as wide, with dark spines on green skin. The fruit turned yellow as it ripened. Many varieties had hairs or prickles on the surface of the skin, more pronounced on some. The Short Prickly was a hardier variety, one that could be grown outdoors. The Serpentine, or Snake Cucumber, a long green fruit covered with woolly hairs, curled and curved into unusual twisted forms.

"Egg Plant," *Solanum melongena* L., arrived in Europe from the East Indies, via the Near East. It was widely grown in the Mediterranean region, and most recipes using this vegetable have come from that area. The earliest mention of it in Europe was in the sixteenth century when a plant was described having yellow or purple fruit the size and shape of an egg. These plants were treated more as ornamentals than candidates for the kitchen garden. Known in Europe as the aubergine, only in America was it commonly called the eggplant. This is something of a misnomer, for the fruit of most varieties grown as vegetables have either rounded or elongated shapes. In recent years there has been a revival of the small white eggplant by nurseries offering it as a house or container plant.

White Mustard, *Brassica hirta* Moench. (see p. 217) was known as both a wild and a cultivated plant when Parkinson described it in 1629. He wrote of the way the hot-tasting seeds were crushed in vinegar for use at the table. Probably no other condiment is as British as mustard, imperative as the accompaniment to roast beef. The seeds of White Mustard are actually yellowish-red. In most recipes for their use they were mixed with the black seeds from Black Mustard. The leaves of the mustard plant also have a sharp taste and were used to add flavour to salads. They are quick to germinate, and young seedlings were grown on a piece of flannel to add greens to winter meals. When combined with seeds for watercress the mixture was called "Mustard and Cress." Mustard also had its place in the sick room: poultices of mustard seed were used to relieve chest ailments, and ground mustard seed was effectively used as an emetic.

Peas, *Pisum sativum* L., eaten either fresh or dried, were staples in the European diet. Custead's list included eight varieties: Early Frame, Early Hotspur, Dwarf Green, Prussian Blue, Dwarf Prolific or Strawberry, Knight Tall Marrow or Honey Pea, Tall Grey Sugar, and Dwarf Sugar or White Peas. By the end of the eighteenth century there were many different kinds of peas to choose from. There were smooth seeded or wrinkled seeded varieties, and indeterminate or determinate plant types, with seeds coloured white, grey, yellow, or green. Semi-dwarf types had been available for many years, and true dwarf varieties were becoming available in the early 1800s. Wrinkled-seeded peas were sweeter-tasting than the starchy, smooth-seeded kinds, and the Hotspur varieties were considered to be among the best. In the 1780s an English seedsman, Thomas Knight, introduced new varieties of Hotspur peas. Custead offered a Hotspur, probably one of the earlier varieties, still preferred by many, as well as one of Knight's improved varieties. The Prussian Blue, with blue-green seeds, was a popular variety in the United States, mentioned by M'Mahon in 1806. Claus planted marrow peas in 1822.

Left: Peas   *Pisum sativum* L.
Right: Beans   *Phaseolus vulgaris* L.

There were two types of sugar peas, Tall Grey and Dwarf White. Sugar peas were developed in Holland in the late sixteenth century. In the early seventeenth century dishes of green peas became very fashionable at the French court, setting an example for the rest of Europe to follow. This culinary development appears to coincide with the introduction of new varieties, particularly the edible-podded sugar pea, which was eaten fresh rather than dried. Dried peas remained a common dish of the poorer classes. In Catholic Europe dishes of dried peas formed a good part of the diet during Lent, replacing some of the proteins lost when meats were forbidden.

Beans were another dietary staple. Before the introduction of species from the Americas in the sixteenth century, Europeans had only the broad bean, *Vicia faba* L., also known as the fava bean. In 1819 William Claus grew Windsor beans, a white-seeded broad bean. Beans from the Americas were in the genus *Phaseolus*. They were called kidney, snap, or string beans by the English and *haricot* by the French. The new species included both climbing plants and bush types. The seed pods were long and narrow, containing various coloured seeds. The pods were picked when young to be eaten fresh and whole, or left to mature and the seeds stripped from the pods for drying.

All the varieties of beans in the Toronto Nursery catalogue appear to have been the American genus. Nine choices were listed: four dwarf and five vining or pole varieties. The dwarfs included Early Mohawk, Early Six Weeks, Early Dunn, and Early Chince; the pole types were Pale White or Cream Coloured, Purple Cranberry, Scarlet Runners, White Dutch Runners, Asparagus, or Yard Long. The garden bean genus *Phaseolus vulgaris* L. included a great variety of plant types with fruit from two or three inches up to two feet long containing seeds that could be red, brown, black, white, or mottled. Another species, *Phaseolus coccinea* L., included the Scarlet Runner and the White Dutch Runner. This species had showy flowers, and the colour of the flower was the same as that of the seed – the White Dutch Runner had white flowers and seeds, and the Scarlet Runner had mottled red and black seeds. The bright red blooms of the Scarlet Runner made it a handsome garden plant, and it was not seriously considered as a vegetable until Philip Miller placed it in the kitchen garden in the mid-eighteenth century. The pods had a strong string along the side and were tough unless picked very young. Frequent inspection of the plant and repeated pickings were necessary as the pods developed. This made it an impractical choice for market growers but a convenient one for the home gardener and the cook.

Squashes were known as gourds in England, and the American species were often confused with plants from Asia. The American species, *Cucurbita pepo* L., was cultivated by the native peoples who used them in a variety of ways as a vegetable and as a basis for sweetened dishes. Custead listed three American varieties: Early Bush, Early Crook Neck, and Large Green Crook Neck. These were not good keepers and were called summer squash or vegetable marrows. Early Bush was a yellow, scalloped, squat variety. The Crook Neck squashes had a peculiar twisted shape and a warty appearance. These were very productive plants, ripening early in the season. During the summer the inner flesh was used as a boiled vegetable; later in the season when the flesh toughened, it was used for baked pies.

The *Capsicum* genus of peppers was introduced to Europe following Columbus's second voyage to the New World in 1493. One of the spices he had set out to find was Black Pepper, *Piper nigrum* L., a tropical vine from the Far East. Capsicum peppers grew on herbaceous or shrubby plants, widely distributed throughout South America and the Caribbean

Islands. As the pepper plants found their way from country to country in Europe, they were met with various reactions. Hungary, Italy, and Spain adopted them readily, finding ways to use the fruit as a substitute for the more expensive imported Black Pepper. They never became an essential or popular part of the diet in France or England. The seeds were easily transported by trading ships travelling to the Pacific where new varieties developed. It is hard to realize that many of the hot, spicy dishes associated with India

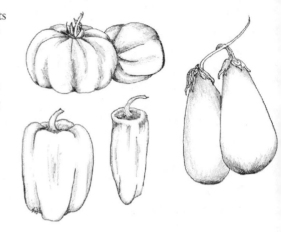

Above left: Tomato   *Lycopersicum esculentum* Mill.
Left: Egg Plant   *Solanum melongena* L.
Right: Peppers   *Capsicum annuum* L.

and southeast Asia were not known before the arrival of the American capsicum pepper.

Two major species predominated, *Capsicum annuum* L., a herbaceous plant, and *C. frutescens* L., a shrubby plant. Custead's varieties were the Long or Cayenne, the Tomato Shaped, and the Cherry Shaped. All were varieties of *C. annuum.*, the genus having many groups. The Long or Cayenne is in the Longum group, the Tomato in the Grossum group and the Cherry in the Cerasiforme group. These three varieties were also listed in the New York catalogue of George Thorburn in 1826. William Claus planted a "very large pepper," probably one of the Grossum group, predecessors of the Bell type, brought to him by a friend in 1823.

Peppers were used in mixed dishes such as ragoûts and stews, and large sorts were stuffed and baked. A condiment or paste was made by grinding together peppers, onions, ginger, and salt. To make cayenne, or paprika, peppers were dried and the flesh pulverized. The grounds were mixed with flour and yeast and baked in small cakes. These were ground again to achieve a powdered consistency. Peppers have an antibacterial property and are an aid to digestion. When rubbed on the skin they act as a irritant, helping to reduce local pain by increasing the blood flow to the area, turning it red. Capsaicin, the active ingredient, is now one of the major ingredients of ointments used in the treatment of arthritis, rheumatism, and shingles.

Indian Corn, *Zea mays* L., a grain all recognize as an American native, was first
seen on the island of Cuba by Columbus in 1492. It was grown as the
major grain product by numerous
Indian tribes throughout North
America. De Candolle found that
more than two hundred indigenous American languages had a
name for it. In 1605 Champlain
saw it growing in what is now
eastern Canada. By that time it had
been introduced to Europe, where
it was known as maize. Europeans found it a poor substitute
for the grains they were cultivating, such as wheat, barley,

Left: White mustard   *Brassica hirta* Moench.
Right: Indian Corn   *Zea mays* L.

rye, or oats. Corn had the disadvantage of a high oil content which became
rancid in long-term storage. European diners have never taken to eating
this vegetable as corn-on-the-cob.

At the beginning of the nineteenth century there were only two varieties of corn known, the Dent and Flint. Sweet corn was an accidental discovery in the United States, and the first seed for it was offered in the 1828
Thorburn catalogue, the only variety mentioned. Custead also offered
only one sort of corn in 1827 but did not identify the specific variety. It
was listed rather casually as "Indian Corn & grass seeds."

Early corn varieties had hard-coated kernels arranged in eight rows. The
flesh was beaten out and ground to make the flour used in Indian baking;
The task was performed as required for daily consumption. Corn meal
was adopted by immigrants in the southern areas of North America who
created recipes such as johnnycake. Grits, or hominy, coarsely ground
corn, became another mainstay in the South but was little regarded elsewhere. Corn was also used as a fodder, the oil content contributing to the
fattening of domestic animals. The production of corn oil later became an
important industry supplying cooking oil for domestic use and as an export
product.

The "Tomato or Love Apple" that Custead knew would hardly be recognized today. Tomatoes were the fruit of *Lycopersicum esculentum* Mill.

which the Spanish took to Europe from South America in the mid-sixteenth century. The botanist Matthiola described them in 1554, calling them *pomi d'oro*, golden apples. This fruit was probably neither red nor round – the shape and colour associated with the modern tomato – but more likely yellow, with a deeply grooved or lobed squat shape, quite small in size. Seeds were sent to Gerard in England from Spain. Two hundred years later Philip Miller called it the "Love Apple," as it had gained a reputation as an aphrodisiac, and some feared that eating it might lead to excessive sexual behaviour.

As a member of the *Solanaceae* family, which included so many poisonous plants, the tomato was for a long time after its introduction regarded with suspicion. In northern Europe it was grown as an ornamental, but in Italy it was eaten as a salad vegetable with oil, vinegar, and salt. It was here that the tomato first gained wide acceptance in Europe. By 1812 it was grown as a field crop in Sicily. In England and North America the tomato slowly gained in popularity, but always as a cooked vegetable, boiled, fried, or baked. It was used in some sauces and baked alongside roasted meats.

Only one entry for the tomato appears in the Toronto Nursery catalogue; the first attempts to breed better varieties did not begin until the 1850s. Today's seed catalogues offer the home grower a bewildering number of varieties often covering several pages, and the American Seed Savers group has assembled upwards of 1,200 older varieties.

The Toronto Nursery provided a range of vegetable seeds or plants for its clientele to meet the needs of most households. For several vegetables the customer was offered choices. A few of the selections were not part of the usual fare at the time; Brussels sprouts and eggplant were not in widespread use, probably unknown to many in Upper Canada. These are now familiar and readily available. However, other vegetables listed in the catalogue are seldom seen today. The modern gardener might wish to try a few old varieties, such as Red Celery or Green Citron melon, to add interest to the vegetable garden and to challenge the adventurous cook.

11

Seeds for Pot and Sweet Herbs
Medicinal Herbs

In the late twentieth century, herb gardens have been revived, and we are again enjoying the decorative textures, tastes, and scents of these historical plants. Herbs have been grown in gardens for many centuries, and most have remained unchanged from the original species form. A number are still in daily use in kitchens around the world, while others have lost their popularity or usefulness for domestic purposes. Our medicine cabinets are no longer stocked with medicinal herbs, although an increasing number of herbal preparations are available today as a result of recent interest in alternative medicine. A large percentage of accepted drugs are derived from plants, yet there is still much to be learned about natural plant chemicals and their effects on the human body.

In the Toronto Nursery catalogue there were two listings for herb seeds, those considered to be of culinary use, "Pot and Sweet Herb Seeds," and those which were intended for medicinal purposes, "Medicinal Herb Seeds." (Neither list included the prices or quantities available.) The medicinal herbs Custead offered included some that were being imported at the time. In providing seed for such plants he may have intended to stimulate the domestic economy, at a savings to both the practitioner and the consumer.

In addition to the familiar culinary and medicinal herbs, the list included other herbs that were useful as insecticides, disinfectants, and dye plants. The nineteenth-century household would have found these plants helpful, if not essential, for maintaining a certain quality of life. Mrs Traill advised prospective immigrants to Canada to bring seeds for the pot herbs sweet marjoram, sweet basil, and balm, "for these are rarely met with here," while seeds for sage, mint, and savory were easily had (Traill 1855/1969:40).

Many plants used as culinary or medicinal herbs belong to the *Labiatae* or Mint family. Plants in this family are easily recognized by their fragrant foliage and square or angled stems. Custead's list included Sweet Basil, Sweet Marjoram, Sage, Summer Savory, Thyme, Moldavian Balm, Hyssop, Horehound, and Balm.

Sweet Basil, *Ocimum basilicum* L., is a herb in common use today as a result of the popularity of Italian dishes in our diet; it is an essential ingredient of pesto sauce. Its affinity for tomatoes has been exploited in many recipes for sauces and salads. It was used extensively by French cooks in the seventeenth and eighteenth centuries in soups and sauces for fish and meat. As the fashion of French cuisine spread through Europe, French herbs and seasonings followed, and in the early nineteenth century egg dishes, soups, and salads were frequently enhanced with basil.

The flavour of basil depends on the concentration of its oil content, which varies according to its growing conditions. A warm, dry, temperate habitat, such as found in the Mediterranean region, provides the optimal climate. The oil is volatile, vaporizing at room temperature. Little remains when the herb is dried, and consequently the flavour is lost. Fresh basil grown in the Mediterranean area is a good deal more pungent than that grown in Canada, but in a dried state it has far less flavour than fresh basil grown here.

Basil originated in the tropics of Asia but is rarely found in the wild today. The early Greeks did not think much of the herb, for Dioscorides wrote that its use would inhibit one's senses, dry up a woman's milk, and might even cause insanity. It was more popular with the Romans, who believed that it was beneficial for those suffering from melancholy. Through the ages it became an aid to digestion, with doses recommended for stomach pain, vomiting, and constipation. Teas made with basil were prescribed in folk medicine to counter nausea and reduce fevers. Recent analysis has shown extracts from basil to be effective in inhibiting organisms that cause dysentery.

Sweet Marjoram, *Origanum marjorana* L., has one of the most delightful fragrances of all plants, an attribute that has ensured its continuous cultivation over many centuries. Early herbals described it as an excellent and useful plant with a strong and exquisite fragrance. The Romans believed it banished sadness, a concept relating the sense of smell to the emotions, as in aromatherapy. The Elizabethans made it into "sweet-bags," and Parkinson

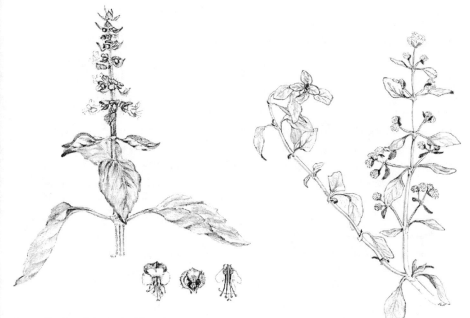

Sweet Basil   *Ocimum basilicum* L.

Sweet Marjoram   *Origanum marjorana* L.

Summer Savory   *Satureja hortensis* L.

Lemon Thyme   *Thymus citriodorus* Hort.

noted that it was "much used to please the outward senses in nosegayes, and in the windows of houses" (Parkinson 1629/1991:452). It was one of the strewing herbs used to freshen the house.

The fragrance of the Sweet, or Knotted, Marjoram was used in cooking as well as bouquets. It was deemed "proper for the kitchen and pleasure gardens" (Perthensis 1807 16:505). It was an important ingredient of sausages and fish sauces. Sweet Marjoram was especially popular with French cooks who use it extensively to this day.

Marjoram tea was taken as a tonic. Mrs Simcoe took a sweet marjoram tea to relieve a headache during her stay in Canada (Innis 1983:166). A preparation of leaves macerated in olive oil was rubbed on rheumatic joints to lessen pain. Sneezing powders made from the dried herb were used like snuff, part of a fashionable social habit in the eighteenth century. Oil extracted from the plant was used externally on sprains and bruises and for toothache. The oil is very fragrant and has been used in the manufacture of perfumes and soaps.

Summer Savory, *Satureja hortensis* L., was, as its name implies, of garden origin. It was probably first grown in southeast Europe or southwest Asia. Its spicy, thyme-like taste was particularly suitable for seasoning dishes of fish, pork, and pulses – staple foods in the winter months for the early settlers in North America. Summer savory has been called the "bean herb" as it not only added flavour to dishes from dried pulses but its carminative action reduced flatulence. Gerard wrote, "it doth marvellously prevaile against winde: therefore it is with good success boiled and eaten with beanes, peason and other windie pulses" (Gerard 1633/1975:577).

The herb was used by the French for flavouring *tortiere*, a kind of pork pie still popular in French Canada, and in seasoning pork sausages which were often smoked for winter provisions. Summer savory should be added toward the end of cooking, for its oil is volatile, and its effectiveness and flavour are destroyed by heat.

The leaves of summer savory were used as a tea to stimulate the appetite and as a remedy for digestive disorders. The warm infusion was helpful for sore throats. In the days when it was fashionable for ladies to have pale, untanned skin, it was also believed that a solution of savory would help lighten the effect of the sun. Savory's aromatic oil has been used to flavour alcoholic beverages and to add fragrance to pot-pourris. In the garden the light purple flowers are very attractive to bees, and should anyone get stung, the plant provides a handy remedy: the pain can be relieved simply by rubbing the foliage on the skin.

Garden Thyme, and Lemon Thyme, *Thymus vulgaris* L. and *T. v. citriodorus* Hort., have been staples on cooks' shelves for generations, popular as seasoning for meat dishes, poultry stuffings, and seafood chowder. Plants in the *Thymus* genus were originally native to the north temperate climate, from Greenland to the Mediterranean. *Thymus vulgaris*, a perennial subshrub, was used extensively in European kitchens for its rather piquant taste before spices from the Far East became readily available. It then lost its place in the kitchen to the exotic herbs, becoming primarily a medicinal herb. Along with sage, it was one of the first herbs to be brought to North America by early colonists.

Thyme's antiseptic properties were long recognized; it was used by the ancient Greeks to treat lung problems and liver complaints and to "expel worms." During medieval times the plant was put among the household linens to repel insects. Thyme oil, known as thymol, was first isolated in 1725, extracted from the plant by distillation. This powerful anti-bacterial and antiseptic agent has proven very useful in preparations for respiratory and gastrointestinal ailments. Used externally, it has been found effective in treating patients for hookworm. The oil is also used in the commercial manufacture of cough drops and as a fragrance in cosmetic products. In recent years thyme has regained its importance as a popular culinary herb.

Lemon thyme has had few of the medicinal applications of the common thyme. While the lemony smell and taste were used to a limited extent in cooking, it has been more suitably used for its scent in pot-pourris and nosegays. Both thymes were used in pleasure gardens as ground covers; in medieval illustrations they were pictured growing on garden seats as soft, thick, fragrant pillows.

Custead's "Moldavian, or Lemon Balm," *Dracocephalum moldavica* L., is another aromatic plant in the Mint family. Grown as an annual, blooming in mid-summer, it is a handsome addition to the garden with its two-foot spikes of pretty violet-blue which are attractive to bees. It has never been one of the popular medicinal herbs, but the dried leaves have a pleasant lemony mint taste that makes an agreeable tea. In earlier times this balm was widely used for a tea served to patients afflicted with one of the many fevers prevalent in the nineteenth century.

Horehound, *Marrubium vulgare* L., has been grown around the Mediterranean for more than two thousand years. Its beneficial qualities as a medicine made it indispensible in the home garden until quite recent times. The Roman writer Pliny recommended horehound as a laxative and a cure for

Horehound   *Marrubium vulgare* L.

Moldavian Balm

Dracocephalum moldavica L.

Balm   *Melissa officinalis* L.

snakebite. These uses continued throughout the centuries, for Mrs Simcoe remarked on the use of horehound for snakebite in Canada in her diary of the 1790s (Innis 1983:55).

Horehound's reputation for healing also extended to the treatment of coughs, lung ailments, and other respiratory problems. These remedies were made from the bitter leaves, harvested just prior to flowering and dried for use in infusions. The plant's curative properties were found in the oil in the leaves. It had a soothing effect on mucous membranes and acted as an expectorant and a mild diuretic which helped to relieve the symptoms of coughs and colds. Throughout the nineteenth century horehound tea was prescribed for children's colds, generally administered at bedtime to reduce distressful night-time coughing. Even more common were the strong-tasting horehound cough drops, sweetened with sugar or honey to make them more palatable. Dried horehound and horehound drops were among the herbal products prepared by the Shakers in the 1820s and sold throughout Upper Canada.

Modern science has supported the use of horehound in treating symptoms of the common cold. *Marrubin*, a chemical compound isolated from horehound, effectively loosens phlegm in mucous passages. In addition, a horehound infusion can be considered a healthful tonic for its high vitamin C content.

"Balm" was a word used for many plants of a soothing, comforting nature. The most common balm in the early nineteenth century was Lemon Balm, *Melissa officinalis* L., appreciated for its refreshing lemony fragrance and taste. Originally from southern Europe and western Asia, the plant has been in cultivation so long that it has become naturalized in many parts of Europe and North America.

Balm was another of the herbs sold in Upper Canada by the Shakers of New York State in the 1820s. In medicine the leaves were used, fresh or dried, in infusions recommended for treating disorders such as melancholy and anxiety. Lemon balm tea was helpful in reducing fever and relieving the discomforts of menstruation. Its general sedative effect could almost be considered a cure-all, for its effect was to relieve the stress of being ill. Fresh-cut leaves were made into poultices for external use in healing wounds or reducing the pain of insect bites. Modern analysis of the essential oils distilled from the leaves has proven the plant to have anti-bacterial and antihistamine properties.

Lemon balm's citrus-like taste has also made it very useful in the kitchen. Recipes for teas, salads, fish dishes, and sauces have employed its lemony flavour to advantage. The leaves were used as a tasty and attractive garnish. The 1772 edition of the *Frugal Colonial Housewife* has a recipe for "Balm Wine," using lemon balm leaves with sugar, egg whites, and yeast. Because of its fresh scent it was a popular ingredient for the "waters" of the seventeenth century, forerunners of eau-de-cologne. Balm oil is still used in the cosmetic and perfume industries. It is now one of the approved ingredients for use in beverages such as bitters and vermouth, and in the manufacture of frozen desserts, baked goods, and candy (Leung 1980:43).

The *Umbelliferae*, or Carrot family, includes a number of plants cultivated as herbs. Caraway, anise, fennel, dill, coriander, and lovage were among the *Umbelliferae* in the catalogue's herb section. This family has supplied many beneficial herbal remedies. The carminative action of teas made from the seeds of caraway, anise, and fennel had the reputation of being "purifiers," relieving digestive distress, cleansing the breath, and acting as mild diuretics.

The Caraway plant, *Carum carvi* L., has a long history of use, being indigenous to the whole Mediterranean region, the area credited with the beginnings of western civilization. Caraway seeds have been found on archaeological sites in the Near East dating back over five thousand years. Egyptian and biblical references recognized both its culinary and medicinal uses. The Romans are said to have ground the roots for a floury substance used in breads, but it has been the pungently flavoured seeds that have given caraway its importance in cultivation. Romans took the plant with them as their empire spread across Europe. Today it can be found growing wild all over the European continent, a common weed as far north as Scandinavian meadows. Caraway is one of the few herbs in which the essential oils tend to be richer in a cool climate. There is now commercial production of caraway in western and northern Europe, Russia, and Morocco.

Caraway   *Carum carvi* L.

The volatile oil found in the seed, judged "highly aromatic and grateful to the stomach" (M'Mahon 1858/1976:344), aids in the digestive process by stimulating the gastric juices. The distinctive flavour is not appreciated by everyone, but the seeds are used to season baked goods, cheese, cabbage dishes, roasted meats, and alcoholic beverages. In the Mediterranean area they are often served with fruit at the end of a meal as a condiment, or "comfits," as Shakespeare called them.

Caraway's medicinal uses took advantage of its effect on the digestive system in prescriptions for flatulence and colic; it was frequently used as an infusion for colicky infants. The nauseous effect of many purgatives was lessened when flavoured with caraway. Catharine Parr Traill recommended the settlers grow it not only because it was "useful" but because the "seed sells well, besides being valuable as a cattle medicine" (Traill 1855/1969:49). This is a reminder that early settlers were often their own veterinarians.

Anise, *Pimpinella anisum* L., another of the ancient herbs from the Mediterranean area, is unchanged since prehistoric Egyptian times when it was known as both a spice and a medicinal plant. In the Bible it was cited as one of the goods accepted as tithes (Matthew 23:23). In medieval times it was an ingredient in aphrodisiac potions.

Anise was cultivated for the seeds, which have a licorice taste when chewed and a spicy aroma when cooked. They were used in baked goods, especially in sweet cakes. The seed and seed oils were used in many medicinal applications. Lung disorders such as difficult breathing and asthma, even the common cold, were treated with anise preparations. Anise-flavoured candies and drops proved helpful in relieving coughs. Anise-water was used from the earliest times to increase milk production in nursing mothers. Seeds steeped in hot milk were effective in treating insomnia. The most important application was in the treatment of digestive disorders; anise taken in a glass of wine increased the gastric juices, improved the appetite, relieved nausea, and acted as a breath sweetener. It has been shown that the medicinal properties of many carminatives are more effective when the oil in the seeds is extracted by alcohol rather than water.

The plant requires a long dry summer period to reach maturity and set seed. In England "the Anise is a very difficult plant to grow with us ... if there happens but a little wet or cold weather in the Summertime, the Plants will rot off and die away ... but this plant is not worth propagating ... since we can have the Seeds much better and at a cheaper Rate from Malta, than they can be produced here"(Miller 1754/1969:104). Today anise is in short supply and has been replaced on many spice shelves by the Japanese Star Anise, *Illicium anisatum* L., which has a similar taste but is from an entirely different plant.

Anise   *Pimpinella anisum* L.

Sweet Fennel   *Foeniculum vulgare* Mill.

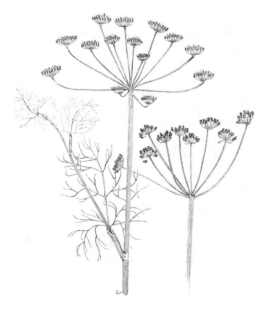

Dill   *Anethum graveolens* L.

Coriander   *Coriandrum sativum* L.

Sweet Fennel, *Foeniculum vulgare* Mill., was one of the medicinal plants the Canadian government encouraged farmers to grow during World War II when imports were cut off. It too was native to the Mediterranean region, where it has been cultivated since ancient times. The Roman writer Pliny had observed that snakes ate the plant when they were in the process of shedding their skins; believing that it improved their eyesight, he recommended it in the treatment of cataracts. A more realistic application of the plant was as a carminative. Physicians used the seeds in the treatment of gastrointestinal ailments such as colic, cramps, and gastroenteritis. The oil in the seeds has now been found to have anti-bacterial properties. Fennel is an ingredient in many Chinese medicinal preparations. In addition to relieving digestive complaints, it is used to tone the spleen and kidneys and improve milk flow in nursing mothers. The fennel flavour is often used to camouflage the strong or nauseous taste of some medications such as laxatives.

In the West fennel is regarded primarily as a culinary herb in salad vinegars, fish sauces, and vegetable dishes. In medieval times, when there were many fasting days in the calendar, the seeds were chewed to relieve hunger pains. They served the same purpose in early America for settlers when they were subjected to lengthy church services on Sunday mornings. Household accounts of the British monarch Edward I recorded as much as eight and a half pounds of fennel seed being required for a month's supply. Just how King Edward used the seed is not known, but fennel tea was known to be popular. It improved indigestion, had a calming effect, and was relaxing taken before sleep, a therapeutic remedy desirable for anyone in a stressful situation.

Today fennel oil is used commercially in the manufacture of soaps and other cosmetic products and is still used to flavour laxatives. It is an approved ingredient for use in baked goods, snack foods, pre-made desserts, candy, and meat products (Leung 1980:169).

Dill, *Anethum graveolens* L., is most familiar today as a flavouring for pickles. It was indigenous to eastern Europe, southern Russia and the Mediterranean region. Many recipes from these areas for breads, vegetables, and fish dishes used it as a seasoning. In England dill was used "to heighten the relish of some vegetable pickles, particularly cucumbers; and occasionally in soups and sauces. The whole herb is also used in medical preparations" (Loudon 1827:666).

Medical preparations containing dill were made primarily from the oil extracted from the plant. One of the many aromatic herbal oils that affected the digestive system, dill oil increased the appetite, aided the digestion, and relieved the stomach and intestines of gas. It has been shown to have anti-bacterial properties and has proven to be a relaxant for muscle tissue (Leung 1980:156). Dill water, an infusion often called "gripe water," or dill oil mixed with sugar and magnesia were used as medicines for children with colic.

Today dill is grown in Europe as a field crop, harvested just before the seeds are fully ripe, with a yield of about five hundred pounds of seed per acre. Dill oil is found as the fragrant component of many commercial preparations such as soaps, detergents, and cosmetic creams.

The recent popularity of foods from Mexico and India have re-introduced the western world to Coriander. *Coriandrum sativum* L. has been cultivated for thousands of years in the East. The seeds have a beneficial effect on the digestive system and were used in medicine to promote the flow of gastric juices; they were of particular use in stimulating the appetite of a convalescent. Their pleasant taste alleviated the bitterness of other medicines. That distinctive taste may be familiar to many as it is used as the centre of "black ball" candy. Coriander has also been used in the flavouring of alcoholic liqueurs.

In medieval Europe coriander was used as a spice in the curing and preservation of meat. The oil from the seed is reported to be anti-bacterial and larvicidal, which would account for its effectiveness as a food preservative. The ground seed is one of the ingredients in curry powders. The oil is used in the manufacture of soaps, creams, lotions, and perfumes. As a medicinal herb "for which there is a considerable demand," it was another of the plants that Canadian farmers were encouraged to grow during World War II.

In Mexico coriander is known as cilantro and in the Far East as Chinese parsley. The taste and smell of the leaves are strong and pungent, quite different from the seed. The fresh foliage of the plant is an indispensible herb in the flavouring of Mexican and Indian dishes.

Lovage, *Levisticum officinale* Koch., had a long history as a culinary plant until the eighteenth century when it was more in favour as a medicinal herb: "It is now almost entirely cast out of the Kitchen-garden and only cultivated for its physical use" (Miller 1754/1969:777). Lovage was grown as early as the eighth century in the physic garden of the Benedictine monastery at St Gall in Switzerland. Such medieval monastery gardens were responsible

for preserving many early species of
medicinal plants as well as perpetuating
the art and science of their uses.

The seeds of the plant were prescribed
to improve digestion and relieve intestinal
gas. The root – thick, aromatic, and mucilaginous – was employed for digestive
ailments as a mild diuretic. As an
emmenagogue, it stimulated the
uterus, relieving menstrual difficulties. (For this reason, lovage should
be avoided by pregnant women.)
Lovage ointments were applied to
skin rashes and bee and wasp stings.
The Shakers of New York State
prepared and sold lovage roots
among their medicinal preparations
and used them for preparing candied
lozenges for breath sweeteners.

Lovage   *Levisticum officinale* Koch.

Lovage leaves and seeds, which have
a taste similar to celery, added flavour to
soups and stews, and the leaves were also cooked as a green vegetable. In
the North American colonies the stalks and roots of the plant were candied
for confections, prepared in the same manner as stems of angelica. The
extracted oil has been used in recent years in prepared foods such as frozen
dessert products and beverages. It has also been employed for its clean,
refreshing scent in soaps, perfumes, and tobacco.

The *Compositae* or Thistle family is the largest family of plants. Included in
Custead's herb list for their domestic uses were "Marygold," tarragon, saffron (safflower) and elecampane.

The "Marygold" offered in the 1827 catalogue was *Calendula officinalis* L.,
now more commonly known as the Pot Marigold or Calendula. (The common garden marigold used today as a bedding plant is a species of *Tagetes*.)
Calendula was well known in the ancient world from Greece to India.
Although it is believed to have originated in the Mediterranean region, it
can no longer be found there in a wild state. The name is from the Latin
kalendae, the first of the month, for in its native habitat it flowers every
month of the year. It also serves as a type of clock, the flowers opening

Marygold   *Calendula officinalis* L.

Tarragon
*Artemisia dracunculus
var. inodora* L.

Saffron (Safflower)   *Carthamus tinctorius* L.

Elecampane   *Inula helenium* L.

in the early daylight hours and closing in the evening. Kitchen gardens throughout Europe grew calendulas for use in both household and medicinal preparations.

Custead listed Marygold under pot and sweet herbs, acknowledging its culinary uses. The flower petals were used fresh in salads, dried for use in soups and stews, steeped in water for a tea, or macerated to colour butter and cheese. The flower heads were used for a golden-yellow textile dye. Medicinal uses included the external healing of lesions, wounds, and ulcers, and relieving the sting of wasp bites. Preparations taken internally were intended to cure digestive and menstrual complaints. The distilled oil was once used in the treatment of eye inflammations. Over the years the calendula provided many benefits to the grower, but today it is grown mostly for its colourful summer blooms, and perhaps to provide a few petals to sprinkle on a salad.

The Toronto Nursery supplied seeds for Tarragon, *Artemisia dracunculus* L., a variety known as the Russian or Siberian Tarragon. The leaves of this plant have been used for seasoning, but the seedlings vary considerably, and the taste of the plants can be somewhat bitter compared to the spicy French Tarragon. However, as the French variety does not readily set seed and can only be increased by vegetative means, early colonists in America may been limited to the Russian variety. It would have been used to flavour vinegars or sauces, but could not have been a satisfactory replacement for French tarragon in fish and meat recipes.

Saffron is included in Custead's list of medicinal herbs, but as the true saffron originates as the stigma of the Saffron Crocus, it is most unlikely that the Toronto Nursery was offering seeds for this bulbous plant. Saffron was, and still is, one of the most expensive spices on the market. Many other plants have been used as substitutes to provide a yellow colour to food preparations, even when they do not provide a similar taste. The most common substitute was the Safflower, or Bastard Saffron, *Carthamus tinctorius* L.

When the Swedish botanist Peter Kalm visited Pennsylvania in the 1740s, he observed that "many of the inhabitants plant saffron, but it is not as good or strong as the French and English variety" (Kalm 1770/ 1966:294). Later, in the nineteenth century, a medical text stated "the excellent saffron collected in Eastern Pennsylvania is known there as American saffron, a term which in other parts of the United States is used to designate the florets of *Carthamus tinctorius*" (Stillé and Maisch 1880:467).

The florets of the safflower were taken from the flower head, shaken free of their pollen, and dried. The yellow colour of the flower turned a brownish-red, with a "rather disagreeable odour and an insipid bitter taste" (ibid.:359). As a medicinal preparation it was administered as an infusion. When it was steeped in boiling water, the resultant beverage caused the patient to perspire, helping to relieve fever. It was also of bene-fit in the treatment of coughs and in reducing the pain of rheumatism. All these symptoms – fever, cough, and pain – were suffered by those who were affected with ague, the malarial illness that plagued early settlers. It might have been thus quite advantageous for the colonial housewife to have a supply of dried safflower on hand.

The plant's name, *Carthamus tinctorius*, refers to its usefulness as a source of dye. Parkinson mentions that it had been called Spanish Saffron as it was exported from Spain "in great quantities to divers countries" to dye silk (Parkinson 1629/1976:329). The Arabs had introduced the safflower to Spain from its origins in Asia Minor in late medieval times. Safflower is cul-tivated in many countries today for medical use and as a dye-stuff, but the principle product is now safflower oil, used extensively for cooking and in the manufacture of paints and varnishes.

Elecampane, *Inula helenium* L., is a tall, coarse plant which bears multi-rayed yellow flowers. Indigenous to Europe and Asia, it has been grown for medicinal purposes for over two thousand years. Its healing properties were found in its roots, dug when the plant was about two years old, before they became too woody, and peeled, dried, and powdered. It was prescribed for lung disorders, administered in a water solution for asthma, coughs, and other breathing difficulties. The bitter-tasting roots were also made into candied lozenges for coughs. Elecampane was one of the ingredients of a medieval wine taken for digestive problems, and used, with *Artemisia absin-thium*, in the liqueur absinthe. It was also highly regarded as a vermifuge, or worm medicine. Stomach ulcers were treated with soothing elecampane palliatives. The plant was commonly known as Scabwort, as one of the most popular preparations was an ointment used externally to relieve itching.

In the eighteenth and early nineteenth centuries large quantities of ele-campane were imported to America as a veterinary medicine. It went under the name Horseheal, used in formulas with other herbs, oils, and soap for "Cordial Pectoral Balls" and "Expectorant Balls." These were administered to horses to reduce the inflammation of pleurisy or asthmatic coughing (Perthensis 1807: 9:394). An elecampane ointment was also one of the most successful ways to heal skin sores on horses. In the early nineteenth century, when horses were essential for transportation and the only veterinary assistance available was from the nearest farrier, elecampane was a useful medication to have on hand. Modern scientific investigation of the plant's chemical properties has shown that the oil contained in the root is antiseptic, with effective anti-bacterial and anti-fungal action.

An early-nineteenth century reference gave instructions for a dye obtained from elecampane: macerated with urine, ashes, and whortleberries, it made a blue dye used for woollens (Perthensis 1807 12:272). Elecampane was certainly worthy of a place in the kitchen gardens of early Upper Canada.

Under the heading "Pot and Sweet Herbs," the Toronto Nursery catalogue listed "Nutmeg, good substitute for spice." This was the Nutmeg Flower, or Black Cumin, grown for its peppery-tasting seed. *Nigella sativa* L., a member of the *Ranunculaceae*, was cultivated extensively by early settlers as a substitute for either pepper or nutmeg, as these spices were imported from the Far East and quite costly.

The seeds of *Nigella sativa* were known in French cuisine as "quatre epices," and in kitchens of the Far East they were one of the ingredients in curry powders. In addition to their use as a seasoning, they were served as a condiment following the meal. Like anise, the seeds act as a carminative and a mild diuretic to settle the digestive system.

Nigella sativa closely resembles its relative *Nigella damascena* L., a garden annual popularly called Love-in-a-Mist. But instead of the many pretty blues or pure white petals of the garden flower, the flowers of Nutmeg have five dull greenish-white petals. Each of the fruit has five sections containing many seeds. These are dull black on the outside, white inside, giving off a camphorous odour when bruised. The strong odour acts as a moth and insect repellant, useful in protecting clothing and household linens in storage. The strongly scented oil contained in the seeds has been used in vaporous inhalations to relieve head colds.

The Marsh Mallow headed the list of medicinal herbs. *Althaea officinalis* L., of the *Malvaceae* family, had been brought to America by the earliest European immigrants. Native to southern Europe and the Mediterranean area, it was cultivated for its medicinal properties since the time of the Egyptian Pharaohs. The roots of this plant have a mucilaginous content which has been used for many purposes, especially as a medication in soothing mucous membranes in the throat and digestive system. The root was peeled and boiled with honey to treat sore throats, bronchitis, asthma, and dysentery.

Marsh Mallow   *Althaea officinalis* L.

Nutmeg   *Nigella sativa* L.

White Officinal Poppy

Papaver somniferum L.

Dyer's Woad   *Isatis tinctorum* L.

It also acted well for external uses, pulverized and applied as a compress or made into an ointment for bruises, sprains, inflammations, abrasions, skin eruptions, chapped skin, and chilblains. While the root was the principal ingredient of most medications, the flowers and the leaves were also used in syrups and teas for treating coughs.

Early nineteenth-century books of household instruction included directions for some rather ingenious uses of the marsh mallow roots. Toothbrushes were made from short lengths pounded to fan out the fibres. Pieces of the root were chewed to calm an unsettled stomach, or given to teething babies for the comforting effect of the juices released as the root softened.

Roots of two-year-old plants were gathered in the fall, when the mucilaginous content was at its greatest, and dried thoroughly, peeled, and stored. Although the marshmallow candy we know today is a mixture of gelatin and sugar, the original sweet marshmallow confection was made with the gelatinous roots of this plant. But in spite of its many uses and widespread cultivation, the marsh mallow has seldom been grown as a commercial crop. It was rather garden-grown in small quantities or picked from the wild: "Every woman wife had it in her physic garden for poulticing, ointments and sweetmeats" (Grigson 1975:110).

During World War II the Canadian government published a pamphlet encouraging farmers to consider growing marsh mallow, as it was in considerable demand and "might succeed in areas of Canada where the winter is not too severe." It suggested that eight hundred to one thousand pounds of dry root could be obtained per acre (Canada Dept. of Agriculture 1940:12). However, there is no evidence that Canadian farmers rose to the challenge. There is still limited demand for the root, as it has been approved for use in various food products such as frozen dairy foods, baked goods, and packaged desserts.

Dyer's Woad, *Isatis tinctorum* L., is a member of the *Cruciferae*, or Mustard or Cabbage family. Woad provided the most common blue dye for woollens until indigo was introduced to Europe from India in the 1700s (Buchanan 1987:112). Significant quantities of indigo were imported into Upper Canada from Asia through the United States in the 1820s, at a cost of twelve shillings per pound, with an added duty of 15 per cent. Indigo was grown as a commercial crop for a short time in the southern United States, but production was abandoned before 1800 as it was cheaper to import it from Asian countries than to produce it in America. The dye obtained from woad is a dull blue compared to indigo, but it gives a more permanent colour. Woad continued to be used in combination with indigo for reasons of economy. Early colonial families in Upper Canada made their own woollen cloth, an important home industry. To have a home-grown source for a dye, especially a popular blue colour, would have been an advantage.

The production of dye from woad is a long and somewhat odoriferous project. As soon as the plant came into flower, the leaves were picked and dried in the sun. A good crop would produce two or three pickings in one season, an acre of woad producing about one and a half tons. The dried leaves were pounded into a pulpy mass and left to ferment, exposed to the air but protected from rain – a process that took about two weeks. After fermentation was complete and the pulpy mass covered with a crust, the woad was broken up and moistened, usually with lime water. Balls of the wet mass were formed once again and left to ferment a second time. When these had dried, the woad was ready for use. The parts of the plant not used for dye were often burned, producing an ash that was a source of lye and potash, two other ingredients used in dye formulas. Today woad is still used by some home weavers but has been replaced in the manufacturing industry by aniline dyes first derived from coal tar by German chemists in the 1830s.

Woad has had limited use as a medicinal plant, mainly in compresses applied to the area of the spleen or in ointments to reduce inflammation (Grieve 1931/1978:853).

Custead's White or Officinale Poppy was *Papaver somniferum* L., of the *Papaveraceae*. Also known as the Opium Poppy, it has been cultivated from prehistoric times in southern Europe and the Orient for its edible seeds, oil, and the drug opium. Large quantities of seed have been found on prehistoric European archaeological sites, leading to the premise that communities may have stored poppy seed in order to survive prolonged sieges. The seeds have no narcotic content. They have been used to flavour baked goods and are still an important ingredient in many eastern European foods. The oil extracted from the seed has been used for cooking and lighting. Today, it is the source of lecithin used in food products and in the commercial production of paints and varnishes.

Because of the abundance of its seed, the opium poppy was represented in prehistoric Mediterranean art as a symbol of fertility. The image of the poppy seed pod was also used by ancient civilizations to represent sleep or death, as ingestion of the milky juices could cause unconsciousness, at times with fatal consequences.

Drugs obtained from the opium poppy have made it one of the most important of all medicinal plants. Analysis has shown the milky juice of the unripe seed pod to contain twenty alkaloids. The most important of these is morphine, the greatest of all painkillers, first isolated in 1816. Before the breakdown of its constituents, the whole raw seed pod was used as a medication, or the the juices from the pod were dried as opium. The effective drug content depended to a great extent on the growing conditions, which varied considerably from place to place. The finest opium for medicinal purposes today is obtained from poppies grown in India. Opium has been one of the most useful drugs ever known, but its narcotic content also led to mind-destroying addiction when used indiscriminately.

In the early nineteenth century the effects of opium were well known, and it was one of the most-used medicinal remedies. Powdered opium in a wine solution, called laudanum, was prescribed by physicians for almost any serious illness. Patent medicines, containing opium in combination with other herbal substances, were popular for treating coughs, diarrhoea, asthma, fevers, and pain. The raw seed pods were given to children to chew on as pacifiers and during teething, or boiled in a sugar solution to make a cough syrup. The juice pressed from pods was used in compresses placed on the head or neck to induce sleep or relieve a fever.

Palma Christi was the common nineteenth century name for the Castor Oil Plant. *Ricinus communis* L., of the *Euphorbiaceae*, is a tropical plant from Africa with a long history of supplying an oil used as a laxative: no other purgative has had such continued and widespread use. The oil is extracted from the seed, which looks like a shiny, mottled, inflated bean. Seeds have been found in Egyptian tombs, dating back over four thousand years (Weiss 1983:31).

In its native habitat the castor plant is a perennial, growing to tree-like proportions. In the north temperate climate it can be grown as an annual, easily reaching a height of eight or ten feet in one season. The seed contains *ricin*, a highly poisonous blood coagulant, in such concentration that one seed can be fatal to a child. In some parts of Africa the seeds were employed as an infanticide. A 1978 murder of a Bulgarian in London, England, was accomplished by inserting a pellet of ricin into the victim's leg by a specially designed umbrella (Weiss 1983:44). Households were rid of cockroaches by putting out leftover food contaminated with crushed castor beans. But the oil of the seed is non-toxic; all the poisonous alkaloids remain in the pomace after the oil has been expressed. The finest quality of oil is cold-pressed from the seed. Castor oil is remarkably stable, does not turn rancid, and remains viscous at both high and low temperatures.

The medical uses of the plant were not limited to its laxative effect. Poultices of the leaves were applied to boils and abscesses to relieve pressure and pain. In its native tropics, the whole plant was employed for a

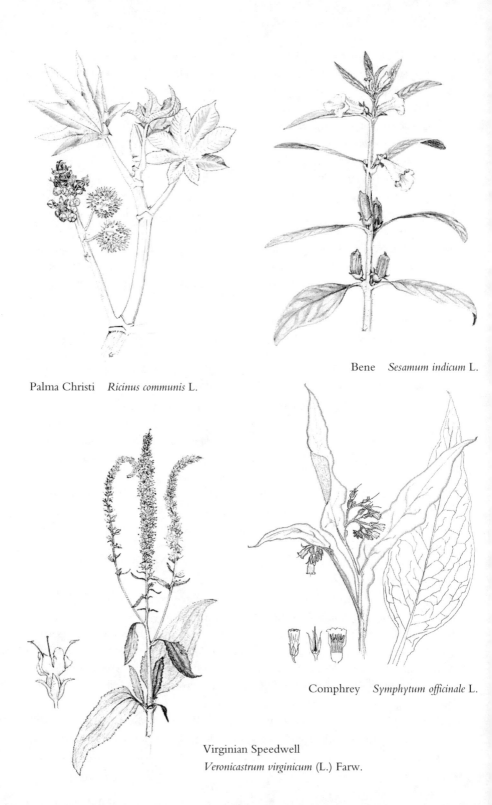

Bene   *Sesamum indicum* L.

Palma Christi   *Ricinus communis* L.

Comphrey   *Symphytum officinale* L.

Virginian Speedwell
Veronicastrum virginicum (L.) Farw.

number of conditions. A leaf worn under a hat was believed to cure fevers and headache. An oiled leaf was applied to arthritic joints and inflamed muscles. Preparations of the root were used to lessen rheumatic pain.

All parts of the plant contain an allergin, which causes severe reaction in some individuals. Factory workers in castor oil processing plants have suffered from a number of disorders including lung, skin, and digestive ailments (Morton 1977:193).

Modern uses for castor oil are many and varied. It has been approved for use in commercially prepared foods. It is used as a base for cosmetic products, particularly lipsticks and soaps. It is also an ingredient for contraceptive preparations. Castor oil does not solidify in extreme cold, nor does intense heat affect its liquid properties; these qualities have made it suitable for industrial uses in hydraulic fluids, as a lubricant for heavy machinery, engines, and aircraft, and as tung oil in the manufacture of wood finishes, paints, and enamels.

Bene, another plant listed in the catalogue with a commercially viable oil was *Sesamum indicum* L., of the *Pedaliaceae*. Commonly called sesame in modern usage, bene (or "Benny") was believed to have been brought to America by slaves from Africa. Throughout its long history of cultivation, dating back to ancient Egypt, it was primarily grown as a nutritious grain product. The seeds contain vitamin A, thiamin, riboflavin, niacin, and a trace of ascorbic acid (Weiss 1983:293). They were used whole, ground into a paste known as tahini, or pressed to extract the oil. This was used for cooking purposes in the same way as olive oil but tends to be less digestible and many find its distinctive taste less palatable. It is widely used today for commercially prepared foods and margarine.

Sesame oil was used as a laxative and an aid to difficult menstruation. The leaves were also credited with healing properties and used as poultices on open wounds. A beverage, made by crushing the leaves in cold water to maximize the mucilaginous content, was prescribed in the treatment of dysentery and in cases of cholera in infants.

The sesame plant needs a warm climate and a long growing period of up to 110 days to set its seed. It has been grown in North America as far north as Philadelphia, but commercial production has never been successful. While the Toronto Nursery offered seed for this plant, Custead may not have been fully aware of its limitations in the Canadian climate.

Virginian Speedwell, or Culver's Root, was indigenous to eastern North America, a member of the *Scrophulariaceae* or Snapdragon family. *Veronicastrum virginicum* (L.) Farw. was brought to the attention of early settlers by the Senecas, who used it medicinally and for ritual purification. Taken to Europe early in the eighteenth century, it was prescribed by physicians as a laxative and an emetic. The root, a blackish rhizome which has no odour but a very bitter taste, was boiled in milk and administered to the patient as a beverage. The plant was also believed to be effective in treating liver disorders and was recommended as "an excellent remedy for the Gout and all Rheumatic Disorders. The Method is, to make a Tea of the dried herb [to be] drunk every morning" (Miller 1754/1969:1441). It was listed in pharmacopoeias until the late nineteenth century when it was regarded as being too violent in its action to be generally recommended. Serious side-effects included severe gastrointestinal irritation.

The common names of Comfrey, *Symphytum officinale* L., of the *Boraginaceae*, quite literally refer to its medicinal uses. Known as Boneset, Bruisewort, Knitbone or simply Healing Herb, it healed broken bones, swellings, and bruises. It had been cultivated in herb or physic gardens since antiquity. Another of its common names, Sarcen's Root, suggests that it may have been taken to Europe from the Mediterranean by Crusaders who had seen it in use in their eastern hospitals. It can still be found growing wild around medieval monasteries and towns on pilgrimage routes in Europe where travellers may have stopped for medical attention. Comfrey has been recommended as a forage crop, as the leaves contain more vegetable protein than any other herbaceous plant. It is said that it grows wild in Europe in places where travelling gypsies stopped to water their horses. Wherever it has been grown, even in America, it eventually becomes a wild plant as its deep rooting habit is persistent and the plant is difficult to eradicate.

Comfrey root is very mucilaginous, which partly accounts for its use in medicine. One of its active chemicals is allantoin, which has been found to aid in cell reproduction and to have anti-inflammatory properties. The roots were dug in late fall or early spring, when the chemical content was most active, ground to a slimy pulp, and strained through a cloth. The resulting fluid was used to wash wounds. In cases of bone fracture, a pulpy mass of the root was pressed around the limb after it had been straightened against a splint, and allowed to dry as a cast. As the pulp does not shrink or warp in drying, or produce heat upon setting as plaster does, it has sometimes been used in modern surgery after delicate bone operations.

Although the leaves and the root have been used in the past for human consumption, there are now grave doubts about these practices. Internal use is discouraged as comfrey contains alkaloids that may be carcinogenic and particularly toxic to the liver (Foster and Duke 1990:180). Several countries, including Canada, have prohibited the use of comfrey in all medicinal preparations for internal usage.

The seed list of herbs offered by the Toronto Nursery could have supplied gardens in Upper Canada with a range and variety of plants to meet many household needs. Two or three plants of each would be more than enough to supply a family's requirements. Produced in greater quantities, they could be sold or bartered for other goods. Growing herbs domestically also reduced the need for expensive imports in the sparsely settled Upper Canada of the 1820s. But usefulness aside, the pleasurable scents and tastes of these herbs were often sufficient reasons for including them in the garden.

12

Seeds for Annual Flowers

Custead's seeds for annual flowers included thirty-two species representing sixteen plant families. The selections included colourful ornamentals, plants with economic potential, and others that were simply "curious" plants. There were tall and short plants and a number of pretty climbers, many with attractive flowers for cutting blooms or dried winter bouquets. Nearly all the annual plants had a lengthy history of cultivation in English gardens. About one-third were native to Europe, many originating in the Mediterranean region. One species was South African; the remainder were introductions from Asia and the Americas. The catalogue gave no indication of the quantities of seed available for any species nor were any prices quoted. Custead could supply his customers with seed for most of the plants that were available and popular in the more established gardens south of the border. Many of the same seed selections were offered in catalogues from seedsmen in the United States in the 1820s and 1830s.

An annual is defined as a plant that completes its life cycle, from germination through growth and flowering to seed production, in a single season. Exotic plants from tropical or semi-tropical areas, which may have been perennials in their native habitat, were usually unable to tolerate the winters of the north temperate climate. These were treated as tender annuals in Britain, and certainly in North America.

Custead offered plants that had the potential of becoming crops of economic value, as has already been noted under other categories in the catalogue. A few of these had a history of cultivation as forage crops or sources of medicinal drugs in their countries of origin. By supplying seeds for plants such as tobacco and Sweet Scented Trefoil, the nursery may have attempted to encourage farmers in Upper Canada to grow these as a measure of crop diversification.

Each of the sixteen plant families represented had its distinctive type of growth. The most numerous species were in the Pea family, *Leguminosae*: Sweet Peas, Scarlet Flowering Bean, Purple Hyacinth Bean, Sensitive Plant, Caterpillars, Snails, and Sweet Scented Trefoil. These plants have papilionaceous blooms bearing a standard, wing, and keel. The fruit is a legume developed from a single pistil. The leaves are alternate, usually compound with an appendage at the base of each leaf stem. Many plants in this family are grown as food or forage crops.

Sweet Peas, *Lathyrus odorata* L., are probably associated with old-fashioned gardens more than any other flower. Yet compared to many other plants grown in early nineteenth-century gardens, they were relative newcomers. Seeds of the original wild plants were first sent to England from Sicily in 1699. The Sweet Pea's original habitat was the highland pasture area of the Sicilian mountains, in a cool, rich soil with good air circulation. Little was heard of this plant until twenty years later, after the English amateur gardener and physician Dr Uvedale had grown it successfully. The flowers were one of the most sweetly scented blossoms known, and the Sweet Pea rapidly gained favour for this characteristic alone, for it was available only in a dull red or purple colour. By 1800, the colour range had been extended to five colours, including two shades of red, pink or rose, purple, and white. The blooms were prized as cut flowers for their scent and long-lasting quality.

The Sweet Pea is a vining plant, with winged stems and leaf stalks. The flowers are borne on a stalk rising from the leaf axil, with one to three blooms on each stalk. The plant adheres to its support by means of tendrils that extend from the ends of the leaf stalks.

Interest in this plant continued to increase during the nineteenth century, and by 1850 it had become one of the most developed of all annual flowers. Up to two hundred varieties were then available, and not only had the colour range increased but so had the size of the blooms. In some varieties the rich perfume had been sacrificed for larger flowers. As the Sweet Pea was so easily cross-bred, it was one of the subjects chosen by Father George Mendel in his famous genetic experiments, published in 1865.

In the nineteenth-century garden Sweet Peas were usually grown separately. A common procedure was to place several plants in a circle around a central stake five or six feet high, with strings attached to the top of the stake for the plants to climb. They were also attractively grown along fences, or in rows where dead branches had been placed for the vines to clamber over (Breck 1866:256).

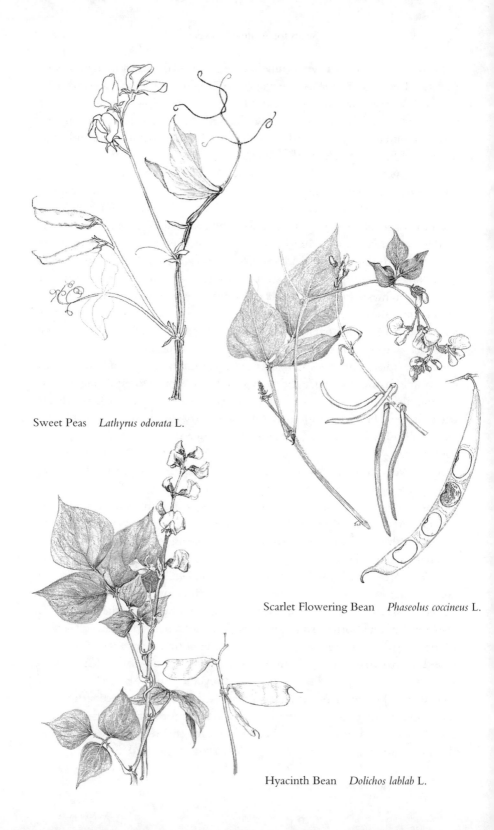

Sweet Peas   *Lathyrus odorata* L.

Scarlet Flowering Bean   *Phaseolus coccineus* L.

Hyacinth Bean   *Dolichos lablab* L.

Seeds for the original species are no longer available, and many modern varieties have lost the exquisite fragrance that brought the Sweet Pea its fame. However, modern gardeners who wish to develop fragrant forms of the plant can do so by collecting their own seed over several seasons. All poorly scented plants must be dead-headed before seeding, and only the most desirable plants allowed to seed.

The Scarlet Flowering Bean, *Phaseolus coccineus* L., came from tropical Central and South America, where it grew as a perennial vine. It may have been the original bean cultivated by the Aztecs, the antecedent of the many garden vegetables in this genus. Its handsome red flowers first attracted the eye of Europeans, who grew it initially as an ornamental. The cut flowers were long-lasting when made into the nosegays and garlands so popular in the early eighteenth century. The vine was less susceptible to air pollution than many other garden plants, and it was recommended to urban gardeners as "it will thrive very well in the City, the Smoke of Sea-coal being less injurious to this Plant than most others" (Miller 1754/1969:1062).

Philip Miller, director and gardener of the Chelsea Physic Garden, was one of the first to recognize the bean's food value in the middle eighteenth century. In the Toronto Nursery catalogue the seeds were offered under both "Annual Flowers" and "Esculent Vegetables," demonstrating its acceptance in both the ornamental and kitchen gardens by the early nineteenth century. Mrs Jameson noticed the vine growing in a Canadian garden when she watched hummingbirds, "two lovely gem-like creatures disporting among the blossoms of the scarlet bean" (Jameson 1838/1972:284).

The rapid, twining growth of the scarlet bean allowed it to run freely in a very short time over whatever support was available. It was used for shade on garden houses and pergolas in large gardens and for screening verandas of smaller domiciles. It climbed over fences, trellises, rock piles, and other unsightly debris on many homesteads where it appeared as a tapestry in red and green. In the North the vine was grown as an annual, sown when the earth was warm, well after the last frost. A white form was available by the mid-nineteenth century and gardeners were told a "very pleasing" effect could be had by planting red and white varieties together. The white form is seldom grown today – it lacks the character of the original red species.

The Purple Hyacinth Bean, *Dolichos lablab* L., is not often seen in gardens today and is seldom mentioned in gardening books or seed catalogues. It was popular in the early nineteenth century as a vigourous vine used to cover bowers, garden seats, and verandah. M'Mahon suggested they be grown "to cover arbours ... or they may be set in neat patches and neat poles placed for them to climb on" (M'Mahon 1858/1976:412).

The plant is perennial in its native tropical environment, where the twining stems will climb to the tops of very tall trees, but it is very tender and will not withstand frost. In temperate climates it can successfully be grown as an annual, for its habit is sufficiently vigorous to produce a vine from twenty to thirty feet long in one season. The botanical name is taken from the Greek for "long," aptly describing its rapid growth. In the Victorian period the Hyacinth Bean was often treated as a stove plant or house plant.

The vine's ornamental value was found in the trifoliate leaves with their deep red veins and stalks and the racemes of violet-purple flowers. The sweet-smelling blooms resemble a miniature wisteria in early summer, followed by dark purple pods containing bean-like seeds.

In the nineteenth century European gardeners believed this plant came from Egypt, where it was cultivated as a crop for the table. The pods were eaten fresh or cooked, and the beans were dried for later use. In tropical countries it was grown as a coarse feed for cattle and horses.

The Sensitive Plant, *Mimosa pudica* L., was introduced to Europe early in the seventeenth century from Brazil where it is a perennial sub-shrub. The leaves respond to any contact, shock, or diminished light condition, giving the impression that the plant is "sensitive." At the slightest touch the compound leaves fold over a central axis and the leaf stalk droops, the whole plant appearing as though it has withdrawn, or is "in a state of repose." This action evolved as a survival adaptation to discourage foraging animals, but in the past other hypotheses were proposed to explain the plant's puzzling behaviour. An Italian philosopher was said to have "flung himself into the sea, because he could not comprehend ... the mysterious nature of this plant." Some thought it had "nerves," or that it was "irritable." The phenomenon of the plant's reaction to touch and light provided another amusing curiosity for plant collectors. The Boston seedsman Breck wrote of growing a number of Sensitive Plants in a frame, four by ten feet, until they filled the space: "It was a source of great amusement to myself and visitors to irritate this mass of plants, which was easily done, by giving the frame a gentle kick. The effect would be to cause every plant to drop its foot-stalks and close its leaves" (Breck 1866:286).

The French Jesuit d'Incarville, an early plant collector, sent many specimens back to Paris from his missions abroad. When in China he won access to the imperial gardens by presenting the emperor with two plants

Caterpillar's Flower   *Scorpiurus vermiculata* L.

Sensitive Plant   *Mimosa pudica* L.

Snail Flower   *Medicago scutellata* (L.) Mill.

Sweet Scented Trefoil
Melilotus alba Desv.

of *Mimosa pudica* grown from seeds sent to him in 1753. The emperor was delighted and "laughed heartily" (Healey 1975:90). No doubt this gift aided d'Incarville in the acquisition of Chinese plants which he sent to Europe. But a regrettable footnote must be added to this story: the Sensitive Plant became such a popular ornamental in the Far East that it now has the reputation of being one of the world's worst weeds, interfering with the growing of twenty-two different crops in no less than thirty-three countries.

"Caterpillar's Flower" and the Snail Flower, *Scorpiurus vermiculata* L. and *Medicago scutellata* (L.) Mill., were very popular plants in the eighteenth and nineteenth centuries. They were "preserved in several curious gardens, for their oddness more than for any great beauty" (Miller 1754/1969:1265). Plants with unusual characteristics piqued gardeners' interest in the strangeness of natural forms. In this case, the seed pods of the Caterpillars and the twisted flower shape of the Snails were responsible for the common names.

Caterpillars were native to the area surrounding the Mediterranean and were cultivated in European gardens by the early seventeenth century. The Latin name *scorpiurus* translates to "scorpion tail," referring to the curved seed pods. The pea-like flowers are yellow, appearing singly on long stems from the leaf axils. The Caterpillar plant was grown not only so that its unusual seed pods could be observed but to entertain those who had a sense of humour and liked to tease. One use of the pods was carefully stated by the seedsman Joseph Breck, who wrote "the pods of these are sometimes placed in dishes of salad to cause surprise to those who are unacquainted with them" (Breck 1866:283). Although this was written in the nineteenth century, it was reminiscent of garden pranks played in earlier centuries when estate gardeners indulged in practical jokes such as fountains that showered unsuspecting garden guests. The practice of putting the seed pods in salad continued into the twentieth century, although the pods are not edible (Bailey 1902:259). Caterpillars are not particularly decorative plants, as their loose growing habit is not suitable for the flower border. However, if the plant has an appeal, surely a corner could be found to try this old-fashioned garden joke.

The Snail Flower, *Medicago scutellata*, is a rapidly growing annual vine, with a twining habit that permits it to climb on any open support. A tropical plant with origins in eastern Asia, it was introduced to European gardens before the end of the seventeenth century. The spirally twisted blooms are similar in appearance to the curves of a snail shell. They are produced on racemes which are longer than the leaves, making the plant quite showy in the late summer. The flowers are variegated purple and yellow, and very fragrant.

Its tropical origins limited the Snail Flower to growing in a hothouse for the best bloom. When treated as a tender annual, the season in the North was too short for the plant to mature. Miller noted that it was grown outdoors in Portugal, where it covered "Arbours and Seats in Gardens, greatly esteemed for its beautiful sweet-smelling Flowers" (Miller 1754/1969:1265). It is rarely seen in North America except in the Mediterranean-like climate of California, where it adapted so readily that it became a troublesome weed, climbing over shrubs and trees, often strangling their growth in the process.

Seed for Sweet Scented Trefoil, *Melilotus alba* Desv., or *M. officinalis* L., was offered under "Annual Flower Seed" in the nursery catalogue. This plant was seldom found in flower gardens even in 1827. It had been grown principally as a forage crop since the early sixteenth century in Europe but was also a very old medicinal herb. Wherever it was grown it escaped cultivation to become a naturalized wildflower. Gerard declared it was a weed found widespread over pasture land in the late sixteenth century. Today it grows in abundance in America, in ditches, along railway tracks, and in any open space, no matter how inhospitable the site may appear.

The pea-like flowers of the trefoil are small, white in *M. alba* and yellow in *M. officinalis*. They are very attractive to bees and butterflies. While it is too weedy for garden borders, the plant can be recommended as green manure for soil improvement.

Trefoil has a pleasant scent, rather like that of new-mown hay. The dried plant was used in herb pillows for its soothing fragrance and set among clothing to repel moths. Since the time of the ancient Romans, it was used in poultices for wounds and swellings. These applications were called "Melilot Plaisters" in the eighteenth century. Recent isolation of plant chemicals trefoil have confirmed its antibiotic properties. The flowers and seed were used for a time in the making of beer, and as a flavouring for cheese, tobacco, and snuff. The scent of the plant is due to the chemical *coumarin*.

During the winter of 1921–22 in Canada, after a season that saw corn crops devastated by corn-borer, many farmers used trefoil, or Sweet Clover, as silage. Veterinarians began reporting an epidemic of cattle deaths due to internal haemorrhaging. The cause was determined to be the highly toxic fermented trefoil (Schwabe 1978:194). It was not until 1941 that the substance responsible for the uncontrollable bleeding was isolated: it was *dicoumerol*, a product of fermented coumarin. This powerful poison is now used in the control of vermin infestations under the trade name Warfarin. Further studies of this plant chemical have led to a better understanding of the processes involved in blood clotting. The research developed the first successful anticoagulant used to control thrombosis and other related heart and blood-circulation conditions in humans.

Three of the annual plants for which seed was offered were in the Buttercup family, *Ranunculaceae*. These were Flos Adonis, Lark's Spur, and Love-in-a-Mist. In these plants the calyx is often coloured like a corolla, and there are many stamens. The plants contain a bitter, colourless juice.

Flos Adonis, *Adonis annua* L., indigenous to Europe and Asia Minor, was one of the European wildflowers to be taken into gardens as Gerard did in the late fifteenth century. He found it growing "in the West parts of England among their corne ... from thence I brought the seede, and have sowne it in my garden for the beautie of the floures sake" (Gerard 1633/ 1975:386). This practice actually extended its range, as the garden flowers escaped back into the wild. The flowers stand erect above the foliage and have deep red petals with bases of either yellow or an even deeper red, numbering from five to fifteen in each bloom. The leaves are delicately divided, similar in appearance to fennel or chamomile. The red flower associated the plant with blood and death. The ancient Greeks named it for the god Adonis who was changed into a flower after his death. The dual colour of the bloom was seen to resemble the eye of a pheasant, accounting for another common name, Pheasant's Eye.

The Adonis does not tolerate hard frosts. In Europe the seed is sown in the autumn, and the plant blooms early the following spring. As this procedure is not possible in northeastern North America the plant cannot be enjoyed as an early spring flower. However, it can be raised as a tender annual, the seedlings put out after the last frost to bloom late in the summer. Unfortunately, using this method the season is seldom long enough for the plant to set seed.

Adonis was listed in old pharmacopoeias as a diuretic to be used in the treatment of heart problems, but it is no longer considered a medicinal plant. The Buttercup family contains extremely acrid juices that cause pain and burning if taken internally. They act upon the body in the same complex way as digitalis and can cause serious reactions in the central nervous system.

Flos Adones   *Adonis annua* L.

Lark's Spur
Consolida ambigua (L.) P.W. Ball & Heyw.

Love in a Mist   *Nigella damascena* L.

The large purple "Lark's Spur" listed in the catalogue may have been any one of three species. The annual larkspurs have a longer garden tradition than the tall perennial species of Delphinium found in our gardens today. The common larkspurs of the early nineteenth century were known as annual delphiniums (*Delphinium ajacis* L. and *D. ambigua* L.) but are now classified under the genus *Consolida*. Both species were indigenous to Europe. As they cross-pollinate readily, many garden hybrids occurred spontaneously. There were many shades of colours, rosy pinks and white, but it was the blue flowers that were greatly appreciated, as the larkspurs had some of the clearest and brightest blues in the garden. Seldom were any of the variations called purple, but violet or lilac-blue were cited in early nineteenth-century catalogues.

President Jefferson had larkspur in his garden, and M'Mahon included it in his garden calender of 1806. As neither of these references indicated the particular species involved, it might be assumed that these were garden varieties. In contemporary American seed catalogues larkspurs were listed as *Delphinium consolida*, but several firms also carried a Bee Larkspur, *Delphinium exaltatum* Ait., a plant native to North America. This was a tall species that bore many-flowered racemes with blooms of a purplish-blue colour. As Custead was offering seeds for a "large purple Lark's Spur," it might well have been this lesser-known plant rather than the more common garden larkspur. The Bee Larkspur was identified in 1758 by William Aiton, an English botanist at the Royal Botanic Gardens at Kew.

Larkspur flowers were valued as cut blooms, either fresh or carefully dried. The whole plant has been used to produce a green dye for textiles. The flowers, macerated and mixed with alum, made a blue ink.

As a member of the Buttercup family, the larkspur contains toxic alkaloids, which had some medicinal applications in the past. The flowers and the seeds were both listed in pharmacopoeias until the mid-nineteenth century when they were no longer recommended for internal use as their purgative action was too violent. The seeds are the most poisonous part of the plant. An ointment, made of ground seed from the larkspur and its wild relative, "stavesacre," *D. staphisagria* L., was used in folk medicine to rid the body of lice and other parasites. This association gave the plant another common name, Lousewort, the louse herb. The ointment was also used to relieve the pain of neuralgia.

Love-in-a-Mist, *Nigella damascena* L., has been appreciated by gardeners for hundreds of years for its pretty, delicate blooms uniquely enclosed in feathery bracts. The botanical name, *Nigella*, is from the Latin for "black," referring to the plant's small black seeds. There are several curious common names for *Nigella* – Love-in-a-Mist, Devil-in-the-Bush, and Fennel Flower – which attempted to describe the many thin bracts and dissected leaves that surround and almost conceal the flower and seed pod. In 1722, the British gardener Fairfield wrote that it was "rather an odd Plant, than beautiful for its Flowers; for the Blossom is of a very pale blue Colour and is encompass'd with shagged Leaves, as if it was ty'd up in a Bunch of Fewel [fennel]" (Dutton 1979:125).

Nigella was a native of the Mediterranean region, including Asia Minor, and was mentioned in early Greek and Roman botanical treatises. Gerard had it in his garden in 1596; Parkinson included it in his work of 1629; and by 1700 it was being grown in gardens in America. The flowers were generally described as light blue, but in 1866 Breck had both blue and white varieties in his Boston seed house (Breck 1866:298).

The flower has five petals and five petal-like sepals set in lacy bracts. The flower matures to an inflated upright capsule with "several cells, which are furnished with Horns on the Top," containing numerous small seeds (Miller 1754/1969:954). The seed capsules were often dried for use in winter floral arrangements. The aromatic black seeds of *N. damascena*, like those of its near relative, the herb *N. sativa*, were used in cooking as a seasoning. At times when black pepper imported from the Far East became excessively expensive, *Nigella* seeds were used to adulterate the more valuable spice.

Two, or possibly three, of Custead's annuals were members of *Convolvulaceae*, a family that contains nine genera, including the genus *Convolvulus* and the genus *Ipomoea*. Custead's *Convolvulus major* is now classified *Ipomoea purpurea* (L.) Roth and the *Convolvulus minor* as *Convolvulus tricolor* L. The Cyprus [Cypress] Vine may have been the *Ipomoea quamoclit* L.

The first two species named were familiar plants in early nineteenth-century American gardens. The *Convolvulus minor* was native to southern Europe, the *Convolvulus major* to tropical America. Both have pointed, heart-shaped leaves. The flower stalks emerge from the leaf axils, three or four blooms on each stalk. They

Convolvulus major
Ipomoea purpurea (L.) Roth.

bloom prolifically, remaining in flower throughout the summer months. Seeds for the original dark-purple *Ipomoea purpurea* are now difficult to find, but many colourful varieties have been developed from this species.

In the *Convolvulus* genus the plants are mostly twining vines with stems twelve to twenty feet in length. The corollas of the flowers are funnel-form to bell-shaped. However, the genus is very confusing, not only within itself but because the *Convolvulus* and *Ipomoea* genera have been integrated in past nomenclature. (The flowers of the *Ipomoea* genus differ from the *Convolvulus* in having one stigma rather than two.) The colours that Custead listed give some clues to their proper identification, but again these can be misleading as there has been so much natural hybridization over the years.

Both plants mentioned above are fast-growing vines that climb by twisting their stems around supports. They can be allowed to clamber casually over fences or shrubs or can be controlled when trained over a pattern of strings or wires. The curious character of these plants is the flowers, which open in the morning and close as dusk approaches. The blooms last only a couple of days, the colour fading with their age. For the most pleasing result the vines are best planted where this morning bloom can be observed, by a window, a doorway, or a path. It has been suggested that the flowering is more profuse when the roots are restricted as in a pot, making it a good subject for a porch or patio container. If left without an upright support the plants will spread out in all directions, interlacing their stems searching for support, forming an effective mass of flowers on a background of dark green foliage.

The "Cyprus Vine" listed in the Toronto catalogue may have been either *Ipomoea quamoclit* L., in the Morning Glory family, *Convolvulaceae*, or an American native, *Adlumia fungosa* (Ait.) Greene. in the *Fumarioideae*, the Bleeding Heart family. Both were known as Cypress Vine.

The *Ipomoea quamoclit*, a vine from tropical America, was grown by many gardeners in Europe and America in the eighteenth and early nineteenth centuries. Joseph Breck of Boston claimed, "No other annual climbing plant exceeds the Cypress Vine in elegance of foliage, gracefulness of habit or loveliness of flowers" (Breck 1866:335). He continued, "the only difficulty in its successful cultivation in our climate, is in the shortness of the

Cypress Vine
Ipomoea quamoclit L.

season." In Boston the Cypress Vine was grown in pots in a hotbed, carefully handled until planting-out time in mid June. With luck and good
weather, the vines would bloom with small, deep-tubed bright red flowers
by August. The foliage was very finely dissected, fern-like, and delicate.
This may have been the plant that Custead had seeds for, but there is
another possibility for the identity of a "Cyprus Vine."

In the *Canadian Settler's Guide*, a "climbing Fumatory, better known by
the name by which its seeds are sold by the gardener, 'Cypress Vine,' " was
recommended for shading a porch or veranda. "This elegant creeper is a
native of Canada" (Traill 1855/1969:15). Mrs Traill noted that this vine
grew over old trees in clearings in the forest, decorating them with lovely
pink flowers. She found the seeds difficult to collect in the wild, but they
were available from local seedsmen and were popular with townspeople
who grew them as shade plants. This plant was the *Adlumia fungosa* (Ait.)
Greene, native to eastern North America from New Brunswick to North
Carolina, familiar today as the Allegheny Vine. It was first identified as
Fumaria fungosa, placing it in the same genus as the common Fumitory in
the Bleeding Heart family, the relationship recognized by Traill. It was
later renamed by the botanist Rafinesque to commemorate John Adlum,
whose contributions to horticulture included the establishment of an
experimental vineyard in Washington, D.C.

Adlumia fungosa is actually a biennial, forming a rosette of delicate leaves
not unlike the maidenhair fern in the first year. Long stems to fifteen or
twenty feet are produced in the second season, bearing loose, pendulous
clusters of small, pink, heart-shaped flowers handsomely displayed. It is
deserving of a place in the garden today, as it was in Custead's time, for its
very delicate texture and pretty flowering habit, but it is seldom offered by
major seed companies.

Which of these two vines was the one offered in Custead's list is conjec-
tural; both were grown from seed, both were garden plants of the period,
and both were delicate in texture, with small bright flowers. The *Ipomoea*
species, being of tropical origin, had to be treated as a tender annual or a
pot plant, while the *Adlumia* is hardy and could be sown in place.

In the *Compositae*, the Daisy or Thistle family, seeds were available for
China Aster, Sweet Sultan, Chrysanthemum, African Marigold and Mexican Ximensia. The blooms of the *Compositae* are compound flowers set in
a common receptacle, surrounded by an circle of bracts called an involucre. The corolla of each flower can be flat, strap-shaped, or tubular. The
flat "petals" are rays or ray-flowers; the tubular flowers usually form a

central disk. In some genera the outside bracts of the involucre appear prominently as scales.

Seeds for the China Aster, *Callistephus chinensis* (L.) Nees., were sent from China by the Jesuit priest Father d'Incarville to the Jardin des Plantes in Paris in 1728. Philip Miller of the Chelsea Physic Garden in London obtained seed from Paris in 1731. Four years later Peter Collinson, the British plant collector, sent seeds of China Aster to John Bartram in Philadelphia, calling it the "noblest and finest plant ... sent per the Jesuits from China to France; from thence to us" (Leighton 1986:401). The fact that these seeds travelled over such a long distance in so few years revealed much about the enthusiasm for plant and seed exchange among botanists in the eighteenth century and clearly demonstrates the close relationship between gardening aficionados.

There is only one species in the genus *Callistephus*. The first plants raised in Europe had single, flat-petalled, purple flowers. Miller was persistent in his propagation, and by 1753 he had made selections from his seedlings which included a blue single and red and white doubles. In the mid-nineteenth century the *Callistephus chinensis* became a favourite of German breeders, who developed new strains including quilled varieties, which were very popular in Victorian borders. In the early twentieth century, since much of the seed on the market was provided by German growers, this plant was equally well known as the German Aster.

Innumerable varieties have been developed since then, including dwarf forms and those with various shaped petals. The doubles were considered the only ones worth having: "no others should be tolerated," gardeners were advised (Breck 1866:141). To maintain specific colours or flower forms, the different varieties must be grown separately to prevent cross-pollination; plants grown for several generations from seed formed by indiscriminate pollination will eventually revert to a single purple flower.

China Asters have always been appreciated for their showy flowers, all the more because of their late summer blooming period. Until quite recently they were among the most common annuals grown in Canadian gardens. In recent years a virus disease, called "aster yellows," has devastated many plantings. The disease is carried from plant to plant by the leafhopper insect, and there is no known remedy. The disease turns the leaves yellow and distorts the shape of the plant. When this disease is noticed, all affected plants have to be destroyed. But virus-resistant varieties are now on the market, and these should be considered when purchasing seed for China Asters.

China Aster   *Callistephus chinensis* (L.) Nees.

Sweet Sultan   *Centaurea moschata* L.

Chrysanthemums   *Chrysanthemum coronarium* L.
Chrysanthemum segetum L.

The original Sweet Sultan, *Centaurea moschata* L., came from the Near East, which accounted for the oriental flavour of its common name. Parkinson introduced the "Sultan's Flower ... but lately obtained from Constantinople, where ... the great Turk wore it himself" (Parkinson 1629/ 1976:327). It quickly became an admired garden plant among seventeenth-century gardeners. It was one of the commonly grown annuals in America by the end of the eighteenth century, mentioned in several garden records and included in the garden calender by M'Mahon in 1806 (M'Mahon 1858/1976:364). The blooms were found to be "so exceedingly sweet," but the scent was "as disagreeable to many as it is grateful to others."

The flowers are quite distinctive, composed of a dense group of florets encased in a series of pointed bracts. The central florets are tubular, the outer ones thin and ray-like. In the early nineteenth century only purple and white forms, the two varieties offered in the Toronto Nursery catalogue, were available. Today the colour range has been increased to include red, yellow, and pink flowers.

Two colours of *Chrysanthemum* were listed in the catalogue, a white and a yellow. It is not clear whether Custead was offering one species or two. The *Chrysthanthemum coronarium* L., the Crown Daisy, generally had white flowers, but a lemon-yellow form was also known. The *Chrysanthemum segetum* L., the Corn Marigold, had a bright yellow flower, although it was much less popular as a garden annual, regarded more as a weed.

The Crown Daisy was native to the Mediterranean area but does not seem to have reached English gardens until the seventeenth century. Parkinson called it the "corn-marigold of Candy [Crete]" (Parkinson 1629/1991:295). Miller listed the White Corn Marigold and the Yellow Corn Marigold separately, even though "some botanists reduce them to one [species], tho' from repeated trials I have never found that the Seeds of the white Sort have produced yellow Flowers, nor the yellow Sort produced the White" (Miller 1754/1969:323). A seed list from Boston in 1842 listed a white sort as *Chrysanthemum coronaria*, and a yellow sort as *Chrysanthemum fl. lutea* – which was not an acknowledged species but simply indicated that the flower was yellow (Breck 1842:11).

Double varieties were available by the middle of the eighteenth century, and from then on seedlings bearing singles were "cast away as good for nothing" (Miller 1754/1969:323). The doubles, considered appropriate for the pleasure garden or the courtyard, were often kept in pots and prevented from growing too tall by frequent pinching, thereby ensuring a continuous show of flowers. Cuttings were taken from the finest of the double sorts for wintering indoors in the "greenhouse or sitting room," a practice that also preserved the more desirable varieties for the next garden season (Breck 1866:159).

Colours of the annual chrysanthemums range from white through creamy hues to a pale yellow. Of the many new cultivars today, all have cheerful, daisy-like flowers with large golden centres. In addition to the single and double flowered varieties, there are also variations in the forms and height of plants.

It must be noted here that the fall-blooming perennial chrysanthemums grown in modern gardens are hybrids derived from the *Dendranthema X grandiflorum* Kitam. (syn. *Chrysanthemum sinensis X indicum*) from China and Japan. These plants were first sent to England in the nineteenth century and raised by florists as hothouse plants until the 1880s. Intensive breeding in the twentieth century has produced many hardy garden hybrids.

Custead's "African Marygold" and the "Orange Quilled African Marygold," *Tagetes erecta* L., were the ancestors of the garden marigold of today. The modern forms are highly bred hybrid varieties which are relatively recent introductions. The Spanish found the African Marygold in Mexico during their earliest explorations of America and took it back to Europe. It escaped from Spanish gardens and spread so rapidly along the African coast of the Mediterranean that it was thought to be a native wildflower. These wild-growing plants were spread to the rest of Europe by the troops of Charles v, King of Spain and Emperor of Rome, after the capture of Tunis in 1535, when it was known as *Flos Tunetanus* (Parkinson 1629/1991:750). The free-flowering habit, golden coloured blooms, and lacy dark green foliage of the plant quickly assured it of a place in European gardens.

The species form of *Tagetes erecta* is quite variable. Gerard mentioned both single and double flowers growing in his late sixteenth-century garden. By 1807 five varieties of the African Marygold were described in gardeners' calenders. The differences were based on the colour of the flower, which varied from a sulphur yellow through stronger yellows to orange (Perthensis 1807 22:110). Variations included three forms of flowers: a single, a double, and the "fistulous" blooms. The latter term referred to the tubular shape of petals, more frequently termed "quilled" as the shape resembles the hollow stem of a feather. The double forms were much preferred over the single, and gardeners were instructed to pull out all singles from their seedlings as soon as they bloomed to avoid cross-pollination with the less desirable forms (Miller 1754/1969:135).

The early nineteenth-century forms of the African Marygold were large branching plants up to five feet in height, with blooms two inches in diameter. They were planted in borders or in parterres, later becoming favourites

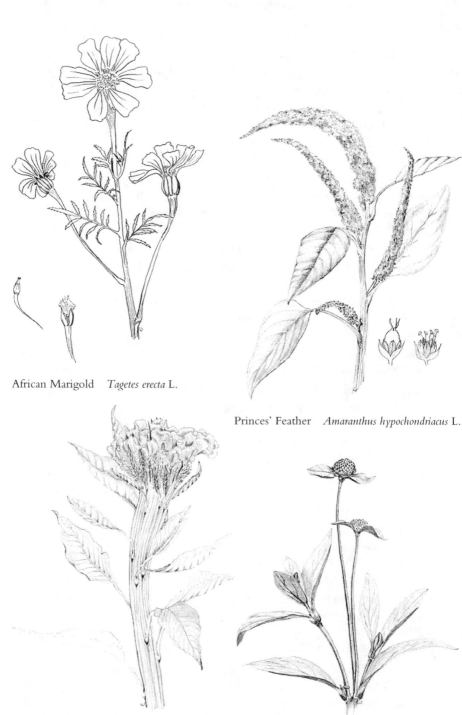

African Marigold   *Tagetes erecta* L.

Princes' Feather   *Amaranthus hypochondriacus* L.

Cock's Comb
Celosia argentea var. cristata (L.) Kuntze

Globe Amaranthus   *Gomphrena globosa* L.

as Victorian bedding plants. An American firm specialized in breeding *Tagetes* in the twentieth century, producing a very wide range of plants with varying heights and flower types.

The whole plant is aromatic, but to some the odour is too pungent for pleasure. At one time it was thought this smell indicated the plant was poisonous, and the marigold was "not to be smelled into, much lesse used in meat or medicine" (Gerard 1633/1975:751). The plant exudes a particularly potent scent upon cutting, and few can tolerate the stench of cut marigolds left standing in water: "These Plants have a strong disagreeable Scent, especially when handed [cut]; for which reason they are not so greatly esteemed for planting near Habitations" (Miller 1754/1969:1353). Today the plant is recommended for the control of soil nematodes, and for this reason it is often planted in the vegetable garden.

Mexican Ximensia, *Verbescina enceloides* A. Gray, was the last annual cited in Custead's list. Now more commonly called Golden Crownbeard, it is known only as a wildflower of the southwestern United States and northern Mexico and is seldom found as a garden plant. The plant was originally named *Ximensia enceloides* by the Spanish botanist Antonio Cavanilles in 1793, in memory of the Spanish monk Joseph Ximenes, author of a treatise on Mexican plants written in 1615. In the eighteenth century it was prized for its late-blooming period, in the season when there was the least colour in most European gardens. By the early twentieth century many more late summer flowers had been introduced, and "the competition of yellow flowered autumn blooming composites is so great that the Verbescinas have little chance" (Bailey 1902: 4:1917). At a time when so many plant species were being cultivated and hybridized for "improved" garden varieties, it appears the *Verbescina enceloides* was ignored. Perhaps there were just too many yellow-flowered annuals available, as Bailey suggested, for these American natives to gain attention.

This *Verbescina* species does not appear in the popular horticultural literature of the early nineteenth century. In 1811 President Jefferson received seeds for it from Andre Thouin, curator of the Jardins des Plantes in Paris, who called it a "*belle grande plante annuelle d'ornement*" (Betts 1986:78). Jefferson planted some and gave the remainder of the seeds to American botanical gardens and to the seedsman M'Mahon. In the 1830s it was included, as Mexican Ximensia, *Ximensia enceloides*, in a number of American seed catalogues: Landreth's in Philadelphia, Thorburn's in New York, and both Ellis's and Breck's in Boston. It is likely that Custead's seeds for Mexican Ximensia were supplied by one of these American seedsmen. Whether or not all were the progeny of those sent to Jefferson, this is another fascinating story of international seed exchange. The transfer of seeds from continent to continent two hundred years ago, in this case from southwestern North America or Mexico to Spain, then to France, back across the Atlantic to eastern North America, and from there to a nursery in Canada, took place in spite of political boundaries and conflicts. (In the 1820s the entire southwestern part of the continent was part of the Republic of Mexico).

In the Amaranth family, *Amaranthaceae*, three species were offered: Prince's Feather, Cock's Comb and Purple Globe Amaranth.

All members of the Amaranthus family are tropical annuals. Prince's Feather, *Amaranthus hypochondriacus* L., was a popular garden plant in European gardens as early as the sixteenth century. The flowers are produced in large handsome plumes, which gave the plant its common name, as they resembled the feathers on the heraldic shield of the Prince of Wales. (Other plants with large flowering plumes were also called Prince's Feather, e.g. *Polygonum orientale*.)

Spanish explorers had found *Amaranthus* species grown as cereal crops by the Aztecs in Mexico. Offerings of the life-sustaining plant played a symbolic role in ceremonial rituals. It has been said the Roman Catholic church prohibited its cultivation in the Spanish colonies in an effort to suppress indigenous religions, but it is more probable that it was replaced by the introduction of European grain crops. Today it is again being grown as a crop in Central America, much valued for its protein-rich seed. The tender young leaves are used fresh as a culinary herb in many Mexican dishes.

Folk medicine made use of the leaves to prepare an astringent wash to bathe wounds and skin irritations. An infusion also served as a rinse for mouth and throat infections.

In garden history the Prince's Feather was grown primarily as an ornamental. During the early nineteenth century, before the idea of the flower border was common, the plant was recommended for the shrubbery, where it added colour and interest. The large inflorescence of dense spikes of blood-red plumes borne above the luxuriant purplish-green foliage guaranteed it to be a favourite of gardeners. The plant is handsome at all times during the growing season because of the distinctive colouring of the leaves, and the late summer flowering period is an added bonus.

One of the features of the *Amaranthus* genus (the name was taken from the Greek for "never fading") is the retention of the vivid colour in the blooms when the plant is dried. The longevity of the blooms made them symbols of immortality and valued for winter bouquets.

The gaily coloured Cock's Comb, *Celosia argentea var. cristata* (L.) Kuntze, has been grown in British gardens since Elizabethan times. In eighteenth-century America it was considered among the most popular and widely cultivated of all garden annuals. The plant was native to tropical Asia, and was known in two varieties. The inflorescence of one variety was a pyramidal form, the other had a curiously crested bloom reminiscent of a cock's comb. Its flower head could attain shapes that were called monstrous or grotesque, but these strange and wonderful flowers were probably the very reason they fascinated gardeners. They could be grown to enormous sizes: in 1820 one was presented to the London Horticultural Society that was a deep purple-red, eighteen inches in diameter and seven inches high (Breck 1866:154). In the late nineteenth century Cock's Combs were favourites at horticultural fairs. They were grown in pots, the object being to produce the largest possible crest on the smallest plant (Bailey 1902:272). A good plant was no more than nine inches high, bearing a bloom at least the same width, as dense as possible and intensely coloured. Like other members of the Amaranthus family, the Cock's Comb held its colour when dried, the brightly coloured, curiously formed flowers providing unusual shapes for winter bouquets.

Eighteenth-century garden guides advised that as "these Plants perspire very freely [they] must be every Day refreshed with Water" (Miller 1754/ 1969:65). Given a warm, moist situation with plenty of light they will bloom in the garden from July to September. The crimson, red, and yellow of Custead's day remain the most common colours, but plants are now available in a wider colour range. In the garden they may need frequent spraying to avoid loss to thrips and red spider mite.

The Globe Amaranthus, *Gomphrena globosa* L., was another of the popular "immortelles" used for dried winter bouquets. The long-lasting blooms could retain their colour for several years. The small ball-like or globose flowers, somewhat resembling those of red clover, were very decorative and have remained one of the all-time favourite everlasting flowers. In the eighteenth century they were "very proper Ornaments for Ladies to wear in their Hair ... far preferable to any artificial Flowers whatever" (Miller 1754/1969:62). Miller also mentioned that great quantities of Globe Amaranths were used in Spain and Portugal "for adorning their places of Worship in the Wintertime."

The original species from tropical Asia had deep violet flowers, which may have been the sort Custead was offering in 1827. By 1866, purple, white, and streaked varieties were available, and in that year a reddish-orange species was reportedly discovered in Mexico (Breck 1866:232).

Since that time there have been many additions to the colour range, but the general appearance of the plant has not changed significantly. Its much-branched, low-growing habit makes it an excellent choice for edging a flower bed.

Two members of the Poppy family, *Papaveraceae*, the Horn Poppy and the Carnation Poppy, were listed. Regular poppy flowers have four to twelve petals and two sepals which fall as the flower opens. Plants in this family have milky or coloured juices which are very bitter or narcotic.

The Horn Poppy, *Glaucium flavum* Crantz., was native to seashores in many parts of Europe, including Great Britain. Gerard described the plant in the late sixteenth century, giving it the botanical name *Papaver cornutum flore luteo*, the "horned poppy with yellow flowers." The word *glaucium* refers to the silvery-bluish green – or sea-like – colour of the plant, derived from the name of the Greek sea-god, Glaucus. The Greek myth tells of how a fisherman observed his catch of fish leaping back into the sea after consuming a plant on the shore. Following their example he too ate the plant, leapt into the sea, and was transformed into a sea deity, half man, half fish, with sea-green hair. Whether or not the plant he ingested was the Horned Poppy, this plant honours him in name.

Few specific references to the Horned Poppy exist in North American garden records, but it must have been introduced quite early in colonial times as it was found wild along the Atlantic coast from Rhode Island to Virginia by the mid-nineteenth century and can still be found there today. The plant is a biennial in its native habitat but cannot tolerate frost. In the North it is treated in the garden as a tender annual, as it can flower and set seed in a single season.

The whole plant, including the root, has a deep-yellow sap that contains poisonous alkaloids. In the past when the Doctrine of Signatures dictated the medical uses of a plant, the yellow juice was used to treat jaundice. It has a strong cathartic action and can produce a narcotic effect on the central nervous system. At one time it was believed the poisonous juice from this plant was used by witches in their incantations to produce madness (Breck 1866:230). When touched or bruised, the foliage of the plant may cause dermatitis in sensitive people. Today there are no medical applications for the Horned Poppy; the only commercial value is found in the oil from the seeds, used in the manufacture of soaps.

The Carnation Poppy, *Papaver somniferum* L., is one of the many forms of the opium poppy. Several forms that bore double flowers were named after a resemblance to another flower; the most common were known as the Pi-

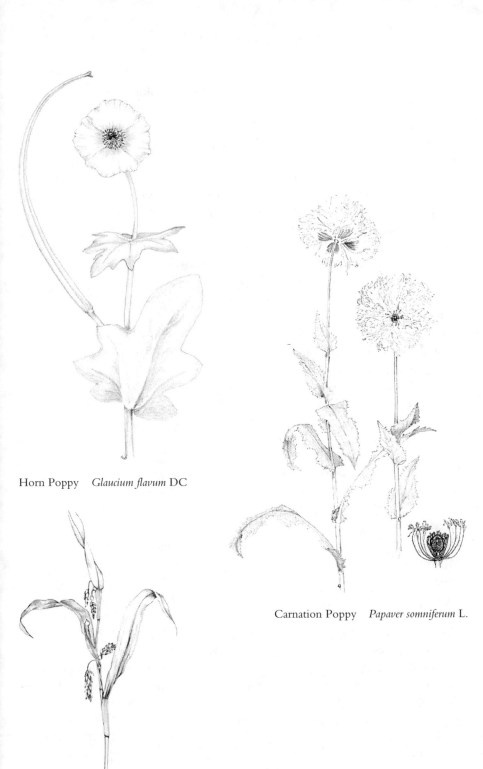

Horn Poppy   *Glaucium flavum* DC

Carnation Poppy   *Papaver somniferum* L.

Job's Tears   *Coix lacryma-jobi* L.

cotee, the Peony-Flowered, and the Carnation-Flowered. The Picotees were double white flowers, splashed with a second colour, usually purple or red. The Peony-Flowered had large double flowers in white or intense hues of red, pink, or purple. The Carnation-Flowered forms were similar to the peony sorts in size and colour, but the petals were notched or fringed. The double poppies had blooms up to four inches in diameter and made a striking flash of colour in the garden. No gardener could "gratify his taste ... and love of colour so cheaply and so fully" than by growing "a good selection of poppies" (Bailey 1902:1206).

The poppy plant grows through several phases, each interesting to observe. The emerging leaves and stems are a distinctive grey-green colour. The thin flower stem rises above the foliage, bearing a terminal drooping bud. As the flower opens, the bud turns upright, eventually opening to a full, luxurious bloom. The flower matures to a cup-like seed pod with a scalloped lid, which becomes rather woody upon ripening. Its many cells contain a prolific quantity of seeds, the reason the plant was adopted as a symbol of fertility in early Greek art. The decorative seed pods were often used in dried floral arrangements.

Archaeological evidence shows that poppy seeds, which are nutritious and contain an oil similar to olive oil, were used as a food since the neolithic period in Europe (Merlin 1984:89–91). In Poland "the common Carnation Poppy is grown for the seed, which is taken when beginning to ripen and strewed on a sort of milk-porrige made from the meal of buck-wheat" (Loudon 1827:63). The seed is still used in many bread and pastry recipes from central and eastern Europe.

The opium poppy has given medicine several of the most valuable drugs for the relief of human pain, but it has also been abused, causing much human misery. Its cultivation is now prohibited in many countries; seed for the ornamental poppies are often sold under a named variety and not as *Papaver somniferum*.

One plant in the grass family, *Gramineae*, Job's Tears, *Coix lacryma-jobi* L., was grown in the eighteenth century as yet another curiosity. The plant bears glossy, pearl-grey seeds shaped like tear-drops. The weight of the seed clusters bear down the stems, creating an arching effect. The nodding stalks have a novel appearance, but unfortunately the summer is not always long enough in northern climates for this tender annual to mature.

This grass, originally from tropical Asia, is still grown in India and the Philippines as a coarse cereal food. In times of famine, flour made from the ground seeds was used for bread (Hedrick 1919/1972:184). In European gardens during the nineteenth century, it was grown simply as another of the "curious" plants. The hard, silvery seeds were used in craft work, made into beads for necklaces and rosaries. They are still available in craft supply houses for home-made jewellery. And with renewed interest in decorative grasses, Job's Tears have seen a revival in popularity, both in landscaping and in dried flower arrangements.

The Evening Primrose, *Oenothera biennis* L., is a member of the *Onagraceae* or Evening Primrose family. All species in this genus are indigenous to North America. The first examples known in Europe were taken to the Padua Botanical Garden and rapidly became naturalized in the Italian countryside. The plant was originally introduced as a food plant and grown for the root, which was eaten as a boiled vegetable, raw as a salad served with a mustard dressing, or prepared as a pickle.

The Evening Primrose was growing wild in abundance in Canada when Peter Kalm travelled here in the 1740s: "An old Frenchman, who accompanied me on a walk collecting its seeds, could not sufficiently praise its properties of healing wounds: the leaves of the plant must be crushed and then laid upon the wound" (Kalm 1770/1966 2:538). The leaves and stems, which have a mucilaginous content, were dried, cut, and boiled to make an astringent solution for the treatment of skin diseases and eruptions. A similar decoction was used for asthma and intestinal disorders. Although the plant is not accepted in modern pharmacopoeias, recent research has shown one of the component chemicals to be effective in controlling blood clotting. The oil expressed from the seeds is being intensively researched as a nutritional supplement and as a relief from premenstrual syndrome.

Evening Primrose   *Oenothera biennis* L.

A biennial plant, the Evening Primrose forms a basal rosette the first year and grows to a height of four feet in the second. The tubular flowers are yellow, with four soft petals that open at dusk. The late-day flowering is necessary for the plant's survival as it is pollinated by nocturnal moths. It self-seeds readily, as its rapid spread in Europe and its widespread geographical range in North America suggests.

The fascinating feature of the Ice Plant, *Mesembryanthemum crystallinum* L., in the *Aiozaceae* or Carpetweed family, is the glistening appearance of its leaves. In the past the plant was described as resembling ice-crystals, rock candy, or crystal gems, or looking as though covered with hoar frost, appearing brilliant in the sunlight. The effect is created by small light-reflecting pustules on the leaves, an environmental adaptation of the plant to retain moisture. The genus *Mesembryanthemum* included many fleshy-leaved desert plants, most originating in arid areas of South Africa. The name, taken from the Greek, means "midday flower," as the blooms open during the day and close at night.

The date of the original introduction of the Ice Plant to Europe is not clear, but its popularity was assured by the late eighteenth century: "The oddness of the whole Plant renders it worthy of a place in every Curious Garden" (Miller 1754/1969:504). Gardeners in the United States initially grew it as a pot plant, but it soon found a place as a border annual, in the greenhouse, and as an indoor plant for window gardens and hanging baskets. It was the only species of the large genus *Mesembryanthemum* to be mentioned in horticultural books of the early nineteenth century.

The peculiar leaves were used on the table for garnishing salads and desserts. Juice expressed from the leaves was for a time used in Europe as a medicine in the treatment of dysentery and incontinence, but the practice had been discontinued by the late nineteenth century (Stillé and Maisch 1880:915).

The Ice Plant was introduced to California in an effort to stabilize sand dunes in coastal areas. It has taken well to its new environment and has become so prolific that it is now crowding out and replacing species of the natural vegetation. Many native Californian wildflowers are now on the list of endangered species, resulting from the risk taken when exotic plants are introduced in wide-scale planting programs.

Custead's Heart's Ease, the little *Viola tricolor* L., of the *Violaraceae*, or Violet family, was a popular plant in the Elizabethan era. It was common practice during this period to give favourite plants affectionate or amusing nicknames. This small plant had more than its share of such terms – Three-Faces-in-a-Hood, Call-to-Me, Pink-of-My-John, Love-in-Idleness, to name but a few. The three colours in the petals, purple, yellow, and white or blue, were related symbolically to the Christian Holy Trinity, but the herbalist Nicholas Culpeper thought the medieval name *Viola trinitatis*

Ice Plant   *Mesembryanthemum crystallinum* L.

Heart's Ease   *Viola tricolor* L.

Balsamine   *Impatiens balsamina* L.

Marvel of Peru   *Mirabilis jalapa* L.

was blasphemous. By the nineteenth century Heart's Ease was the favoured name – in the popular language of flowers, signifying the happy memories that eased the heartbreak of separated lovers. Today the plant is more familiar as Johnny Jump-Up, no doubt referring to the way it appears spontaneously in the garden year after year. Its free-blooming habit and cheerful upturned flowers have endeared it to gardeners, in spite of its having no scent. The colours in the petals are not distributed in exactly the same way in every flower, and sometimes individual petals may have more than one colour.

The *Viola tricolor* grows wild in the north temperate regions Europe and Asia and is the ancestor of the garden Pansy. Early in the nineteenth century Lady Mary Bennet grew two wild species of Heart's Ease in a heart-shaped bed in her garden southeast of London, England. She happened to notice that there were interesting variations in the flowers, and with the assistance of her gardener and the nurseryman James Lee, several cultivars were developed. By 1830 other gardeners began to pursue this lead, and the modern form of the pansy evolved, one with a dark patch in the centre of the flower. The humble Heart's Ease had become a "bold, circular, velvety rich flower" (Brickell 1986:226). Later in the century the pansy was used extensively as a bedding plant in formal garden arrangements and is now more common than Heart's Ease in western gardens.

Several members of the Violet family have been used medicinally over the centuries, primarily as an expectorant and antiseptic, but these practices had ceased in the West by the late nineteenth century. The plant may cause some skin irritation in sensitive people.

The Toronto Nursery offered seeds for a "fine, double Balsamine," *Impatiens balsamina* L. This may have been somewhat misleading to its customers, as Balsamine, or Garden Balsam, did not always come true from seed. The original species was a single-flowered plant from tropical Asia. In the Far East, balsamine flowers were used to make a red colouring, used in textile dyes and for cosmetic purposes, much in the same manner as henna. It was cultivated in Europe in the seventeenth century, and many garden varieties were available by the 1800s. The flowers were mostly pinkish in colour, from a near-white or flesh colour through to rosy-red or purple. The average garden plant was about two and a half feet high, the flowers borne close to the stem in the leaf axils. The seed pods exploded dramatically to the touch when ripe, as though they were "impatient," thus giving the plant its botanical nomenclature.

The double forms of balsam became very desirable border annuals in the late eighteenth and early nineteenth centuries. President Jefferson grew purple, red, and white balsams. The best seed was imported from France (Breck 1866:247). Very showy specimens with two colours in each bloom, called "flaked" or "bizarre," were highly prized. Gardeners kept their own secrets about how to raise a superior plant; one belief was that the seeds which were four to nine years old, taken from semi-double forms, would produce better double specimens than fresh seed (Loudon 1827:865). A plant displayed in England around 1820 was described as having a main stem over two inches in diameter, very branched, forming a small bush. Shortly after, another *Balsamina*, carefully potted up for an exhibition, reached four feet in height and five feet across "covered with large double flowers." Eventually the plant's popularity was responsible for it becoming commonplace, and by the late nineteenth century it had lost its appeal for many gardeners.

The forms of balsam available today are limited by comparison to those grown in the early nineteenth century, and modern seed tends to be quite variable. Unless the grower has been careful not to allow varieties to cross-breed, and specifies a particular variety, the seedlings resulting from a packet of seed will vary in both the colour and form of the blooms. The plants bloom consistently throughout the summer, but in many examples the flowers are concealed beneath the leaves. The thick, succulent stems are quite brittle and require support to prevent breaking in a wind.

The Marvel of Peru, *Mirabilis jalapa* L., is more familiar today by the name Four O'Clock. The colonial Spaniards introduced the plant to Europe from South America in the sixteenth century. The names *Mirabilis* and "Marvel" refer to the plant's unusual characteristics. Its blooms – it can bear more than one colour on a single plant – are so light sensitive that they do not open until late in the day, flowering all night and closing in the light of the next morning. The night-blooming habit was called "very clever" by President Jefferson, for the flowers attract night-flying moths which are responsible for their pollination. The plant has been used in botanical studies of genetics because of the varying colours of the flowers.

The tubular flowers appear in groups of two or three blooms at the ends of the stems. There are no petals; the coloured part of the bloom is a calyx, not a corolla. The common colours are vivid reds and yellows, but white and pink forms are known. A few varieties have blooms with stripes of a second colour along the length of the flower tube. The Marvel of Peru is easily grown from seed and will form thick tuberous roots in the first season, which will provide good plants for up to another five seasons. In northern gardens the tubers must be treated much as those of the dahlia, dug out in the fall and replanted the following spring.

Another of the "curious" plants in the catalogue was the Proboscis Flower, *Martynia annua* L., known today as the Unicorn Plant or Devil's Claw, classified in the *Pedaliaceae* (Griffiths 1994:727). The plant has had a number of botanical names applied to it, for example, *Marynia proboscides* and *Proboscides louisiana*, incorporating the word proboscis (meaning trumpet-like) to describe the unusual form of the seed pod. The name for the genus *Martynia* was selected to honour John Martyn, a botany professor at Cambridge and editor of the 1819 update of Miller's *Gardener's Dictionary*.

The Proboscis Flower was native to central North America, in an area stretching from the Mississippi basin to Mexico. The southwestern Indians used it as a food plant, picking the fleshy green immature seed pods as a vegetable (Hedrick 1919/1972:356). They were introduced to early settlers, who pickled the young seed pods. When the pods mature, the fleshy covering is shed, revealing a woody core that splits into two long curved hooks or prongs to release the seeds. The ornamental quality of the seed pods used as decorations and in dried arrangements accounted for its great popularity. It was widely planted and has escaped to the wild in some areas of the northeastern United States. However, the plants were deemed "not suitable for bouquets." Planting instructions in gardeners' almanacs implied that they belonged in the kitchen garden, where they were to be cultivated in the same way as tomato plants. The plant is clammy, covered with soft sticky hairs, and has a sprawling habit. Some find it to have an unpleasant scent, not unlike the British yeast spread called Marmite. The flowers are exceedingly attractive, opening wide with five lobes of light bronzy-pink petals with darker lines in the throat. Racemes carrying several blooms grow out of the leaf axils. This remarkable and handsome plant is seldom grown in modern gardens, but seed is available from several major seed houses.

Scarlet Flowering Havannah Tobacco, *Nicotiana tabacum* L., is a member of the *Solanaceae*, or Potato family. A number of genera from this plant family originated in South America and were destined to gain worldwide economic importance. When Columbus sailed into the West Indies, he observed the native peoples smoking the rolled leaves of the tobacco plant.

Proboscis Flower   *Martynia annua* L.

Scarlet Flowering Havannah Tobacco
Nicotiana tabacum L.

Red Persicaria   *Polygonum orientale* L.

Tobacco was introduced to Spain, named *Tabacum* by the botanist Nicholas Monardes, whose *Plants from the Newe Founde World* contained the first illustration of it. The French ambasasador Jean Nicot, now commemorated in the name *Nicotiana*, later took the plant to Paris. Less than a hundred years after its initial introduction, tobacco was being cultivated all over Europe and had become an important commercial product. When Peter Kalm travelled in French Canada in the 1740s he noted that "every farmer plants a quantity of tobacco near his house ... it is necessary ... because it is so universally smoked by the common people. Boys of ten or twelve years of age, as well as the old people, run about with a pipe in their mouths" (Kalm 1770/1966 2:510).

Tobacco contains nicotine, one of the most poisonous narcotic substances, which can be fatal even in moderate doses. Extracts from the plant have been useful as insecticides in horticulture and agriculture and in controlling parasites on both humans and animals; it was especially effective in the control of scabs and ticks on sheep. Tobacco has proved effective as a contact insecticide to control aphids, scale, and leaf hoppers. It was of value in the orchard to reduce the damage caused by the plum curculio. The methods used to control insects involved burning the powdered leaves or spraying with an infusion; the first horticultural references for spraying dates to the late seventeenth century. In the transatlantic seed exchanges between Collinson and Bartram, leaves of tobacco were wrapped around packages of seeds to resist insect damage (U.S. Dept. Agriculture [1950]:774–5).

Recently the dangers of smoking tobacco have become recognized, and the practice has been prohibited in many places. The hazards of tobacco use were expressed by Breck in 1866 when he wrote "It would be well if the plant were raised only for the destruction of insects, rather than, as I feel is the cause, for the destruction of human beings" (Breck 1866:297). Extracts of tobacco were being used medicinally in the nineteenth century as an emetic and diuretic, although it was declared "hostile to all forms of life."

A pharmaceutical reference commented that "the imposts upon tobacco furnish the largest item of national revenue, and ... it is one of the most important articles of commerce" (Stillé and Maisch 1880:1406). When Custead offered his seed for *Nicotiana tabacum* in 1827, the custom duties on imported tobacco were 20 per cent of its value, and large quantities were being imported into Upper Canada. Records of custom seizures show that additional quantities were being smuggled into the country. The interest in raising tobacco in Upper Canada as a cash crop was reflected in a pamphlet *Directions for Those Who Raise Tobacco in This Province*, printed in York in

1828; Dr Baldwin bound a copy of this treatise in the same volume as the Toronto Nursery catalogue.

Red Persicaria, *Polygonum orientale* L., was the only plant in the *Polygonaceae* or Buckwheat family listed among the annual plants. This was a popular hardy annual in the early nineteenth century, and the seeds were sown out in the spring with larkspur, nigella, and sunflowers (M'Mahon 1858/1976:312). Many of the flowers mentioned in M'Mahon's *American Gardener* are still seen in our late twentieth century gardens, but the Red Persicaria is not often among them.

The plant was first described in 1707 when it was brought to England from the East Indies. The seeds of the "Great Oriental Persicaria" were sent to the American botanist John Bartram in 1737 from his English correspondent. The plant we now know as *Polygonum orientale* was a "noble annual ... six or seven feet high and makes a beautiful show with its long bunches of red flowers" (Leighton 1986:464). It "makes a very grand Figure in the Borders of large Gardens, late in the Season, when few other Plants are in Beauty" (Miller 1754/1969:1054). Its pendulous flower stems gave it another popular name – Prince's Feather – and its height gave it the whimsical name Kiss-Me-over-the-Garden-Gate. It does look well alongside a fence, where it aptly demonstrates the latter name. Although the plant grows to a fair height, it seems able to resist strong winds. The stems are curiously knotted or jointed where branches and leaves occur, a characteristic of many plants in the Buckwheat family.

13

Afterword

A thorough examination of William Custead's Toronto Nursery catalogue of 1827 has revealed that in the first few years of settlement in Upper Canada there was an ardent interest in gardens and a quite sophisticated knowledge of horticulture. The Toronto Nursery could provide a variety of plants and seeds to grow the basic requirements for food, home remedies, shade, and shelter, and in addition to these necessities, ornamental plants for the most ambitious of pleasure gardens and interior decorations.

When I first discovered the Toronto Nursery catalogue in the Toronto Metropolitan Reference Library, I felt challenged not only to identify the plants listed but also to reproduce a garden using those plants. The task of identification was, for me as an amateur gardener, quite daunting. It became essential to research garden literature from the seventeenth to the nineteenth centuries and to locate as many early nursery catalogues as possible for comparison. Finding the current nomenclature for each plant also involved consulting modern references, as a great many plants have been reclassified. A search through contemporary nineteenth-century garden literature yielded most, but not all, of the Latin botanical nomenclature for the English common names. For the remainder I looked at earlier sources such as Parkinson and Gerard to find some of the more unfamiliar plant names. Even so, a few remained elusive. For these I consulted plant taxonomists for their assessment and for confirmation of my interpretations. Overall, I had to admire the accuracy and consistency demonstrated by the eighteenth and nineteenth century botanists in their identification and classification of plants. Although there have been many changes over the years, and some plants have been renamed time and time again, the great majority were initially ascribed to the same family, and frequently to the same genus and variety that is accepted by modern taxonomists. Tracing the changes in botanical names remains a challenge for today's gardeners, as many modern garden centres do not always use the most recent appellations in their labelling practices. It appears we are often confronted with the same inaccuracies in nomenclature that Custead experienced.

Once I had established the modern classification of each of Custead's plants, the next hurdle in creating a garden was to find sources for appropriate plants or seeds. A large number of the original species Custead knew are no longer available from major seed houses or nurseries. Locating sources for live plants was impractical; the solution was to grow the majority from seed. Seed catalogues by the dozens piled up year after year in the hope of finding specific plants. This stage of the project wasn't easily accomplished, for modern seed houses and garden centres cater to present-day trends and fashions, with the latest in genetic breeding for the largest blooms and most unusual or brightest colours predominant in their presentations. Among the most difficult to find were seeds for native American plants, as these are often ignored as garden material here in North America. Even seed houses specializing in wildflower seed couldn't, or wouldn't, supply seeds for native plants if they had the reputation of being "weedy." A number of American native species I ordered from Great Britain, where many North American plants have been grown in gardens since their original introduction.

Herbaceous plants, even some that are tender and not winter-proof, turned out to be the most successful introductions to my garden. I grew a number of tender perennials as annuals. Woody plants presented a more complex problem; those that were hardy took several years to mature, but those that were native to warmer climates were difficult, even impossible, to grow out-of-doors. Some of these are known to survive in the most southerly areas of Ontario, however, and may have proved hardy in Custead's nursery.

In order to illustrate the tender woody plants, I took several trips to photograph them in historic gardens in the United States. A small number of Custead's plants such as the double hyacinth and the American chestnut have become extinct in the years since he published the catalogue. For these it was necessary to study illustrations in historical botanical works. I often consulted old drawings like those in early issues of *Curtis' Botanical Magazine*, to ensure that the selection I made was correct for the period. Flower paintings and photographs were seldom satisfactory sources, as I initially intended all the illustrations to describe the leaf, bloom, and seed of each plant. As this was possible only when I could observe live plants throughout their growth cycle, not all my drawings met my original concept.

Many of the botanical drawings made for this study were drawn from live plants grown in my own garden. This aspect of my research began with finding sources for seeds of appropriate plants, propagating them in my little greenhouse, and then transplanting the seedlings into the garden, watching every stage of growth. These experiments continued for several years, as some plants did not flower or mature until the second or third year. Inevitably there were seeds that did not germinate, seedlings that did not survive transplanting, and tender plants that could not withstand the cold and wet of winter. Several were not suited to the climatic conditions of eastern Ontario or the light sandy soil of my garden. For these the drawings were done from photographs taken on excursions to other gardens or from the wild, and others were adapted from eighteenth and nineteenth century illustrations. For example, the Cardinal Flower was photographed in the wild, and the double hyacinth that cannot be matched in modern horticulture was adapted from historical sources. Even this strategy was not sufficient to cover all the plants mentioned in the text, and there were a few that had to be researched in botanical literature. For intimate details I studied numerous botanical texts and spent many fascinating hours picking plants apart under the microscope. The illustrations were demanding but enjoyable work that served to give me a greater appreciation of the intricacies of nature. The variations I encountered in this small selection of plant material were astounding. The experience was stimulating: I became more keenly observant of the structure and detail of each plant, and I have become a "curious" gardener.

The exercise of reproducing a Custead garden introduced me, an avid but amateur gardener, to many plants I had never known before. Some of these, such as the Blackberry Lily, have become favourite features in my garden. Many of the annuals self-seed every year, cropping up in unexpected but often appropriate places, providing new combinations of colour and texture. The hardy perennials provide colour throughout the summer seasons. The herb garden has become a "history garden," for in addition to culinary herbs, it now contains many of Custead's selections grown for dyes and medicinal preparations. Seeds for some of Custead's "esculent" plants were available through gardening associations that organize seed exchanges; several of these groups of "seed-savers" specialize in seeds from old varieties. While some of the vegetables have not been improved upon since Custead's day (the Hollow Crown parsnip is still a standard variety), a great number old varieties have been lost. Indeed, the quality of many vegetables would not meet with present-day standards of taste or texture. In the past vegetable seeds were saved by the grower from year to year. Today many of the improved varieties are first-generation artificially pollinated hybrids that do not come true from seed and must be re-ordered from the supplier each year.

Larger issues of the subject of gardening became engrossing as I worked on this project. It became apparent how important the garden was in providing many of the amenities for maintaining a satisfactory quality of life in early Canada. The contributions made by conscientious gardeners – their exchange of information as well as actual seeds and plants – has played an almost unrecognized role in our past. The history of individual plants, their discovery and introduction to cultivation involves a cultural exchange between many parts of the world. Stopping the continuity of these ongoing processes at a particular point, as I have done in this examination of the Toronto Nursery catalogue, provides an interesting background to social history in this country's formative years.

In tracing the history of garden plants, the "how" and "when" they were brought into cultivation can be told. But the "why," which in so many instances remains unanswerable to historians, here often becomes apparent. It is best understood when plants that filled a specific need were brought from the wild (wherever in the world that might have been) to a convenient place for their ready use. The most obvious of these were plants that supplied edible products – vegetables, oils, and flavourings – and plants containing aromatic and mucilaginous substances that provided relief from physical ills.

Needs for food and medicine were originally the most persuasive reasons for establishing a garden, but plants were also grown for their loveliness alone. The admiration of beauty was not merely a conceit, for flowers, the supreme gesture of nature, have played an important role in human experience. Flowers have served to celebrate occasions since the dawn of civilization, from their use as symbols of the renewal of life in spring to personal adornment for social events. Plant forms and colours have become metaphors for human ideas and emotions. In ancient times flowers were offered as tributes to deities, garlands provided decoration, and floral crowns were worn by honoured persons, and the ceremonial use of plants continues to this day. Flowers and fruit still decorate our places of worship, the selections made according to the season or the significance of a particular religious ceremony: Thanksgiving, Easter, weddings, and funerals are the most familiar of such occasions in America. Bouquets and corsages are still given to people receiving honours, from the Queen on each of her appearances, to the concert performer, to someone celebrating an anniversary. House plants, cut flowers, and dried arrangements adorn our homes as they have for centuries. Here it might be said that the more things change, the more they remain the same.

The art and science of gardening was not limited to providing necessities of life or supplying flowers for delight and pleasure: it was driven by the desire to understand and control nature. The works of Gerard, Parkinson, Miller, and other early English botanists reveal the degree to which these individuals were engrossed in the exploration of the appearance and behaviour of plants. They were fascinated by the way plants differed in growth patterns and the shapes and colours of the leaves, flowers, and seeds. Their close observations allowed them a certain amount of control. Parkinson advised gardeners that while their skill or art was important, nature had to be understood – for gardening was "whatsoever Art, striving with Nature, can cause to prosper with us" (Parkinson 1629/1976:557). Gardeners were counselled on the careful pruning and protection of fruit trees for successful crops and on the destruction of seedlings lacking the desired characteristics to maintain fine-quality plants. Early Canadian gardeners devised such practices to increase their skills, which also gave them some control over nature. It goes without saying that this trend continues today even more dramatically with research into genetic reproduction.

The selection of garden plants, as with so many other cultural expressions, has had to adapt to changing times: the dictates of fashion reach even into the home garden. No sooner has one plant been granted the honour of being the most choice when another has appeared to fill its place. In this way a garden can be seen as a reflection of the many changes experienced by early nineteenth-century society, politically, geographically, and socially. At that time the idea of self-expression was relatively new. The neat, comfortable social structure of the eighteenth century was fast disappearing, perhaps more rapidly in the North American colonies than in Europe, and every aspect of cultural life was affected. Around the town of York in Upper Canada a few estates still employed "old country" gardeners to build and maintain their landscape. However, looking back to the early 1800s we find ornamental gardening beginning to be practised by every class of society, not only the discriminating elite. Not all immigrants to Upper Canada were among the affluent, yet they too mourned the loss of their former gardens, and many tried to reproduce a familiar landscape. Spring flowers were the most lamented, especially as Canadian winters were so much longer and more severe than those to which most newcomers were accustomed.

Almost two centuries later, gardening is one of the most popular of pastimes in North America. Flowering plants now come in many more sizes and colours than were ever found in the original species or their naturally occurring hybrids. Trees and shrubs have been hybridized to modify sizes and shapes and make them suitable for modern urban and suburban gardens. Even the thorns on some species have been eliminated to make them more user-friendly. Numerous tropical plants are no longer limited to the greenhouse; many tropical perennials are now common in gardens as summer annuals – the ubiquitous marigolds and petunias, for example – in a greater range of colours and sizes than Custead could ever have imagined. More importantly, these plants are readily available at reasonable cost from neighbourhood nurseries, garden centres, even supermarkets.

The Toronto Nursery catalogue shows that the trend to provide a service to all classes of society began in Upper Canada early in the nineteenth century. Residents of Upper Canada were already offered an up-to-date and varied selection by discriminating nurserymen like Custead. From trees and shrubs to vegetable seeds, there were choices to satisfy the most traditional and conservative taste, as well as that of the most adventurous or "curious" gardener.

Appendix

━━━━━━━━

For those wishing to pursue the study of garden history or create a heritage garden, the following resources were found to be particularly helpful. Included are gardens at historic sites that interpret a particular historical period, botanical gardens that contain plant species and varieties used in the past, libraries with collections of early botanical publications, sources for seeds of heritage and native North American plants, and horticultural organizations. Many, many more references could be cited, and this list is intended to be only an introduction to some of the major sources.

HISTORIC SITES AND BOTANICAL GARDENS IN ONTARIO

In Ontario, the former Upper Canada, several historic sites open to the public have heritage gardens.

Bellevue House, 35 Centre St., Kingston, ON, K7L 4E5.
Operated by Parks Canada.
Open during the summer season.
The garden at Bellevue, a residence of Sir John A. Macdonald, Canada's first prime minister, represents an example of landscaping in the 1840s. The garden layout and plant selection have been well researched. Careful attention has been given to the garden tools used, as gardeners can often be seen at work during the hours open to the public.

Black Creek Pioneer Village, Jane St. and Steeles Ave., Toronto.
Operated by the Metropolitan Toronto and Region Conservation Foundation.
Open May 1 to December 31. Closed December 25.
Over thirty restored buildings and costumed guides interpret life in the pre-Confederation period. Gardens adjoin many of the period homes, some with herb gardens containing dye and medicinal plants as well as culinary herbs. Gift shop.

Central Experimental Farm, Ottawa.
Operated by the Department of Agriculture.
Open year round.
Public gardens contain horticultural and agricultural plants. Demonstration areas include an arboretum, wildflower garden, rock garden, perennial beds, and collections of fruit trees and shrubs. The greenhouses often have special exhibitions, such as that of Chinese chrysanthemums held in the fall. A comprehensive library is in the Sir John Carling building. A Friends of the Farm organization provides special exhibits, displays, and demonstrations. An annual membership is open to all.

Edwards Gardens and Civic Garden Centre, 777 Lawrence Ave. East, North York, ON, M3C 1P2.
Operated by the Edwards Foundation and a non-profit volunteer organization.
Open year round.
The Civic Garden Centre offers programs, exhibitions, workshops, and seasonal displays and contains a library with 6,000 books. Annual membership available. It is a meeting place for several horticultural organizations including the Ontario Rock Garden Society and the Wildflower Society.

Niagara Parks Commission School of Horticulture, Box 150, Niagara Falls, ON, L2E 6T2.
Operated by the Niagara Falls Park Commission.
Open year round.
The horticultural gardens cover 33.3 hectares of landscaped grounds, with formal gardens surrounding the main buildings. The research facilities include an herbarium with examples of over 3,000 species. The school offers a three-year post-secondary course in horticulture.

Royal Botanical Gardens, Box 399, Hamilton, ON, L8N 9Z9.
Funded by the Ontario Ministry of Culture and Communications and the Regional Municipalities of Hamilton-Wentworth and Halton.
Open daily except Christmas Day.
The Royal Botanical Gardens cover 2,700 acres, with gardens of all sorts, including perennials, herbs, fruits, and shrubs and three miles of nature trails. Seasonal displays are on view in the Nature Interpretive Centre and the Mediterranean Greenhouse. Guided tours are available to bus groups. The Royal Botanical Gardens has one of the best horticultural libraries in Canada with many historical volumes. Gift shop.

Spadina House, 285 Spadina Road, Toronto.
Operated by the Toronto Historical Board and the Garden Club of Toronto.

Open year-round.

The house and gardens are on the site of the early nineteenth-century residence of William Warren Baldwin. The present house and grounds have been restored to the early 1900s, but the gardens are not dissimilar to those enjoyed in earlier times and contain many historical plants. The gardens may be viewed free of charge, but there is a fee for viewing the house. Guided tours take place twice a week during the summer months.

Upper Canada Village, Highway 2 east of Morrisburg.

Operated by the St Lawrence Parks system, Government of Ontario.

Open mid-May to mid-October.

Upper Canada Village contains buildings that were moved from their original locations during the building of the St Lawrence Seaway. Interpreters in period costume staff the site. In general the village represents life before Confederation in 1867. The gardens are varied according to the type and date of the building they accompany: an early flower garden, a doctor's garden, a farm garden, etc. The choice of plants has been well researched, and most are grown in the village greenhouses. The site includes a large gift shop.

HISTORIC SITES AND BOTANICAL GARDENS IN THE UNITED STATES

The longstanding interest of American historians and gardeners in garden history research is well represented in many historical restorations. A number of American horticultural associations have established historic or herb gardens too diversified to list. A few of the more accessible public gardens, particularly those with research facilities, are listed.

The Arnold Arboretum of Harvard University, Jamaica Plain, Massachusetts.

Operated by Harvard University, part of Boston's park system.

Open every day from sunrise to sunset.

The arboretum, designed by Frederick Law Olmsted in 1872, covers 265 acres and contains 7,000 kinds of woody plants. Almost every tree and shrub hardy in this climate zone can be found here. There are also extensive herbaceous gardens. The arboretum's education department offers a wide range of courses and lectures. The Hunnewell Visitor Center gift shop has many books for sale, including the publications of the arboretum.

Colonial Williamsburg, Williamsburg, Virginia.

Operated by Colonial Williamsburg Foundation.

Open year round.

Willamsburg was declared the capitol of the British colony of Virginia in 1699. Gardens typical of the early eighteenth century surround many of the restored buildings, from practical home gardens with herbs and vegetables to the formal grounds of the governor's palace. There has been substantial garden research here, much of it documented by archaeological investigation. The nearby restorations at Jamestown also have well-documented gardens associated with early plantations.

Genesee Country Village and Museum, 20 miles southeast of Rochester. Box 310, Mumford, New York, 14511–0310.
Operated by the Board of Regents of the State University of New York.
Open mid-May to mid-October.
The village on the 200-acre site reflects the changing architecture throughout the nineteenth century. The gardens are carefully planted to be compatible with adjacent structures, reflecting the changes in gardening over a period of 100 years. These include kitchen gardens, herb gardens, fruit trees, and decorative Victorian gardens. The museum carries on a research program for the heirloom vegetable gardens, and seeds for selections grown in the village are available in the gift shop. Bordering the village is another museum project, the Nature Center with wildlife trails.

Hancock Shaker Village, west of Pittsfield, Massachusetts, on Route 20. Box 898, Pittsfield, MA 01202.
Operated by Shaker Museum Foundation Inc.
Open end of May to end of October.
The village illustrates the Shakers' simple lifestyle in this rural agricultural setting. The Shakers were known for their production of garden seeds during the nineteenth century, for this was one of the major sources of income for this community. The Shakers also sold herbs and herbal remedies, and a large herb garden is maintained on the site to illustrate this aspect of their horticultural practices. There is a gift shop in the museum. The library and archives are open by appointment.

Longwood Gardens, Box 501, Kennett Square, Pennsylvania, 19348–0501.
Operated by non-profit organization.
Open year round.
While Longwood has no specific historic garden section, the extensive grounds of this outstanding public garden contain many plants grown in earlier periods. A research library includes many early American horticultural publications. A well-stocked gift shop offers a wide selection of publications and heirloom seeds.

Mount Vernon, Mount Vernon, VA, south of Washington, DC.
Operated by the Mount Vernon Ladies Association of the Union.

Open year round except Christmas Day.

Mount Vernon, the home of President George Washington, has extensive gardens demonstrating Washington's interest in horticulture, as a farmer and a gentleman. A walled vegetable garden and an ornamental garden with an orangerie reflect the British traditions followed by early settlers in America. The restorations demonstrate historical garden technology from grafted and espaliered fruit trees and the preparation of organic fertilizers to the heating methods used in the orangerie.

National Arboretum, 3501 New York Ave., North-East Washington, D.C. 20002–1958.

Operated by the United States Department of Agriculture.

Open year round except Christmas Day.

The arboretum covers 444 acres, with nine miles of paved roads. The emphasis is on woody plants and the arboretum carries on a research program on trees and shrubs. Among the research holdings is a herbarium with over 500,000 dried plants. The well-organized herb garden, planned to display plants according to their uses, is sponsored by the Herb Society of North America. The gift shop carries arboretum publications.

Old Sturbridge Village, 20 miles south of Worcester. Sturbridge, Massachusetts, 01566.

Operated by a non-profit organization.

Open March to November.

The village contains early buildings from New England, dated from 1790 to 1840, many with surrounding gardens including a large herb garden, vegetable gardens, and orchards. Excellent craft and educational programs are offered. Sturbridge issues a catalogue of heirloom seeds, available through the mail. It also publishes many titles on historic subjects, sold in the gift shop.

Thomas Jefferson Center for Historic Plants

Monticello, Box 316, Charlottesville, Virginia, 22902.

Operated by Thomas Jefferson Memorial Foundation.

Open daily except Christmas Day.

In addition to maintaining the gardens at Monticello, the home of President Thomas Jefferson, the Center for Historic Plants is the first of its kind in the United States. It collects, preserves, and distributes historic seeds and plants, many of which can be seen on Monticello's grounds. The center publishes an annual newsletter, *Twinleaf*, which includes a list of plants and seeds for sale. Jefferson was instrumental in introducing many plants from Europe to America as well as sponsoring botanical exploration on this continent, and the vegetable and ornamental gardens reflect his work. There are two shops on the premises, one run exclusively by the Center for Historic Plants.

SEED SOURCES

Chiltern Seeds, Bortree Stile, Ulverston, Cumbria, LA12 7PB, England.
Chiltern's has an annual catalogue of almost 300 pages. The listings include a description of the plant and germination information. There is a small section on vegetables and herbs as well. This is a good source of seeds for both European and American native plants.

Heritage Seed Program, RR 3, Uxbridge, ON, L9P 1R3, Canada.
The Seed Program, an outgrowth of the Organic Growers, offers a quarterly publication and an annual meeting. The concentration is on vegetable and herb preservation, and there is an annual seed exchange.

J.L. Hudson, Seedsman, Box 1058, Redwood City, CA 94064, U.S.A.
Hudson publishes an annual *Ethnobotanical Catalog of Seeds*, which includes those from tropical and semi-tropical Central and South America. Descriptions and germination advice is given, in addition to interesting information on plant uses.

D. Landreth Seed Co., 180 West Ostend Street, Box 6426, Baltimore, MD 21230, U.S.A.
Landreths, "America's Oldest Seed House" founded in the year 1784, is still in existence and publishes an annual catalogue. A few flower and vegetable selections are offered in packages; most are listed as bulk seed. A number of heritage seeds are offered.

Ontario Rock Garden Society,
Box 146, Shelburne, ON, L0N 1S0, Canada; and
Ottawa Valley Rock Garden Society
25 Crystal Beach Drive, Nepean, ON, K2H 5M6, Canada.
These two societies are affiliated with the North American Rock Garden Society (NARGS) (Box 67, Millwood, NY 10546 U.S.A). The rock garden societies offer lecture programs, newsletters, borrowing libraries, plant sales, and seed exchanges for members. Many rare and select species, difficult to find in commercial outlets, are available in the seed exchange. (Note: these addresses are subject to change.)

Richters, Goodwood, ON, L0C 1A0, Canada.
Richters has an international reputation as one of the largest and most reliable suppliers of herb seeds and plants. Their detailed catalogue lists many rare, difficult-to-find plants and seeds, including Oriental species. The catalogue descriptions include the uses, both culinary and medicinal, for most selections.

Seed Savers Exchange, and *Flower and Herb Exchange*
3076 North Winn Road, Decorah, IA 52101, U.S.A.
These two seed exchanges were pioneer organizations for the preservation of old plant varieties in America. The Seed Savers Exchange now deals exclusively in vegetable seeds; the Flower and Herb Exchange is an offshoot of the original exchange. Members list surplus seeds during the winter months for publication in the annual catalogue in early spring. Seeds are cross-referenced, giving both common names and Latin nomenclature where possible, although not all old varieties have been classified by taxonomists.

Bibliography

UNPUBLISHED SOURCES

National Archives of Canada (NA)
MG19 F1. Claus Family Papers.
MG24 D5. Account Book of Stephen Conger, 1803–1828.
MG24 H13. Letters of Margaret Hall, 1827–1828.
MG24 H16. Journal of Rev. Patrick Bell, 1833–1834.
RG1. Township Papers.
    Land Books.
RG16. Customs Records for Ports of Entry, 1820–1828.

Public Archives of Ontario
B70 Series D-5. Home District Directory, 1836.
Land Book vol. 5. Land Record Index.
Land Petitions, Upper Canada.
RG1 L3. #1097. Township Papers, Toronto Township.
Pamphlet 1857. Traill, Catharine Parr. *The Emigrant Housekeeper's Guide to the Backwoods of Canada*, part 2.

Metropolitan Toronto Reference Library, Baldwin Room
Baldwin, William Warren. Papers [1798]–1844.
Custead, William Ward. *Toronto Nursery Catalogue*. York, Upper Canada: William Lyon Mackenzie, printer.
Goldie, John. Papers, 1822–1866.
Robson, William. Three Letters to William Robson from Alexander Davidson, 1838, 1843, and 1845.

PUBLISHED SOURCES

Abercrombie, John, and Thomas Mawe. 1776. Reprint 1822. *Everyman His Own Gardener*. Edinburgh.

Bailey, Liberty Hyde. 1902. *Cyclopedia of American Horticulture*. 2nd ed. 4 vols. New York: Macmillan.

– 1925. *Manual of Gardening: A Practical Guide*. New York: Macmillan.

Betts, Edwin M. 1986. *Jefferson's Flower Garden at Monticello*. 3rd ed. Charlotteville, VA: University of Virginia Press.

Bianchini, Francesco. 1977. *Health Plants of the World: Atlas of Medicinal Plants*. Translated and adapted by M.A. Dejey. New York: Newsweek Books.

Bourne, H. 1833. Reprint 1988. *Flores Poetici: The Florist's Manual*. Guilford, CT: Opus Publications.

Breck, Charles H.B. 1842. *Catalogue of Vegetable, Herb, Tree, Flower and Grass Seeds for Sale at New Seed Store, no. 45 North Market Street, Boston*. Boston: Tuttle and Dennett.

Breck, Joseph. 1866. *New Book of Flowers*. New York: Orange Judd Co.

Brickell, Christopher, and Fay Sharman. 1986. *The Vanishing Garden: A Conservation Guide to Garden Plants*. London: John Murray in association with the Royal Horticultural Society.

Bridgeman, Thomas. 1829. Reprint 1864. *The Kitchen Gardener's Instructor*. New York: C.M. Saxton.

Britton, Nathaniel Lord, and Hon. Addison Brown. 1913. Reprint 1973. *An Illustrated Flora of the Northern United States and Canada*. 3 vols. New York: Dover.

Buchanan, Rita. 1987. *A Weaver's Garden*. Loveland, CO: Interweave Press.

Canada Department of Agriculture. 1940. *Medicinal Plants and Their Cultivation in Canada*. Publication 484. Ottawa: Department of Agriculture.

Carson, Jane. 1968. *Colonial Virginia Cookery*. Charlottesville: University Press of Virginia.

Child, Mrs. 1833. Reprint 1965. *The American Frugal Housewife*. 12th ed. Worthington: Worthington Historical Society.

Claus, Edward P., and Varro E. Taylor. 1968. *Pharmacognosy*. Philadelphia: Lea & Febiger.

Clinch, George. 1919. *English Hops*. London: McCorquodale & Co.

Coates, Alice M. 1956. *Flowers and Their Histories*. London: Hulton Press.

The Cook Not Mad. 1833. Reprint 1982. Toronto: Cherry Tree Press.

Crawford, Pleasance. 1985. "Some Early Ontario Nurserymen." *Canadian Horticultural History* 1, no. 1.

– 1984. "Boulton's Garden: Fifty Years in the Landscape of the Grange, Toronto." *Canadian Collector*, July/August.

Curtis' Botanical Magazine. 1787–1984. London.

de Candolle, Alphonse. 1886. Reprint 1964. *Origin of Cultivated Plants.* 2nd ed. New York & London: Hafner Publishing.

Dirr, Michael A. 1983. *Manual of Woody Landscape Plants.* Champaign, IL: Stipes Publishing.

Dutton, Joan Parry. 1979. *Plants of Colonial Williamsburg.* Williamsburg, VA: Colonial Williamsburg Foundation.

Erichsen-Brown, Charlotte. 1979. *Use of Plants for the Past 500 Years.* Aurora, ON: Breezy Creeks Press.

Everett, Thomas H. 1982. *New York Botanical Gardens Illustrated Encyclopedia of Horticulture.* 10 vol. New York and London: Garland Publishing.

Ewan, Joseph. 1969. *A Short History of Botany in the United States.* New York and London: Hafner Publishing.

Favretti, Rudy J. 1964. *New England Colonial Gardens.* Stonington, CT: Pequot Press.

Firth, Edith G. 1962. *The Town of York, 1793–1815: A Collection of Documents of Early Toronto.* Champlain Society for the Government of Ontario. Toronto: University of Toronto Press.

Foster, Steven, and James A. Duke. 1990. *Eastern/Central Medicinal Plants.* Peterson Field Guide Series. Boston: Houghton Mifflin.

Freeman, Margaret B. 1979. *Herbs for the Medieval Household for Cooking, Healing and Divers Uses.* New York: Metropolitan Museum of Art.

Garden Club of Toronto. 1979. *Plants of Pioneer and Early Days in Ontario.* 3rd ed. Toronto: Paragon Press.

Gerard, John. 1633. Reprint 1975. *The Herbal, or General History of Plants.* Revised and enlarged by Thomas Johnson. New York: Dover.

Godfrey, Charles M. 1979. *Medicine for Ontario: A History.* Belleville, ON: Mika Publishing.

Greenoak, Francesca. 1983. *Forgotten Fruit: The English Orchard and Fruit Garden.* London: Andre Deutsch.

Grieve, Mrs M. 1931. Reprint 1978. *A Modern Herbal.* Harmondsworth, Middlesex: Penguin.

Griffiths, Mark. 1994. *Index of Garden Plants: The New Royal Horticultural Society Dictionary.* Portland, OR: Timber Press.

Grigson, Geoffrey. 1958. *The Englishman's Flora.* St Albans, Herts: Granada Publishing.

Grigson, Jane. 1975. *Jane Grigson's Fruit Book.* Harmondsworth, Middlesex: Penguin.

Harvey, John. *Early Nurserymen.* Chichester, Sussex: Phillimore & Co.

Healey, B.J. 1975. *The Plant Hunters.* New York: Charles Scribner's.

Hedrick, U.P. 1933. Reprint 1966. *A History of Agriculture in the State of New York.* American Century Series. New York: Hill & Wang.

– 1950. *A History of Horticulture in America to 1860.* New York: Oxford University Press.

Hedrick, U.P., ed. 1919. Reprint 1972. *Sturtevant's Edible Plants of the World*. New York: Dover.

Henery, Blanche. 1975. *British Botanical and Horticultural Literature before 1800*. 3 vols. New York & Toronto: Oxford University Press.

Herman, Samuel. [1868]. *Paxton's Botanical Dictionary*. London: Bradbury, Agnew & Co.

Holm, Leroy G. 1977. *World's Worst Weeds: Distribution and Biology*. Reprint. Honolulu: University of Hawaii Press.

Huxley, Anthony. 1978. *An Illustrated History of Gardening*. New York and London: Paddington Press in association with the Royal Horticultural Society.

Innis, Mary Quayle. 1983. *Mrs. Simcoe's Diary*. Toronto: Macmillan.

Jabs, Carolyn. 1984. *The Heirloom Gardener*. San Francisco: Sierra Club Books.

Jameson, Mrs Anna. 1838. Reprint 1972. *Winter Studies and Summer Rambles in Canada*. 3 vols. Toronto: Coles.

Jones, Robert Leslie. 1946. *History of Agriculture in Ontario, 1613–1880*. Toronto: University of Toronto Press.

Kalm, Peter. 1770. Reprint 1966. *Travels in North America*. 2 vols. New York: Dover.

Langdon, Eustella. 1972. *Pioneer Gardens at Black Creek Pioneer Village*. Toronto & Montreal: Holt, Rinehart and Winston.

Leighton, Ann. 1986. *American Gardens in the Eighteenth Century: "For Use or for Delight."* Amherst, MA: University of Massachusetts Press.

– 1987. *American Gardens of the Nineteenth Century: "For Comfort and Affluence."* Amherst, MA: University of Massachusetts Press.

Leung, Albert Y. 1980. *Encyclopedia of Common Natural Ingredients*. New York: John Wiley & Sons.

Lewis, W. 1748. *Pharmacopoeia of the Royal College of Physicians at Edinburgh*. 4th ed. London.

Loudon, John Claudius. 1827. *Encyclopedia of Gardening*. 5th ed. London: Longman, Rees, Orme, Brown and Green.

M'Mahon, Bernard. [1858]. Reprint 1976. *McMahon's American Gardener*. 11th ed. New York: Funk & Wagnalls.

Merlin, Mark David. 1984. *On the Trail of the Opium Poppy*. London & Toronto: Associated University Presses.

Michaux, André. 1803. Reprint [1974]. *Flora boreali-americana*. New York: Hafner Press.

Miller, Philip. 1754. Reprint 1969. *The Gardener's Dictionary*. Abridged ed. Herts & New York: Wheldon & Wesley.

Millspaugh, Charles F. 1892. Reprint 1974. *American Medicinal Plants*. New York: Dover.

Moodie, Mrs Susanna. 1832. Reprint 1974. *Roughing It in the Bush*. Toronto: Coles.

– [1854] *Life in the Clearings versus the Bush*. New York: De Witt and Davenport.

Morton, Julia F. 1977. *Major Medicinal Plants: Botany, Culture and Uses*. Springfield, IL: Charles C. Thomas.

New England Farmer. 1871–2. Edited by Simon Brown and Stilman Fletcher. Boston: R.P. Eaton & Co.

New York State Fruit Testing Cooperative Association. 1986. *New and Noteworthy Fruits*. Geneva, NY.

Nicholson, George, ed. 1887. *The Illustrated Dictionary of Gardening: A Practical and Scientific Encyclopedia of Horticulture for Gardeners and Botanists*. 7 vols. London: L. Upcott Gill.

Nuttall, Thomas. 1818. *The Genera of North American Plants, and a Catalogue of the Species, to the Year 1817*. Philadelphia: printed for the author by D. Heartt.

Ody, Penelope. 1993. *The Complete Medicinal Herbal*. Toronto: Key Porter.

Ontario Historical Society. 1989. *Consuming Passions: Eating and Drinking Traditions in Ontario*. Papers presented at the 101st Annual Conference of the Ontario Historical Society at the Radisson Hotel, Ottawa, May 4, 5, and 6, 1989. Meaford, ON: Oliver Graphics.

Parker, Asa. 1851. *The Canadian Gardener*. Aylmer, ON: Thomas Watson.

Parkinson, John. 1629. Reprint 1991. *Paradisi in Sole Paradisus Terrestris: A Garden of Pleasant Flowers*. New York: Dover.

Pennsylvania Horticultural Society. 1976. *From Seed to Flower: Philadelphia 1681–1876*. Philadelphia.

Perrot, Emile. [1971]. *Les Plantes médicinales*. Paris: Presses Universite de France.

Perthensis. 1807. *The New Encyclopaedia, or Universal Dictionary*. 23 vols. London and Perth: Vernor, Hood, and Sharpe, R. Morison.

Pesman, M. Walter. 1962. *Meet Flora Mexicana*. Globe, AZ: Dale S. King.

Pirone, Pascal P. 1978. *Diseases and Pests of Ornamental Plants*. 5th ed. New York: Wiley.

Pizzetti, Ippolito, and Henry Cocker. 1975. *Flowers: A Guide for Your Garden*. 2 vols. New York: Harry N. Abrams.

Prince, William Robert. 1846. Reprint 1979. *A Manual of Roses*. New York: Earl M. Colman.

Pursh, Frederick. 1814. *Flora Americae Septentrionalis*. London: White, Cochrane.

Reader's Digest Association. 1978. *Reader's Digest Encyclopedia of Garden Plants and Flowers*. 2nd ed. London: Reader's Digest Association.

Reaman, G. Elmore. 1970. *A History of Agriculture in Ontario*. 2 vols. Toronto: Saunders of Toronto.

Rennie, James. 1833. *Alphabet of Scientific Gardening*. London: William Orr.

Reynolds, J., and J. Tampion. 1983. *Double Flowers: A Scientific Study*. London: Polytechnic of Central London Press.

Schwabe, Calvin W. 1978. "Cattle, Priests and Progress in Medicine." In *Wesley W. Spink Lectures on Comparative Medicine*, vol. 4. Minneapolis: University of Minnesota Press.

Somer, Margaret Frisbee. 1972. *The Shaker Garden Seed Industry*. Old Chatham, NY: Shaker Museum Foundation.

Stearn, William T. 1967. *Botanical Latin*. London and Edinburgh: Thomas Nelson & Sons.

Stewart, John, and Susan Buggey. 1975. "The Case for Commemoration of Historic Landscapes and Gardens." *Bulletin, Association for Preservation Technology* 7, no. 2.

Stillé, Alfred, and John M. Maisch. 1880. *The National Dispensatory*. Philadelphia: Henry C. Lea's Son & Co.

Stuart, David, and James Sutherland. 1987. *Plants from the Past: Old Flowers for New Gardens*. London: Penguin.

Stuart, Malcolm, ed. 1979. *The Encyclopedia of Herbs and Herbalism*. 2nd ed. Rexdale, ON: Classic Bookshops.

Taylor, Norman. 1961. *Taylor's Encyclopedia of Gardening*. 4th ed. Boston: Houghton Mifflin.

Traill, Catharine Parr. 1855. Reprint 1969. *The Canadian Settler's Guide*. Toronto/Montreal: McClelland & Stewart.

– 1836. Reprint 1989. *The Backwoods of Canada*. Toronto/Montreal: McClelland & Stewart.

– 1840. *The Backwoods of Canada*. 5th ed. London: Charles Knight.

– 1857. *The Emigrant Housekeeper's Guide to the Backwoods of Canada, Part 2*. 7th ed. Toronto.

Transactions of the Massachusetts Horticultural Society for the Years 1874, 1875, 1876. Boston: Tolman & White, Printers.

United States. Department of Agriculture. [1951]. *Crops in Peace and War*. U.S. Government Printing Office.

van Ravenswaay, Charles. 1977. *A Nineteenth Century Garden*. New York: Universe Books.

von Baeyer, Edwinna. 1983. *A Preliminary Bibliography for Garden History in Canada*. Ottawa: Parks Canada.

von Baeyer, Edwinna, and Pleasance Kaufman Crawford. 1995. *Garden Voices: Two Centuries of Garden Writing*. Toronto: Random House.

Webber, Ronald. 1968. *The Early Horticulturists*. Newton Abbott: David and Charles.

Weiss, E.A. 1983. *Oilseed Crops*. London and New York: Longman.

Wood & Bache. 1858. *United States Dispensatory*. 11th ed. U.S.A. Hospital Department, Philadelphia.

Index